VIRTUS

THE NEXT FRONTIER

EVOLUTION AND RENAISSANCE OF THE ECONOMY AND DEMOCRACY

CREATING NEW JOBS, BUSINESSES, INVESTMENTS
GENERATING VALUE HOLISTICALLY AND SUSTAINABLY

BEHRAD FOROUGHIZADEH

Order this book online at www.trafford.com
or email orders@trafford.com

Most Trafford titles are also available at major online book retailers.

Print information available on the last page.

ISBN: 978-1-4907-5225-9 (sc)
ISBN: 978-1-4907-5224-2 (hc)
ISBN: 978-1-4907-5226-6 (e)

Library of Congress Control Number: 2014921827

Trafford rev. 06/27/2015

www.trafford.com

North America & international
toll-free: 1 888 232 4444 (USA & Canada)
fax: 812 355 4082

Contents

PART 1
Game-changing and Disruptive Variables

PART 2
VIRTUS—a Possible Solution

PART 3
Applicability: 19 Examples

DISCLAIMER NOTICE AND RELEASE OF LIABILITY

Please read, understand, and agree to this disclaimer before buying or reading this book or using any of its data or information. The word, concept, model, theory "Virtus" in this book - is not to be confused with, or assimilated to any other, eventual, equally respectable concept, theory, model, description, organization, and so on, which might use this same word.

Please note well:

The material in this book represents an introduction to a new economic model (theory) and concepts and that it has no political or ideological ends. The use of the material and information provided herein is the sole responsibility of those who so choose to do so—hence, the reader/user/utilizer/etc. (henceforth user(s)) agrees that the author cannot be held responsible or liable for this.

Through use of this book and or the material and the information provided herein, the user fully agrees to hold the author, his family members, their extended family, their interests, etc. (henceforth, the author), harmless and completely to release him/them from any and all liability that any users(s) may claim to incur directly or indirectly.

Users of this book and its information are advised that this book and the information it contains are issued solely to represent a possible alternative or at best a different perspective. It is to be used for informational purposes only and is a general introduction to the subject matter. Neither the information presented nor any statement or expression of opinion, or any other matter herein, directly or indirectly constitutes a representation by the author of, or a solicitation to use, this for any other purposes other than that of reading about a different perspective on the matters covered in the book or an invitation or solicitation to decide, act, or take action in any way, shape, or form.

The user agrees that the information contained herein is based on referenced sources, which in most cases are generally accepted as being authoritative and reasonably reliable, but is not guaranteed by the author, as he is not the owner or creator of such data and does not purport this to be a complete summary of the available data. The author, publisher, editor, and their associates are not responsible for errors, omissions, deletions, changes, and or redirections to/in links, references, archiving or inaccessibility of data, especially if it is web based.

The author does not take any position with regards to any political, religious, ideological, social, etc., viewpoints or formulate any judgment whatsoever concerning any of the subject matters covered in the book (e.g., immigration, speculation, reforms being enacted, emerging nations, banking, China, India, etc.) independent of their origin or subject matter.

Any opinions expressed are solely opinions. The author encourages readers to supplement the information in this book with independent research. Readers should not rely solely on the information presented. Rather, they should use the information provided as a starting point for additional independent research on the subject matter.

Most of the quantitative and empirical data provided in the book is available from public sources. The author makes no representations, warranties, or guarantees as to the accuracy or completeness of the information and data provided by the referenced sources. The reader is advised that this data and information is subject to change or unavailability without notice and is not within the author's control.

It is hereby noted that statements contained in the book that look forward in time, including everything based on historical information, involve uncertainties and are prone to change, which may affect underlying assumptions and conclusions.

The user fully accepts that the book and/or any or all of its information and or data must not be used in any way, shape, or form to make financial, investment, business, employment, or any other decision of any kind anywhere in the world. The use of the information and data provided in this book to any end is the sole responsibility of those who freely elect to do so, releasing the author from any eventual liability of any nature and holding the author harmless.

The information presented in the books, papers, articles, etc., and web sites referenced in the book are not the author's responsibility. The author does not control, endorse, or guarantee information and content found in such sources and/or their continued availability, accessibility, or updating (fully or partially). Users agree that the author is not responsible for any content, associated links, resources, or products or services associated with third parties that may appear on the sources' material or their web sites or any additional recommended reading—this is not a solicitation to use or promote these in any way. Users further agree that the author is not and shall not be liable for any loss or damage of any sort associated with the use of this or third party content. Any links to web sites are provided to credit the source and for the reader's sole convenience only. The author does not own third-party components, information, data, etc., or their content included in the book. The author therefore cannot warrant or guarantee that the use of the content contained in the work will not infringe on the rights of third parties. The risk of claims resulting from such infringement rests solely with users.

The author does not guarantee the accuracy of the data included in this work. Boundaries, colors, denominations, and other information shown on any map (taken from official public domains) in this work do not imply any judgment on the part of the author concerning the legal status of any territory or the endorsement or acceptance of such boundaries. The author does not suggest, promote, set a preference for, or provide ideological, religious, cultural, or political views or any economic models these might represent. Any conclusions derived from this work are the sole responsibility of the users and those that arrive at such conclusions.

The author also disassociates himself from and refutes and repudiates any type of thought and or idea related to, associated with, or linked with any notion of violence, xenophobia, offensive, stigmatizing, diminishing, etc., and in general any other form of hate-related, discriminatory, sectarian or segregational, denigratory, extremist, gender-, cultural-, or origin-related arguments, etc., including any ideological thought processes or ideas, opinions, etc., whatsoever and/or that may lead to such things.

To the contrary, a life lived internationally has made the author extremely sensitive to and appreciative of different cultures, diversity, and to the immense wealth each perspective has added to the author—and adds to humanity.

The real intent of this book and the author is to highlight the potential risks the economic impasse and the current unsustainable global imbalances might pose to peace and prosperity internationally and to provide a possible solution that might allow to step to a higher level of civilization that makes treasure of peace and diversity and promotes healthy and balanced international trade, exchange of ideas, and the free movement of people among nations.

The user also agrees that this book represents a mere introduction to a possible new/evolved set of concepts, theories, notions, and perspectives among many others and that there is no suggestion that this is the only solution, the best solution, or one with all the answers. The user agrees that what is being presented here is at best a baseline framework that, if validated, accepted, and concurred with by a pool of experts in all fields necessary and ratified as a possible way forward by any organization, state, or government will need to receive the contribution of many before it can be completed, rolled-out, and implemented. The author's central concepts, theories, notions, models, and opinions have been presented are a product of his intuition, developed in good faith, and after more than reasonable research and hence to the author's best knowledge have been genuinely developed by the author. The user also understands and agrees that it is objectively impossible to verify all possible viewpoints at any point in time; hence, any eventual similarities are to be considered solely and purely coincidental and anyway only an additional perspective and opinion. Consequentially the author does not accept any eventual claims or liability for this.

The author's hope through this work is to add a further, perhaps an infinitesimally small, contribution to how we might wish to bring about productive change and maybe through small pragmatic steps, perhaps, contribute to rendering the world a better place to live for as many as possible independent of citizenry, age, or gender.

Dedication

To my wife, Anna Maria
To our son, Daniele

To current and future generations

Acknowledgments

This work would have not been possible without the continued and sustained trust and motivation I received from my wife, Anna Maria, and our son, Daniele, throughout the development of this new book and the many difficult moments it involved. I owe sincere gratitude to my parents, retired admiral M. Ali and Maria Luisa Foroughizadeh, who gave me the opportunity for an education, travel, see the world, and develop an appreciation for different cultures, perspectives, windows on reality, and viewpoints and to my sister Desirèe for her support.

Many thanks also for the valuable contribution of the thousands of professionals[1] internationally behind the studies, research papers, reports, data, databases, blogs, websites, and textbooks referenced in this book, especially to those who contributed behind the scenes. To the valuable, publicly available information, provided transparently by agencies of the United States Government, international organizations such as the United Nations (UN), the World Bank, OECD, the International Monetary Fund (IMF), and the European Central Bank. To the many international news and information providers around the world and the professional men and women who contributed to them but whose names might not appear in these works.

A special recognition goes to my dear friends Kuroush Raffie and Claudio Giorgini whose advices I treasured. To be earnest, I must also include the many teachers, professors, mentors, colleagues, and friends. This includes all those I was lucky to encounter, even for a brief moment, during the twenty-seven international relocations in my personal journey through this amazing experience called life. Each added personal and intellectual wealth. Sincere acknowledgment and gratitude goes toward Dr. Marc D. Baldwin PhD and Dr. Gordon PhD for the demanding editorial work.

---

[1] From economists, to memebers of academia, consultants, reaserchers, and scientists.

Prologue

An increasing number of signs indicate we may have reached an exceptional historical crossroad in the evolution of our ways of doing things, models, economy, and societies—but even more so in losing sight of the vital importance of centrality of mankind, inaliable rights, freedoms and true democracy. Every time this has happened in the past no political, economic, military power or business or economic model has been able to stop the inevitable momentum towards change. America and post-war Europe were founded, shaped and forged by these quintessential human needs.

On the dawn of the twenty-first century, notwithstanding the levels of advancement and progress humanity has achieved to date, important challenges need to be addressed. Among these are the impact of new technologies and innovations, a structural economic impasse of planetary scale, the generational dilemma and prospects for the young, families, and those in critical age groups; loss of source(s) of employment and income, business closures, instability; the accelerated depletion of natural and energetic resources; population growth and mass immigration, rising levels of poverty and new forms of slavery; volatility of markets, irresolvable public debts, insecurity of hard-earned savings, investments, pensions, retirement and wealth—together with their consequent effects on health, well-being, and peace of mind of entire generations.

Unfortunately, we also face exposure to seemingly more frequent, more powerful, and more destructive natural calamities that seem to be ever more ruinous, costly, and devastating in their impact. Yet these represent only a few of the trials we face and not necessarily the ones posing the most immediate and proximate threat to our evolution and continued survival as species. We live in a time of stalemates, turmoil, and uncertainty, important and preoccupying geopolitical instability, shift in influence, power and new international expansions, virulent failed-state scenarios, and the breakup of entire socioeconomic systems in a growing number of counties. Whether we may be on the brink of defaulting economic systems, societies, nations, escalating social unrest, new forms of extremisms, induced xenophobia, and terrorism, perhaps even war are legitimate questions that loom.

Historical evidence only confirms that continuing down this path will, among other things, ultimately lead to the loss of sovereignty for a growing number of countries, independence, and the need for dependence on others by those exposed to such risks. The contribution of each of the above elements or a different combination of these to the demise of entire states, economic systems, empires, and civilizations (Greer and Lewis 2001) is still a much-debated subject among economists, scholars, and historians. But this is not the main issue.

The *main issue* is that these events are unfolding right now, accumulating greater force, destructive potential, and with increased frequency. No matter how it's put, we are facing a socio-economic deadlock and unpredictability of formidable and unfathomable dimensions. A problem driven and exacerbated by a vacillating economic model that might no longer be able to provide answers and that may initiate (or may already have initiated) a countdown toward a spiral of unknown consequences, exposing the levels of civilization and development reached through millennia of human evolution and or to a totally new world order—but not necessarily the one envisaged by some.

From an evolutionary point of view, this time seemingly had to come—a time that is exerting extreme hardships on growing numbers of people and other concerns; a time when existing models no longer seem to provide answers; a time of great irresolvable systemic blocks, paradoxes,[2] and dichotomies;[3] and one that demands evolution toward something that can provide lasting solutions.

Closed-looped models, convictions, restraints, preconceptions, and economic dogmas are objectively impeding governments, policy and key decision makers, from finding concrete new ways of undertaking greater endeavors, addressing new challenges, leveraging countless new possibilities, and opening roads toward new frontiers. Senseless and counterproductive, continuing down a path that inhibits the realization of dreams of individuals or of millions of people. The young must have the chance to realize their aspirations, ambitions, and futures. The middle-aged have the right to finalize and crown their endeavors, honor

---

[2.]   Inconsistencies, impossibilities, absurdities

[3.]   Irreconcilable differences and contradictions, e.g., increasing taxes while sources of income disappear

their responsibilities to their families, and allow their children to develop into adults. The young-at-heart have the right finally to reap the rewards of their hard-earned accomplishments in relative peace and serenity, allowing them to leave an honorable legacy of their life achievements.

No aspiration, person, enterprise, business, employment, or opportunity to progress should be sacrificed on the altar of models that might have reached their maximum potential and might no longer be able to provide answers, but that need to be updated, modernized and allowed to evolve.

Could we be trapped in a logic bubble? Fearful, too conformant, or lacking vision in confronting and tackling the issues at their core, uncertain of our individual responsibility, or unable to undertake the resilience our ancestors demonstrated? Every person has his or her own respectable view on this. But one fact remains—this course cannot be maintained for too much longer.

Notwithstanding, every problem, viewed from another perspective hides an opportunity. As a species that has gone to the moon and Mars, reaching the outermost corners of our solar system, and delved into the smallest particles of matter, we can achieve many feats. We have an opportunity to resiliently address the challenges we face and to open a new chapter in development and prosperity.

In an era of many game- and paradigm-changing, dimensions, variables, and challenges (natural and human-made) that impact different domains of our lives, mankind is on the verge of making the biggest leap in our advancement. We can open an era of unprecedented possibilities and prolonged prosperity, undertaking a step-level move toward new plateaus of a more evolved society and civilization and greater personal, scientific, and spiritual enlightenment; or we may confront immeasurable multiple structural, systemic, and economic meltdowns with unpredictable consequences.

The ability to evolve towards a sustainable economy, improve our quality of life, preserve our ecosystems, and enhance the societies we live in, are quintessential to prolonged survival, success, and prosperity. This ability has and will continue, allowing us to open new windows on reality and to tap into opportunities that will otherwise remain invisible, uneconomical, improbable, impractical, and/or unimaginable under the existing model(s).

Seeking to fulfill our aspirations both as individuals and a society, finally going beyond the obvious, sets the stage for increased potential for optimism, confidence, and hope.

Paradoxically, many of the tools and the means to move to a more sustainable approach are already available. However, the will to make the necessary changes beyond known frameworks, thresholds, and comfort zones, currently seems sadly lacking. Incredibly our ancestors overcame relatively comparable challenges (for their time), with much less knowledge, technology, resources, and capability.

Legitimate Questions

Though some the questions we hear or read might be provocative and or rhetorical, they do convey a growing, legitimate concern among experts, policymakers, economists, businesspersons, and individuals. Let us see some of the more recurring. What is happening to markets, investments, banking, businesses, trade, and prospects, our hard-earned money and savings? How might businesses be transformed? Will new technologies replace everything? For how much longer will we allow otherwise successful enterprises to vanish under the avalanche effect that stems from an increasingly predominant cost-focused paradigm, leaving wasteland and economic and employment destruction along its path?

Net of recurring mini-recoveries from time to time, how will governments address and resolve the growing challenges? Do the currently adopted solutions work, do they have lasting structural effects, or are they just temporary patches? How will dichotomies and forces that pull in diametrically opposing directions be addressed? Are developed countries destined to remain *in bilico*,[4] between potential defaults and ever-increasing debts? Will they be exposed to financial speculation and/or undeclared economic conflicts? Will eventually recurring austerity measures ultimately strangle and suffocate any remaining vital signs of economic activity in countries where these are enacted with possibility of spillover? Are uncontrolled speculation and unsustainable taxation going to bring about additional strain? Will the developed world become the backyard of emerging nations, with jobs, businesses, production, ideas, and human intellect moving away from the developed nations to other parts of the world; or will emerging nations face the same crisis and the same dilemmas advanced economies are facing in less time than is politically comfortable, or will they remain immune? Are the vast majority of the seven billion souls who inhabit this minuscule and statistically unique planet destined to mass poverty? What is happening to the world around us, to our communities, which seemed to function properly until very recently? It is not hard to remain flabbergasted that only few years ago there was an economy made

---

4. In frail balance

of non-precarious real needs, real exchanges, real trade, real returns, and real jobs. What happened to these real needs? Is there no stopping this? Is it possible to reverse this self-consuming paradox?

In searching for answers that provide temporary personal relief and peace of mind, our self-survival mechanism activates the logical and rational part of our brains. We articulate hypotheses, reasoning, for example, "surely the mini-recoveries we are witnessing are testament that it is all over." We reassure ourselves that "we are finally out of the tunnel. It must finish. There is too much at stake." In other words, we force ourselves to acknowledge that the answer to these questions has an outcome that appeals to us. And then we are hit (again) by the question many fear the most, one that haunts us before we go to sleep and one that we try to push aside in the remotest synapses of our cerebral cortex. Are we sure that our business, job, family will remain untouched by the impasse? For how much longer will we avoid the next list of bankrupt investors and entrepreneurs, closing businesses; layoffs; companies that need to sell off their technology, innovations, advanced machinery, trademarks, or patents; businesswomen and men who see their investments evaporate; or simply the growing number of those who step into oblivion?

These lines are written with the hope, drive, and passion of a father who wishes to see the best for his son and his future; a businessperson who witnesses current events unfolding before his eyes without being able to contribute, to control, or at least effectively to voice concerns to make a difference; a person among the billions of inhabitants of this singular planet; and a person who is bewildered at how fast we are going toward possibly the largest precipice humankind has ever faced on a planetary scale and apprehensive as to why no one seems to be able to intervene effectively to turn the car around, stop it, or at least slow it down. Are there any answers for any of the above questions? Is the current economic scenario similar to that of a patient who is no longer responding to treatment?

Are we sure we are looking at the problem from all perspectives—the right perspectives—or are we fixated on looking at it from known perspectives? Do we—as adults and a society of free men and women from every walk of life—wish to take on the challenge of leading the opening of a new era and taking responsibility for its design, development, and steering? In short, what we are going to do about these problems, how are we going to resolve them, in what timeframes, and at what opportunity, cost, etc.—these are the main issues.

Premises

This book has an important set of premises. It is an introductory book on a new and evolved economic model that is *ideologically free*, with no bias toward or a choice between current or historic ideologies—be they liberal or conservative—capitalist, socialist, communist, or any other "isms" or versions in between that have left their mark on history or are currently being adopted. As with any historically successful framework, the prosed solution and the new economic theory discussed in this book is designed to evolve upward from the existing economic model.

This book is not intended to be politically correct or its inverse, but has objectivity as one its primary goals and is designed to go beyond the layers, clutter, and filters of accumulated complexity. It does not set preferences toward, espouse, choose, promote, or judge different political views or the views of any one of the many economic schools of thought, international agencies, or government and nongovernment departments or organizations, nor is it meant to validate or antagonize any of the above, the perspectives they might represent or people who work in them. However, it does start off with the existing market-based economic model as it is the result of thousands of years of human evolution, and it is where we stand today. It is not about east or west, north or south, or even the middle. Should this book ever be associated with a sense of direction or motion, it would only be that intrinsic to natural evolution and progression—the immediate and long-term future. It is not about controversy, rhetoric, speculation, utopic concepts or conspiracy theories.

It is not meant to convey arrogance by claiming to provide the answer to it all, a suggestion that this is the only solution or the best solution. Rather, it is designed to provide a starting point, a baseline model, a framework, a transition and conversion protocol, and related tools, making available a common ground on which policymakers, economists of different creeds, professionals from various walks of life, scholars, business leaders, strategists, international organizations, and specialized NGOs[5] and government agencies can develop, contribute to, and finally

---

[5.] Nongovernment organizations such the UN, IMF, World Bank, OECD, etc.

complete these notions, arriving at a concurred solution through a consensus-driven approach. In fact, for any model to work, it has to consider all stakeholders and concerns making up the current economic framework without prejudice—independent, that is, of their role or market sector. We cannot think, for example, of an economy without banks or investors, just as we cannot do without either employment and industry or a system that fails to address hard or controversial issues no matter how much frustration these issues generate.

It is not about promoting revolution, anarchy, chaos, extremist, fundamentalist ideas, nor is it about unrealistic, nonpragmatic, impracticable solutions, drastic change, about turns, or elaborate complexity. This book goes beyond the existing, the given, the accepted frameworks, the paradigms, the assumptions, and the boxes in which they have been contained and outlines a possible solution. The current economic impasse potentially touches the majority of people who wake up each morning and need to provide for their families, develop and grow their businesses and investments, make a living, realize their dreams, and have the opportunity to set the foundations for their families, improve their lives, generate new ideas, reach challenging new objectives, and procure a future and a deserved retirement—to live their lives.

Hence, this book cannot be limited to focusing only on quenching the justified technical nature of demanding, exacting, professional, and intellectual curiosity of a few readers in one or two fields; it must address the varied needs of a broader audience with expertise in as many other fields as possible. Any next model will in fact need the contribution, involvement and collaboration of expertise from as many fields as necessary. Arising from a very strong intuition in early 2006 about an evolved model, this book is the result of a multiyear endeavor in analyzing data from many different renown and authoritative information sources (henceforth sources),[6] not only to verify the validity of the premises, but also to corroborate the applicability of this possible new model. This book is not about enforcing a single viewpoint, but about providing different perspectives, allowing ample room for readers to arrive at their own conclusions. There is, however, one element to keep in mind

---

6. Government agencies, Central Banks, and national statistical offices (US, EU, and emerging nations); United Nations NGO's, top-ranking universities, think tanks, top ten conlusting firms, authoritative economic, financial journals, and media)

throughout the book: all models are the result of human intellect. As such, all models have a limit, an Achilles' heel—a set of weak points.

Though these weak points might differ, there is one trait that seems to be common to most models—namely, their capacity to evolve and adapt to new variables, forces, and challenges over time. This is one trait that the proposed model is designed to address, simply because any model that follows must be able to evolve at least as rapidly as the growing technological, human, and natural challenges it will face.

As for the shortcomings of the proposed model, it is clear that a utopian, error-free, or fail-proof model is unrealistic. What can be done, though, is to open the model to allow the contribution of expertise and find new ways to mitigate these shortcomings in the best way possible.

In essence, this treatise provides a new and innovative baseline framework that is open, evolvable, and scalable allowing ample room for improvement and possibility to address as many concerns as possible from experts in all fields. The natural equidistance and/or independence of the solution from existing "isms" will become self-evident.

Disagreement

As a final premise, it is of fundamental importance to appreciate that, for centuries, economists, philosophers, sociologists, and thinkers in a variety of fields have developed contrasting economic models. They have written extensively about their ideas and the intricate ways they should operate, explaining their advantages over their historical counterparts.

Disagreement on models lies even among those that declare their allegiance to the same general model, generating many differing schools of thought. *Yet it is difficult to know how many times we were saved by the contribution of conflicting points of view.*

As a society, we still have not configured a model that could finally put an end to a debacle that seems to repeat itself *ad infinitum.* In all historical periods, the way human societies were configured and the economic models they used involved compromises incorporating many opposing viewpoints. The current economic model is at best the result of compromise among differing points of views. The scope here is not to judge any of the existing models, but to see if there is a solution. Is there a different approach, or are we condemned? Additionally it is to confirm that any new model must benefit from different legitimate viewpoints.

Choices

In laying the foundations for this book, several choices had to be made. Some were very hard, others were challenging, and still others required a considerable will. This book will predominately concentrate on the solution rather than repeating the detailed (structural and systemic)[7] cause-and-effect analysis that precede the introduction of the new model. The focus of this book presumes reader general knowledge of the many structural and systemic dichotomies and blocks, problems, and challenges our current models face and value the possibility to validate this analysis with freshly updated data and information from different authoritative sources.

The first most arduous choice was to assure objectivity and provide different perspectives throughout. It would be tremendously easy to fall into the trap of demonizing or victimizing entire subsectors of society for the challenges we face today. It is too easy a task for a book to judge the other, to accuse, for example, the politicians for their inability to bring about desired outcomes or the bankers for their greed.

Similarly no data was sought either to confirm or to deny the existence of phenomena such as strong lobbies that push toward achieving particular interests in particular areas; common sense suggests that this often happens: when money is involved, the merging of interests becomes reality. These relations, however, might not endure the test of time simply because they respect the nemesis of the same axiom that greed and self-interest eventually lead to a conflict of interest. Much time and many pages can be dedicated to these matters, but they cannot be part of this book.

---

7. e.g., public debt, deficit, monetary, and fiscal policy, taxation, central and general banking, pensions, (un)employment, population growth, delocalization, generational turnover, retirement and pensions, mass migration, mass migration, poverty, slavery, piracy, and increase in criminal activity, population growth, and exposure to health risks; climate and geological change and increased exposure to their effects; exposure to effects of failed states, social unrest, geopolitical imbalances, extremisms and new forms of terrorism, regional wars and their spillage; exposure to new bubbles (economic, markets, banking, real estate); sustainability; etc.

The problem does not stem from one person or group of people, but more likely from our collective way of going about our business. Additionally, it would be too easy and banal to write a book that fills our lives with additional anger, frustration, and possibly revulsion, disgust, or animosity—mostly unessential to finding a viable solution. This, however, does not excuse or justify those who have acted with criminal intent and affected the lives of thousands. We also need to be reasonable. Many people of all occupations contribute with sincere goodwill and do the best they can. This includes the majority of those trying to find a solution to this very deep and serious crisis, most likely inhibited or limited by the gridlocks of current reality.

The second choice was remaining focused on the main issues and identifying a new model framework and protocol that contain a possible set of solutions to address the different challenges we face. Equivalently, a substantial effort had to be made to get rid of the preconceptions and biases with which we are bombarded on a daily basis and which could inadvertently permeate the source data, the material collected, analyzed, and elaborated and, hence, presented herein. This book looks at the many dimensions of the issues—with particular focus on sustainability, advancement, innovation, and technology and is not limited to seeing things from one national perspective as the problem is now planetary—it concerns all of us.

This treatise is not about quick fixes but about lasting yet time-sensitive and realistic modular rollouts with positive knock on effects, not about piecemeal, or void slogan-based remedies, but about systemic turnaround; nor inventing continuous means to come up with structurally empty mini-recoveries such as the ones witnessed by a few countries—that though welcome, helpful, and necessary these have not, and most likely might not provide lasting solutions, but about structural prolonged remedies that generate constant virtuous cycles of economic traction. Nor is it about promoting the frail models on which neoeconomic giants rely, but a systemic, long-duration, and sustainable economic evolution.

The third choice is one about how to proceed. One of the choices is a natural continuation of things as they are. Continuing on this road, the most probable outcome is more of the same. On the other hand, there is a distinctly different alternative. We cannot appreciate the full extent of the new dimensions it provides, somewhat like the game-changing enterprise the likes of Christopher Columbus[8] undertook: he might have been convinced to have circumnavigated the globe reaching the Indies (though not the ones he thought) or maybe even new land, but he had no clue as to the majesty of this finding, that lay just a few hundred nautical miles due west, northwest, or southwest of his position—a continent spanning nearly the whole longitudinal axis of our planet. It is the same type of feat and challenges pioneers such Isaac Newton, Ferdinand Magellan, James Cook, Vasco de Gama, Adam Smith, Thomas Jefferson, initiated and faced in opening new eras of opportunity. This new road offers potential for advancement, an opportunity for evolution.

The fourth choice was with regards to the modality whether to fix the existing models, replace them completely with others, or evolve them. Using an analogy, a tremendous amount of effort seems to go toward patching up the growing number of cracks and holes that are appearing in a structurally weakened, ecosystem-destructive dam (the current economic model) instead of addressing the real issue, the dam itself and the imminent risk it poses.

Do we wish to continue to focus our thoughts, energies, and resources on continuously mending this dam (i.e., bolting down the turbines or carrying out maintenance on each element of the dam)? Or is it time to ask ourselves if we can expose the cities and its inhabitants in its wake to imminent destruction and satisfy the primary needs for which the dam was created using other methods that might also remove the hazards, and render the end result a viable and sustainable one and one that creates value for all stakeholders?

Many dedicate much effort, all driven by perfect goodwill, to study for example the best forms of austerity measures—repayment timetables, appropriate financial instruments, the best government policies and reforms, the effects of a possible spillover, the spread, increased taxes, mass layoffs, etc. But is this losing sight of the bigger picture? Everything is now interconnected; everything is reliant on everything else, producing additional layers of complexity and dichotomy. If a structural and systemic solution is sought for sustainability; prolonged and profound economic impasse, mass unemployment, financial market instability, public debt, etc.—this needs to be addressed outside of the straitjackets of the existing models.

[8.] Or his predecessors

The forces that impede current models from working properly are increasing, shaping, and fomenting the current standstill. They will continue doing so with greater virulence. As enormous pressures build up behind these dams, exerting growing pressure on their structures, these forces will ultimately find their way to the weakest points. Once they reach the structural point of failure, some of the dams might burst.

Should this happen, the extent of immediate damage, its propagation, and its effects on other financial systems, businesses and entire economies around the world will be very hard to fathom. It would not be hard to guesstimate, though, that they might be much bigger than what the world witnessed with the 2008 near-systemic meltdown. Some already have coined different names, such as mega tsunami, reminiscent of environmental disasters.

Whether or not this might happen is not the goal of this book. What is important is being cognizant that, in the eventuality of implosive or explosive phenomena, independent of their causes, i.e., speculative markets, emerging markets, or defaulting developed countries; there could be severe systemic effects, only adding complexity to the many challenges already being faced.

Objectives

This treatise is about the introduction of a new paradigm-, game-changing, evolutionary theory/concept. Any possible solution that could affect the lives of millions, if it is meant to work, should be shared, and divulged. If found reasonable, it will need to be developed further and improved by many others and only then can it be considered valid for use in part or in whole.

The book focuses on reaching three fundamental objectives, each presented in a distinct part of the book.

First, it explains why the existing model might have reached its maximum capability in responding to new challenges and why new variables such as innovation, new technology, and sustainability cause wide-ranging problems and contradictions that cannot easily be resolved, adding to those already forming in the fundamental building blocks and cornerstones of the existing models.[9]

It is important to understand that the elements and dimensions covered here are by no means the only contributing factors to the economic impasse. Part 1 also provides insight into the reasons why the existing model can no longer be fully effective in managing growing short-, medium-, and long-term needs and challenges.[10]

Part 2 of the book introduces a possible solution. For the solution to be practical and effective, it must have the potential to be applied in relatively short timeframes and be able to jump-start economic revival structurally and systemically—reasonably in much less time that has already passed since the beginning of the crisis through small quick-win modular roll-outs.

This, however, is based on the willingness to bring about *lasting*, resilient, and "future-able" evolving reforms—on a new model that is able to effectively leverage these. The paradigm shift toward a possible solution

---

[9] e.g., public debt, pensions, monetary policy, business models, employment covered in readily available information on websites and other media such as those of the IMF, UN, and renowned economists

[10] e.g., distributed economic traction and economic revival, employment, climate change, sustainability, population growth, mass migration, etc.

might be equivalent to that faced by humanity as it migrated from the barter- to the currency-based economic model, though the effect might be much larger due to the size of the economy, extent of the problem and the numbers involved. While this shift could be perceived as the economic equivalent to a renaissance or an evolutionary big bang, from a purely conceptual point of view, the model's rollout instead requires a step-by-step approach, benefiting, if implemented correctly, from quick wins and from leveraging domino effects.

This part of the book provides a conceptual and introductory description of a new theory with a possible solution through a new model:

- Modernizing, redefining, and realigning the economy—in line with twenty-first century needs, requirements, and challenges

- Virtus—the "Value-Based (Generating) Baseline Evolutionary Economic (Prosperity) Model (BEM^{HESD})"—its makeup, primary components, and how it evolves from modern market-driven philosophy but goes far beyond it, creating a new level (plateau)—opening a totally new chapter in the evolution of the economy and economics, and their dynamic interaction with innovation and the evolving ecosystems that surround us. "Virtus" in this book - is not to be confused with, or assimilated to any other equally respectable concept, theory, model, description, organization, and so on, which might use this same word

- The necessary governance and a balancing framework essential to providing equilibrium in the system

- The transition and conversion protocol (the Alpha-e Protocol) to facilitate evolution, together with migration concepts and tools that will enable the transition from the current model to a new, open, evolutionary, and sustainable prosperity model

In essence, this book aims to offers a baseline framework to harness a new economic plateau(s) for lasting, sustainable economic advancement and prosperity, opening up potential that would otherwise not be visible, viable, and/or available under current models.

Third, in part 3, this treatise provides concrete examples of applicability in different market sectors. It explains how these concepts can be leveraged and implemented to deliver not only near-term opportunities but also those that provide possibilities prolonged and over long-term horizons.

These areas can activate structural economic traction, systemic recovery, prolonged, and long-lasting sustainable development of investments, business, employment, new prospects, innovation, etc., exploiting the underlying potential of the new variables (such as game-changing innovations) and allowing a new chapter in the evolution of humankind to be opened with a dynamic evolutionary economic model conceptualized to address today's challenges and the evolving needs of the of our century.

PART 1

Game-changing and Disruptive Variables

In this part of the book, the short-listed disruptive, game- and paradigm-changing new technology related subject matters, such as innovation, advancement, and new paradigms such as the web and nanotechnology will be analyzed. The next chapters explain the reasons why we might have reached a moment of maturity and saturation in the evolution of our current economic model(s); one of those unique moments in history where a step-level move to the next plane(s)/plateau(s) is necessary.

There is a fundamental premise that needs to be made about this part of the book: the considerations underlying the technological advancements covered herein, are based on current knowledge.

The reader is invited to actively think beyond these known thresholds, extrapolating these concepts further, considering wider areas of impact, and seeking new dimensions. This not only helps in creating a virtual interaction with the ideas of the book, but allows for a better appreciation of the material covered in part two of the book; an active involvement in the generation, enhancement, suggestion of ideas and concepts for the continuous development of the solution—and understanding how to leverage the result of this interaction.

In the following chapters many new concepts will be introduced. To offer the best possible balance between synthesis and readability, technical and non-technical representation, a preference was given to comprehension throughout. The use of new concepts required the use of new acronyms to reduce repetition, and wordiness of otherwise long descriptions. The reader is invited to appreciate that an ideal number of new concepts/acronyms is probably impossible to reach as it is subjective to different individual needs.

Innovation

This chapter is not about a judgment on innovation and technology, as they have brought us to where we are today. Rather, it is an attempt to shed light on the different perspectives, opportunities, and critical issues that we will be facing and to address a future that surprisingly is not very distant; in many cases, it is already here. Understanding trends will allow us to possibly turn critical issues into opportunities. Innovation covers all areas of human activity; consequentially, it will be impossible to cover all areas that are affected by innovation. Hence, as a matter of synthesis, the focus here is on those that are more overarching, influencing more domains. Additionally, the following chapters do not concentrate on a single element (e.g., the benefits derived from these developments), but focuses on the areas worth consideration and highlighting as these need to be addressed to find a possible solution.

Not too long ago, a dear friend noted, "I found myself laughing about a statement my brother made regarding his use of the Internet. The Internet sort of feels like having Aladdin's lamp. . . . You put a question to it in simple language, and instantly, it comes back with a thousand answers. Most of the time you find what you are looking for among the first two pages." It gathered a laugh or two. My friend mentioned he felt his brother was exaggerating. Only a couple of months later, no one was laughing any longer. This conversation took place only a decade or so ago. Similarly, a few years back, many entrepreneurs, executives, and super-consultants were struggling to understand how they could make money from the Internet. Many investors threw massive sums of money at it to the point that a gigantic speculative bubble burst under its own weight, creating one of the biggest financial black holes in stock markets globally. As in many new fields, numerous suffered multiple defeats. Some became frustrated and went to the other extreme, predicting the fall of the new economy, the virtual Promised Land, and the unavoidable return to the old brick-and-mortar economy. The truth usually lies in between. When things are new, our eyes are not trained to look beyond the apparent. We fail to see things beyond the adopted models, limiting their real potential view. Consequentially, some only focused on being the first, others in obvious niche areas while many others still took a watch-and-see approach, especially after the first big bust. Notwithstanding, only a few years later, there is hardly anything one cannot buy or do on the Internet. You can purchase anything from shirts to pants, pots, pans, pins, paints, paper, sushi, and your favorite vacation, even choosing your room and taking a virtual tour beforehand in order to know exactly where you are going. Nothing is out of reach. But even more surprisingly, business models such as social networks, that only a few years earlier seemed improbable, impossible, had been shunned as having no business sense, nonviable, or beyond imagination emerged. Those who were born after 1990 might say, "So what?" Yet most of this was, at best, science fiction to the majority of those born before that date. And it all happened in just a few years.

What is the Internet today? Is it truly very far away from the concept of Aladdin's lamp? Where is it headed? Where is it taking us? Where do we want to go with it? What do we want it to become? To increase its potential benefits, advances and breakthroughs must be managed productively. Nothing can be left completely out of control, at least not for long. Indeed, nature works within the framework of very complicated systems that keep it always in balance, throughout its many cycles. Our planet responds to the universal laws of physics. The universe(s) and the microcosm of quantic particles also adhere to many yet-to-be-understood laws. Any attempt to leave anything human-made alone to manage itself for long has proved to be, in most cases, unproductive, while in others destructive.

Among the many advancements, the Internet is no exception to this. While it should remain an accessible and free domain—what we could call a knowledge, economic, and social (*KES*) platform open to all—without some fundamental rules, it might be growingly prey to those who hack it, phish it, etc., and use it for purposes that instead of producing benefits might produce damage and harm, potentially on an unpredictable scale to millions. Some sources estimate that there are more than two billion Internet users across the planet to date. True or not, that is nearly one third of the planet's total population. Many more are said to own a mobile phone. This interconnection among people, in such short time frames, has never been reached in human history. The implications of just these variables are still to be fully appreciated. In an effort to start this investigation, let us focus on some of the more meaningful aspects of KES (or KES[A] as we will see shortly).

KES^A

Thousands of new websites pop up every day while others disappear just as rapidly as they emerge. The Web essentially revolves around four paradigms. The first three are of human origin while the fourth might not be, at least not fully:

- **K**nowledge—are sites that provide/share/disseminate information/data/news.

- **E**conomic—are sites that have an economic end (i.e., selling, buying, promoting).

- **S**ocial—are sites that have a social/interactive/networking objective.

- **A**wareness—is a variable that goes beyond artificial intelligence or super intelligence.

In the next sections we will examine each in detail and provide an appreciation of their singular nature, their impact and possible challenges that will need to be addressed.

The *K* in KES^A

Many aspects of knowledge are taking form, and they are bound to shape and transform the way we live. Knowledge has many dimensions to it, and it is not limited to Internet or other new variables such as *Web inclusivity* (discussed later). Let us analyze the major ones here. One aspect of knowledge is the raw information/data in itself and anything digitally stored (e.g., your name and birth date, the formula for calculating the orbit of Mars, the definition of legal terminology, highly sensitive government data, the molecular composition of elements, the wealth of streamed data, and so on).

The second aspect of knowledge has to do with not only how information, data, and knowledge are processed, but also the results of this elaboration. Raw data gives way to databases and their management. Elaborations use the raw data to process information, and the results of this elaboration, together with a third aspect—the results of the elaboration of a human brain—all need to be stored in databases or clouds. Software and applications are moving away from the need to be associated physically with the personal medium of connectivity that processes the data it receives. Computers once needed software physically purchased and installed to process data, which henceforth resided on the computer.

This concept has evolved, and today your preferred medium (e.g., tablets, smartphones) can download the applications you need or run them remotely in a cloud. This model, however, is already old news despite its recent commercial availability. Clouds, as they exist today, are virtual places on distant servers that run applications and provide storage space.

In the not-too-distant future, there will probably be no real need for the smart media in use today since everything necessary might reside in the cloud(s)—literally everything from personal, professional, and business applications to work data, personal data, photographs, films, to music (and even deleted data). It is only logical to think that, as time goes by, each element in the cloud or other storage media, might end up having a price tag associated with it, even your own data in many ways it already has to a growing number of concerns—incredibly with the exception of the true owner of this data—the individual or the entity to which this belongs.

Clouds in cyberspace make sense commercially, because they are children of the same paradigm: *Web inclusivity*. In the not-so-distant future, the medium might probably move toward becoming a mere instrument for sending and/or receiving data about all matters concerning one's life. This medium might not even need to be visible in its standby state, or when not necessary, as we will see later. This knowledge dimension also includes something extremely important. It forms the repository of all thinking and its evolution, a place where all human knowledge, know-how, ideas, inventions, thoughts, strategies, perceptions, feelings, moods, fears, hopes, rage, doubts, questions, and movements reside.

How will this enormous repository influence our lives? What implications might these events have on existing models, lives, interactions, businesses, jobs, investments, markets, and economies? Just to provide a small example of the wide-range of possible implications and exposure to unforeseeable risks; in proving their concerns, recently two biologists made headlines by disclosing how easy it had been for them to download all the information necessary from the Web to reactivate the poliovirus using every day, easily acquirable lab machinery. The other aspect of knowledge deals with the third dimension of data, information, results of elaboration, and in general *inclusive information* (henceforth II) or better yet its

- denial/access—e.g., II can be rendered fully or partially unavailable without prior notice with incalculable domino effects on systems, applications, and reports that depend on it. A good example here is citations used in academic work. Increasingly often previously available sets of data/information are inadvertently deleted, readdressed, removed, archived, etc.—rendering the citation ineffective and potentially leading to a plethora of unknown consequences—in full transparency this book has also been victim of this uncontrolled denial/access;

- manipulation—e.g., II is exposed to manipulation in ways that physically printed data could not be, whereas a single modification from a single input source can;

- visibility—e.g., visibility over II can be controlled providing different perspectives over II; selectively assigning different levels of detail and views of data to different users, customers, stakeholders. Individuals, businesses, organizations could become prey to profiling and filtering according to dynamically changing needs of different players.

- completeness—e.g., the level of comprehensiveness of II can be controlled;

- original source validation/verification—e.g., as everyone relies on potentially the same subset of II—this becomes an assumed truth;

- accuracy—e.g., the previous point gives way to exposure to inaccuracy;

- veridicity (truthfulness) e.g., II under KES^A increases exposure to the possibility of falseness and false positive phenomena;

- II overkill e.g., exposure to an abundance of II and phenomena such as big data makes it hard to find what is relevant;

- time theft and focus inhibition—e.g., the above points could lead to exposure to wanted or unwanted unproductive time spent in searching, being detoured to unnecessary II, dispersion of energies, and inhibiting focus and concentration;

- etc.

Extrapolating this concept to higher levels, if the axiom that has held true throughout human history—that information is power—remains valid, will whoever has access to segments of the overall KES^A, its transportation and distribution means, and its elaboration or storage unequivocally hold power? The difference with the past is the exponential amount, quality and detail of data and information, which will be available to those that hold it.

The *E* in KES^A

Here we talk about the economic aspects of KES^A.

Think of the interactions that lead to business opportunities and their development, the joining of forces that create investments, returns on investments, how they translate into sales, revenues, profits, expenses, and compensation, etc. All of these will be impacted. Moreover, think about the dynamics and processes that currently translate into offers, orders, production, and payments. To what extent might these evolve? What about hard-earned savings?

Who will produce what? Where? How? With what? With whom? For whom? This also includes everything that governs the most critical of economic variables—banking, markets, and market transactions worth trillions of dollars, euros, sterling pounds . . . daily, equity and bond values, checking account transactions, pension funds, insurance and mortgages, and much more. There is much more to be said here also, but given the book's central theme, it is best to elaborate this in the manner it deserves in a specific book and/or paper.

The *S* in KES[A]

Let us now touch on the S in KES[A]: the social dimension. This concerns the world of social networks, in which many interact with others. This dimension does not touch on website content (e.g., photos, opinions, conversations) because these belong to the knowledge domain. What is discussed here is subtler. It is about the choice of whom one connects with, the quality of the interaction, the purposes of the interaction, and the type of the interaction, among other things. Actions and reactions provide stimuli with reference not only to the impact between the two or more connecting people but also to the cascading effects that they have on the general behavior of the masses or subsegments of it.

There are already applications that sense the general mood or communication trends of society and subsegments of it (e.g., applications that hone in on communications among the hacker communities to anticipate attacks on certain websites). The reasons for such sensing and the material in question may vary, but this also is beyond the scope of this book. This raises the question of what effect this has on everything else. And are current governance and socioeconomic models geared to face these additional variables and challenges? With what instruments? How? To reach what objectives?

Social networks are currently the property of companies that have for now a purely lucrative scope. Legitimate questions posed by experts include such things as the unlawful or uncontrolled use or divulgation of this information or the sale of these companies that manage and "own" this data (your data). These are just a few of the appropriate and rightful questions that need to be addressed sooner rather than later.

The *A* in KES[A]

The last element composing KES[A] is awareness. I have elected to discuss this only very briefly in this book, not only because it will fill a paper of its own, but also primarily because the risk associated with it is not yet seen as imminent. Rightly or wrongly, it is not the central theme because for now it is only a thought, although one worth initial investigation. I have not seen much evidence of it in recent literature, except possibly some notions of it in science fiction—or I might not have looked in the right places. Yet there are elements all around us that might suggest the possibility of such an eventuality not being too far-fetched after all or at least worth reflection.

While navigating the Web in the early days (only a couple of decades ago), each search was a unique transaction, building only a singular, bidirectional connection and creating rudimentary synapses between two elements, which probably quit existing the moment the transaction ended. This happened in closed/limited-network environments, involving relatively very limited resources and connecting to a single server or a limited number of rudimentary servers/PCs, for a determined timeframe. Today, at an increasing rate, each search is more of a stream of information and connections rather than a unique query/response episode. It feels, looks like, and is a flow, an interaction with one or more applications, creating an incalculable number of synapses even after the session ends.

Transactions are anticipated during the search, producing responses even before there is time to finish typing or voicing the first letters of a query. The Web today is linked to mobile applications, creating numerous additional connections to yet other servers and more intelligent applications that are growing and sharing data each day. Today data continues to be elaborated, and additional intelligence is developed even when we are not actively using the system, we think we have deleted or trashed the data, or we are completely disconnected. This information flows and its eventual elaboration occurs without human intervention or control, creating new nodes of interconnecting II, its further elaboration, and something beyond meta-intelligence building.

This is not limited to personal data, which might reside on social networks or our laptop/tablet/smartphone or the sum total of KES. It includes data, applications, the results of elaborations, cross-elaborations, reactions and feedback to it, etc. (II), that are kept on servers across the world. It goes from the II generated/provided by the grocery store down the street, to the company that produces buttons, to those that produce light-bulbs, to the banks, to the company that produces electricity, to the one that controls the local power grid, to the accountant, to the law-enforcement agencies, to the ministries of finance, to the aircraft manufacturer, to the shipbuilder, to the defense contractor, to the intelligence community, to the country's most sensitive data, to the office of the highest-ranking public officials, and to the office of the president—and the interaction between them.

In this process, the number of connections and synapses is probably incalculable as it grows exponentially with each second. A growing number of industrial and nonindustrial processes are being linked up to Web-based applications that serve to control them (e.g., presses, robotics) and to produce data from these processes. These applications are, in most cases, linked to others that govern other areas within a company, such as finance and senior management decision-making cockpits. The applications are also connected to a growing number of outside concerns, such as suppliers, customer systems, and other industrial processes, which are connected to other applications and servers both within and outside their companies—in a virtual link that could go around the world, creating more connections and more synapses. This connectivity enables the purchase of something online that is produced from scratch and invoiced immediately. This interconnectivity also allows the use of data by many concerns.

The *A* in KES^A refers to awareness. It is an awareness acquired by humans who use the systems. Yet is this the only type of awareness possible? This notion goes beyond a new concept called "super intelligence (artificial intelligence)" or of a new variable that could be called *mocynet* [mobile, cyber, Internet] and anything electronic. We need to be aware that in 1997 a computer called Deep Blue beat Garry Kasparov, one of the world's best chess players, at his own game. What today is called the dimension of digital minds could theoretically be superseded by *(KES)* awareness.

This level of awareness includes the convergence between man, what is man-made, no longer human intelligence, and the interaction between man and the world that surrounds him/her providing a new levels of conscientiousness and capabilities among which could be *mind-activated activities* (representing only the tip of the iceberg of new possibilities and dimensions) that will change our way of thinking, perceiving, communicating, doing things, and relating with one another for the foreseeable future.

Web Inclusivity

Whatever the paradigm on which new sites are founded (KES[A]), most websites are rapidly superseded by others that use what can be called a more inclusive paradigm. Websites lose uniqueness and innovation to the more inclusive websites and paradigms that replace them in ever-shorter timeframes due to a phenomenon that could be named "Web inclusivity." The more a website provides generic "me too" data, the higher its chances of demise and becoming a victim of Web inclusivity. To clarify this, the following example may be helpful. Not long ago (even as recently as the latter half of the 1990s), physical distance often separated people from their dream destinations due to lack of access to information, leading to the necessity to use the services of expert intermediaries. In many cases, people who dedicated their lives to becoming experts in the travel industry journeyed to offer their hands-on expertise.

The choices in many cases were limited to selecting a carrier (land, sea, or air) to get you to your desired destination and, in some cases, not even that. You needed to rely on the expertise of a trustworthy travel agent who could provide you with added-value experience that went beyond the few fancy photographs in glossy brochures. In other words, you needed someone with real hands-on experience with that destination. Your only source of real feedback on a hotel's true adequacy, for example, was by word of mouth from friends or from trusted travel professionals. After much thought and comparison, you literally took an act of faith, hoping for the best.

Unless you were a seasoned traveler, before the 1980s, questions that would seem banal today were potential showstoppers. How do you estimate your expenses? How much in traveler's checks do you need? Where do you get cash if you run out of money (this is before the dissemination of ATMs)? What are you going to eat (before fast-food globalization)? How do you get about town (before navigators)? Will there be car-rental companies (only major cities were equipped with such facilities)? If so, will you be able to drive with your state's driver's license? Do you need to obtain an international driver's license? In case of emergency, where is your country's nearest consulate? In terms of language and cultural issues, what happens if you need medical assistance? It might sound strange, but these questions were still relevant until the midnineties. In such a short time, technology has evolved. The travel industry, in ways unthinkable until a few years ago, has also addressed many dilemmas that impeded travel. Arranging a trip is within everyone's reach nowadays; to such an extent, that tourism's numbers across the globe have grown n-fold since the 1980s.

Since the invention of the Internet, the concept has evolved dramatically. In the beginning, you had to create a vacation, putting all the elements together. You searched for your preferred destination on a limited number of specialized travel websites. Data was not organized in standard formats, as we find today, and much time was lost finding comparable information. For example, you first investigated websites that talked about your destination. Then you browsed the websites of the airlines that flew there, checking them one by one. Hence, you looked at each hotel website individually (if you knew which ones were available), then you looked at the car rentals, and so on.

It was an exhausting experience, and it sometimes took days. At the end, you had to go back to your travel agent with the pieces of information that you gathered to make the booking because in the majority of cases there were no online booking or payment facilities. If there were, the majority of people did not feel secure making payments online. And even after checking availabilities, more often than not you ended back at the drawing board or gave up and asked your agent to create the package for you.

In the early days of the Internet's real diffusion (the late nineties), these different/unique websites were competing against one another, providing alternatives on the Internet. As months progressed, some entrepreneurs started "bundling" websites containing the same type of complementary services, acting as a virtual search engine (e.g., creating the first level of Web inclusivity, putting together a limited number of airlines, hotels, or car-rental companies).

It is very difficult to come by data to evaluate whether these businesses even had time to benefit from an adequate return on these investments because in no time, others reached a higher level of Web inclusivity. They enclosed all-inclusive sites under one umbrella, also allowing you to choose your seating on an aircraft, an operation only possible on the airline's site until only a few months earlier.

The reason for this long description is for a purpose; it is to emphasize how fast and deeply single elements of innovation impact real lives, entire business models, possibilities, prospects, and an unquantifiable number of other variables and elements of our existing models (not just economic).

Coming back to Web-inclusivity, at this rate, is there anything stopping someone/entity from reaching the ultimate level of Web inclusivity, one that will allow users to fulfill all needs (business or otherwise), for example, to create a wish list and let the Web do the rest? Order their choice of dessert on the third evening of their hotel stay in a restaurant outside of their hotel? Have their houses cleaned, decide the best house insurance for their families, and the best deal for the tires on their cars that need replacement, all before they leave on vacation? Yet these possibilities are already reality in a growing number of solutions, situations, and places across the globe.

Innovation and Web Inclusivity will touch everyone, especially those generations that will follow. If it only took two decades for game-changing, technological breakthroughs that needed to be understood, accepted, implemented, etc., to substantially change the nature, timeframes, media, modalities, processes, and entire economic models that humanity has used for millennia, imagine how geometrically faster future sets of variables and innovations will affect individuals, interactions, processes, models, and so on, by the day.

Is Web inclusivity only affecting the travel sector though? Web inclusivity is not sector-specific. In the real world, things are aggregated into the Web inclusivity paradigm faster than what we might wish to consider. It is happening across all sectors. Web inclusivity is no longer confined to imaginary lines that separated distinct economic sectors (e.g., travel, retail, banking, real estate, construction) in our existing models for centuries.

In theory, this is great. Why go back and forth between many sites when one site can do all? But what does this imply? At what cost does this come to individuals, society, jobs, business, and the economy? Additionally, Web inclusivity also encompasses the many apps that are being developed and that are still separate distinct modules.

Taking into account the massive numbers of apps inundating the market, we may not be too far away from a scenario whereby the end user might just want a fully inclusive bundle of enabling apps for whatever he or she needs to do, based on their profile or historic usage, through his or her preferred medium (tablet, smartphone, etc.). This may include profession focused apps, to those for opening a hotel room door, to using it as a full-remote controller (to manage just about everything from toys to air-conditioning), etc., growingly replacing fully or partly many previously tools, media, human-run or managed processes, chores, or activities. Some of these technologies are already here.

Is this all though? Not long ago, visiting different sites meant obtaining different prices and choices. Higher levels of inclusivity may mean one can instantly assess market demand and supply. Could this impact the availability of prices and real choices? To what degree? In what time frames? What then? But more importantly, how will these affect individuals and their possible sources of income, business, investments, etc.? Will this also put challenges on the business models of suppliers, customers, and services unknown until recently, exerting the self-consuming "cost centric"–only logic paradigm (discussed later) even further? How far are we truly from that all-inclusive Web inclusivity paradox?

MOBINT: Mobile and Internet Convergence

Mobility is probably the true step-level revolution within the Internet revolution. It gave the Internet its legs to walk and be present virtually everywhere with its owner.

At this rate of convergence, when will we end up needing only one medium that does it all, one that can change its shape to fit different needs? "Mobint," we could call it, is the convergence between mobile technology and the Internet. For now, it provides directions to restaurants and access to online books or movies. It gives access to e-mails without the need for a PC. It enables online airline check-ins. In can even show if the refrigerator is running out of milk or open a garage door with a simple app.

It is clear that Mobint will evolve everything we currently know in ways still beyond our understanding. Its evolution might also foresee an additional new variable that could be called *media inclusivity*, i.e., the convergence of currently separate forms of media (PC, laptop, tablet, smartphone, gaming console, music, and video streamer emergency services radio and displays, military grade digital and communications equipment, etc.) into one multipurpose medium that can be physically transformed in size and shape to fit different needs.

A group of professors and researchers at the Massachusetts Institute of Technology are working on a new concept called "reality mining." The applications they have developed are based on the movements of cellphones. The apps can tell not only where users went but also how long they stayed in a particular room of a house, at what exact time they walked out of a room to walk into another room, with whom they might have been (if other phones were being tracked as well) and when they stepped out of the house. Among other things, the apps can tell if users were running, jogging, or walking.

What is fascinating is that, for those who sign up for the program on a voluntary basis, the researchers can predict future movements with a declared accuracy of around 95 percent. In conducting their study on a group of volunteers, they noticed common behavioral patterns of people who did not know each other. In the long run, for example, these patterns could make them prone to health problems such as diabetes. They maintained that if you share your movement information, they can advise you on potentially hazardous behaviors that increase your risk of and exposure to certain health problems.

The main concern is around privacy and the ability to exercise one's rights. That should include using one's proprietary data as one pleases. The paradox here is that our private information is already available to those who want to access it and use it. But what if they can change it, modify it, or distort it? People have a growing number of questions. For instance, can we change the model? If others are free to sell our information, why are we not benefiting from this or managing its distribution?

There are many schools of thought here. Some argue it would be a source of income. Others argue that if one has nothing to hide, one should not be worried. Still others argue that one's perception of oneself might be one thing, whereas the way the information is used or elaborated—and, hence, the way one ends up being perceived and exposed to judgment by others—might be a totally different story. How many people have lost their jobs because of what they deemed a perfectly normal life routine posted on the Internet?

Yet what is even more intriguing and requiring much more thought, reflection, and concern is that all the above considerations have been made with the underlying premise that internet will not be superseded and replaced by game-changing technological innovation beyond our current knowledge and perception. As with everything else man-made, Internet is bound to be superseded and replaced by a newer paradigm. At the current pace of innovation it is reasonable to think that this might occur sooner than we currently can guesstimate.

Additionally, the convergence of many "things" that today are still physically separated and activated via applets or programs on physical media, into a state of growing virtualization, interconnectivity, and inclusivity - in a not so distant future, might give way to new levels of convergence with our brain and or body, and simply become thought, voice or movement activated. What new worlds will this scenario open, what challenges will it entail, and what opportunities might it conceal?

Without being either too naïve or extreme, there is an objective need to concretely address issues such as human governance, exposure to the risks associated with of a state of *general inclusivity, virtuality, awareness,* and control on behalf of individuals, organizations or digital entities as described in previous chapters, is of strategic and fundamental importance.

Theoretically, for the first time in history, an *interconnected network of things* that could include hardware, software, machines, robotics, circuits, sensors, CPU's, memory, data, networks, switching, robotics, systems of industrial production, inventory, accounting, transaction, defense . . . and its possible continuous independent or guided mutation into something different, with no identifiable, specific, central reference point (e.g., location of its primary functions), might be able to have unlimited control over, and access to, all sources of human knowledge from the beginning of recorded human history, independent of language, level of encryption and secrecy, type and complexity of algorithm, topic, and level of detail of this knowledge; processes; activities; transactions; production; sources of energy, utilities (production and distribution); telecommunications, logistics, transportation, defensive, news, and information . . . all personal data of all individuals, all and everything human made anything that has interfaced with a computer since the beginning of the digital age. If one were to include the wealth of social media data which many today freely, and willingly, provide, share, and produce; this might create a material exposure to other possible risks involving human thought, emotions, interactions and behavior. In theory, there is no limit to what this scenario might be able evolve into.

Objectively, this scenario might also mean needing to factor-in and address eventual risks associated with its repercussions on employment, business processes, markets, control over strategic infrastructure and life support systems (i.e., food production, utilities) and so on.

To assure proper (human) governance, its onus and responsibility must be distributed over many individuals, entities and organizations at all levels within society.

Virtual Money, e-Money, and e-Wallets

Before we discuss these forward-looking elements, we should form an appreciation for how we got here from the physical to the virtual nature of money in a matter of only a few decades. So how is money generated in the current system? Thought there is much-heated debate and disagreement among economists, the prevalent description seems to be the following: one of the primary ways money is generated through the banking system is when money is created at a commercial bank level, when a bank grants a loan (McKenzie and Tullock 1978).

Every time a bank approves a loan, it provides funds via a cashier's check, a credit on an account balance, or an electronic fund transfer directly to an account—the bank creates new money. This action instantly increases the amount of money in circulation in an economy by the same amount. It is for this reason that many economists say that banks generate money when they give out loans.

The only thing stopping banks from going overboard with this (i.e., generating all the money they want) is that banks are restricted by two factors: the total amount of deposits they hold for customers and reserve requirements. The reserve requirement is usually expressed as a percentage of a bank's total demand deposits that cannot be loaned out and must be held on deposit with the Federal Reserve or in cash in the bank's vault.

Reserve requirements can be changed by the central banks at any time. Reserve requirements have nothing to do with the financial standing of banks or ensuring that banks can meet demand deposit requests. They simply exist to restrict the amount of money banks can create.

But if this is true, then is the system continuously generating money? Acting as counterweight to the money generation process—on the exact opposite end of the scale—as money is generated in the system, money is also eliminated by the system each time a loan is paid back, be it as an installment or in a lump sum. As absurd as it might sound, if a bank receives more loan repayments than it has requests for loans in particular periods, it will not be able to create as much money as it could. In fact, some bankers and economists dispute the necessity for reserve requirements and affirm that banks' restraints in generating money should be limited only to their profitability and credit standing.

Each loan generates a demand in the system that goes up the chain to the ultimate level of the central bank or the Federal Reserve. The demand for the loan (together with the aggregated demand for all other loans in the country) generates digital accounting entries upstream in the accounts of banks that are members of their relative central banks/Federal Reserve.

This process allows the central banks/Federal Reserve Banks that accumulate this data to control the flow of money into the economy (theoretically in line with a country's monetary policy) through a number of ways, increasing or casing the legal reserve requirements, as previously stated.

The money creation process is prone to problems. The control of the money supply in an economy is not as easy as it might sound. Central banks/Federal Reserve Banks have three main tools at their disposal to control money generation and availability:

- modifying the reserve requirements of commercial banks

- limiting the value of loans that central banks can make to commercial banks at discounted rates

- purchase or sale of government bonds or notes by a central bank/ Federal Reserve

De facto, the two key assumptions behind the balanced functioning of the system are that loans are continually issued in a normally functioning economy and that these loans are ultimately paid back. Do these underlying assumptions, though, still hold validity today? For example, if central banks or the Federal Reserve provides the banking system with injections of money, why then are these increasingly not reaching the real economy, as they used to not so long ago? This is yet another systemic dichotomy. The effects are visible all around the world.

The underlying message is not to jettison everything; instead, it is to ask ourselves what can be done better: *to find a solution, a better model, one that could be more beneficial and remunerative to all stakeholders whilst putting much needed systemic stability and credibility back into the system. The virtuality of money and its current generation modality are not a problem, but a key to the solution.*

Fortunately it is occurring at the right time from an evolutionary standpoint, facilitating the path toward a solution and apt to address the new challenges and variables. Just to provide an example, the emergence of new phenomena such as Bitcoin represent just a mere beginning of a much larger more important evolution taking place in the banking and financial industry. Would the virtuality of money not create the basis for a different rapport between different stakeholders (customers, banks, etc.)? Virtual money and its ramifications into e-money and e-wallet concepts is already an actuality.

If not already available in some parts of the world, in the imminent future a growing number of individuals and businesses will also be able to pay with their smartphones at the supermarket, movie theater, etc. Will this mean the end of credit and debit cards? What happens to many other processes that revolve around payments, transactions, and exchange of money? What about everything associated with the current physical nature of money, its management, security, distribution, and supply?

Will all this entail more synergies, mergers, cuts streamlining in businesses, processes, models, Web and media inclusivity, and Mobint? Will it force more businesses to close, generating more job losses? What impact will new models of virtual money have on existing and future business models?

Though no one has that sort of a view into the future, it is highly likely that the impact on the financial industry, and markets in general, will be profound, and transform the fundamental paradigms, models, and operations to their very core. Brute pragmatism of market logic dictates that only those firms and institutions that perceive this change, adapt, and adopt new business algorithm(s), paradigms and strategies will remain standing.

Next Generation Banking Finance and Markets

If we look at the growth of the primary market (to date) indexes around the world over a five-year historical horizon, a curious pattern seems to be forming. Each of these primary indexes seems to indicate that it has reached the same level as before the financial crisis in 2008 in a near-perfect V-shaped format. This could be good news and the auspice is that it is exactly that. Yet it is possible that we could be in front of yet another bubble. One of the differences between 2008 and today is that in 2008 there was still a real economy. Many businesses were still open, and they provided today's unemployed with real jobs.

Additionally, more and more financial experts and analysts have lately noticed a curious and alarming similarity between the trends of the stock market in the periods leading to the 1929 crash and the Dow Jones's performance index (e.g., McLellan n.d.).

What then? Governments have taken many steps to introduce mechanisms and instruments to reduce these eventualities. In the United States, for example, some of these have translated into the Dodd-Frank Wall Street Reform and Consumer Protection Act of 2010 (discussed later).

But in today's economic environment, do we need to arrive at a physical burst of a bubble for the repercussions of the underlying motives to hit the already frail recessive and emerging economies? How far can we stretch the model? Even more concerning, what might the impact of the next bubble burst be—what will it produce and how will it change the world we live in?

"Ouroboros"—The Snake-Beast That Ate Itself

Despite the bad press banks and the financial industry is receiving and the frustration and hard feelings it might spur, *to be perfectly balanced we need to remember that without this system most businesspersons would have never have had the opportunity to create and grow their enterprises, provide jobs, or pay salaries. Investors would have been unable to invest, individuals to buy homes and cars or send their young to university.* Speculation? Conspiracy? The truth might be simpler. For good or bad, all of the above respect what could be called the *fundamental axiom of money: money goes where money is to be made and has a possibility of being better remunerated.* It has always been like this; and historically, no human wall, law, religion, or political system seems to have changed this—for long at least. It is the nature of money. Not all is vice as there are many individuals and entities around the world that will put money to better and more productive uses.

Is it right? Is it wrong? Maybe the real query is whether, with money's intrinsic nature, we can leverage upon this mechanism to reduce its negative impact while improving its positive effect. In an evolved model, this will have nothing to do with a choice between electing one of the "isms" of the past.

Furthermore, if money is generated virtually through a relatively simple process—in a world where technology has eliminated barriers that once provided the foundations and cornerstones for the current model and the proper functioning of the system—would a new, evolved modality that achieves more benefits to the majority of stakeholders be possible? Can such (practical) models that can guarantee the remuneration, security, solidity, and control requirements needed by the system while addressing the shortcomings of the current system, be envisaged?

Reasonableness and impartiality are fundamental in both posing and addressing these tough questions. Undeniably, there is a concrete need for advancement in the current economic model and the banking system is one of its quintessential elements.

Evolution of this system may or may not lead to a possible separation of roles between institutional banks and those that wish to focus on financial markets. In fact, in the medium term, this might not be the central issue at all. In an evolved model, these arguments might not even be as relevant or they might lose their significance altogether.

No matter how we look at the matter, technological advancement, systemic dichotomies, new variables, and the need for an evolved model will bring about a transformation in the banking and financial markets industry, the result of which, in economic terms, will be similar to a renaissance or a big bang for this industry.

The banking system is on the brink of a new step-level evolution that will change its connotations as we know them today, providing greater benefits and new and evolved opportunities (for the market, investments, business, employment, customers, etc.) to many stakeholders and to the great majority of individuals—if planned, designed, rolled out, and managed properly. New enterprises and financial institutions that jump at the opportunity first will occupy the leadership positions. The rest will need to spend a lot of time, resources, and effort before they can catch up or at best become relegated to "me too" paradigms.

Also, because this sector will be hard-hit and heavily influenced by Web inclusivity and many other new and existing variables. Strategies devised to mitigate this phenomenon while harnessing new concepts must be implemented as soon as possible.

The evolutionary enhancement projects to be implemented will enable the financial/banking system to leverage new opportunities available on the new plateau(s).

The progress will be so extensive and profound that it will probably restore much of the needed trust in the real banking system in the eyes of the investors, businesses, and households; but what is more important, it will allow real banking to reoccupy a leadership position in creating business opportunities and value creation in areas that are still unknown.

Taking into account the extent of the changes the design and mechanics the evolved banking model will bring about, the specific argument could be better elaborated separately with adequate focus, diligence, and conscientiousness as the first banks to implement these changes will change the financial system forever, practically overnight and globally.

Banking, financial institutions, personal accounts, savings, financial systems, markets, transactions, and their processes and anything that has to do with money: how it is generated, exchanged, valued, invested . . . will increasingly shift toward new modes, modalities, and dimensions and change our current ways of doing business forever.

Networked Intelligent Systems and Apps

In the not-so-distant future, a company that manufactures widgets and needs fifty kilograms of any specific item will simply need to type in a request for it on the Web-inclusive app to find three suppliers immediately that have confirmed their product availability.

How will these variables impact intermediaries, supply chains, wholesalers, agents, exporters, importers, other websites, and industrial applications? What further implications might this have on known industrial or business models, processes, investments, and employment?

But networked intelligent systems, and applications are not only about things as we know them today, they involve innovations, and their yet to be discovered cause and effect implications in a myriad of other fields. This is probably one of the areas of greatest impact on our lives in the future—in every aspect of it. From the way we communicate and interact to how we think and how we do things.

To provide an idea of what we are talking about, we must make reference to the many advanced studies on the human brain that are being funded by the US and EU governments, just to name a few.

These studies not only serve to map, and understand how the human brain works but also how to leverage cerebral activity to activate, manage and control, embedded (in body) and/or out-of body organs, limbs, software, hardware, machinery, and robotics—currently through nano-sensors, and transmitters implanted in the brain, and other parts of the human body, enabling, among other things, the creation of direct connections to the web, but also interaction with networks of people, software, hardware, and theoretically any other machine, and robotics linked to the network—theoretically, on a planetary scale.

From a purely scientific point of view, the research currently being conducted, does not exclude the capability of integrating this type interaction also to other living beings, and the integration of these advances to human organs, cells, and even genetics. It is estimated that by the year 2020 some of these applications might no longer belong to the realm of science fiction.

Already there are many experiments that have surpassed the "proof-of-concept" phases, and many have translated into real life applications used in different fields.

This scenario adds to the complexity of the concepts of awareness, and the different types of inclusivity thus far discussed, opening a plethora of new areas of investigation, understanding, and concern—especially around those areas that will emerge from these advances and studies. Beyond everything else discussed thus far, we need for example, to understand how this transforms the most disparate things; from the necessity to convene for a meeting, to the need for business travel; from how we find/procure new sources of income, to how we generate sales, and revenues-in a world which is no longer today's world, in an economy that is growingly different from today's reality, in a reality that will increasingly belong to the previous century, the previous millennium, the previous era, and from which we are undeniably navigating away from.

e-Retail

Web inclusivity has impacted the retail business heavily in the past years. The official numbers of Internet sales on Web-inclusive websites are impressive and growing exponentially all over the world. Websites that were originally set up to sell only a specific item (e.g., books) have now become epicenters for just about anything one might wish to buy or sell.

Where is all this taking us? Will physical retail disappear? What could this mean to the current value chain made up of numerous businesses, professions, and stakeholders? To answer these questions, let us extrapolate the current model to a possible not-so-distant future of a type of merchandise that might still be a bit harder to separate from the physicality of a retail store, i.e., clothing.

Unlike a camera that you can buy on the Internet once you have investigated and identified it—not only in your own country, but also in a country that offers it at a substantially lower price (even considering transportation)—in order to buy clothing you are still, even though to reducing extent, in need of a physical store.

This is because you might wish to try on the clothing, compare it to other items, experience the joy of shopping, etc. But what if, in the near future, the manufacturer or designer gives you an opportunity to bypass the current retail model that needs your physical presence? Should a shopper wish to purchase nice apparel shown in a Web catalog, an advertisement, or simply seen in a shop, is there any real reason why he/she could not do this, and complete the purchase digitally?

The person would need to provide their digitized body scan directly to the factory with an app on a smartphone using an interactive modality so that she/he can immediately see a digitized version of themselves in the apparel.

This app could also personalize the skirt to fit her specific requirements, with an theoretically endless selection of buttons, zips, colors, accessories, etc., leading to the production (in an unknown location in the world) of a perfectly custom tailor-made skirt, giving no only the perception it is no longer mass produced, but also creating the potential for the individual of becoming a new fashion designer/creator supplanting or creating new competition for business models that took decades to build and defend, bypassing all the existing intermediaries at a considerably lower cost. Incredibly, since I started writing the book in 2006, this business model has already come into its early phases of existence. What will happen to the retail industry? What will be its business model? What might be the *consequences to other industries in the supply chain or adjacent sectors, such as construction and real estate, the publishing and advertising industries, and their supply chains*? What might the impact be in terms of additional business closures and unemployment? What about the investors?

The answers that emerge seem crudely to point toward one conclusion: the gravitational pull of what we could call the Virtus *law of inclusivity* that states that: in the absence of opposing forces such as uniqueness, smaller elements of a paradigm are theoretically bound to group together around ever-larger cores.

In the same way that the gravitational force pulls particles and atoms together to form stars, planets, and galaxies, Web inclusivity seems to be governed by comparable laws, pulling everything together around ever-larger concentrations of Internet matter.

Independently of how many sites we populate the web with in the future, is Web inclusivity the Internet's natural essence? Are the systemic shortcomings and dichotomies of the current model more evident now? And how it will touch everyone in every country? How does this now change the perception of BRIC[11] or other apparently "healthier" economies?

Will this not touch investors as well? Are we not all in similar boats—just distanced temporally? Are the current economic models geared to address these issues or have they provided effective remedies? Can we afford to stick to these existing models? Are we trying to resolve issues and challenges that have a different DNA than our current model?

[11.]   Brazil, Russia, India, China

Nanotechnology

A nanometer is equivalent to one billionth of a meter. A nanometer is so small that it is said to be the size of a handful of atoms. Nanomaterials are not only made by humans. As the GAO report (2010) states, "Nanomaterials can occur naturally, be created incidentally, or be manufactured intentionally.

Naturally occurring nanomaterials can be found in volcanic ash, forest fire smoke, and ocean spray. Incidental nanomaterials are by-products of industrial processes, such as mining and metal working, and combustion engines, such as those used in cars, trucks, and some trains" (1). Human-made nanomaterials instead are developed for a particular application, "such as improved strength, decreased weight, or increased electrical conductivity" (GAO 2010, 1).

Nanotechnology introduces another, extremely impactful, game-changing element. In this context the term "nano" refers to the size of miniaturized technology. Miniaturized technology is best known for things such as the electronic circuit boards that reside in a computer's CPU or other current-day electronic equipment. Nanotechnology, however, will bring the further miniaturization of products and processes down to scales in the nanometer range.

Current technological theorists state that this will dramatically impact the need for resources to build and supply the factories, hospitals, offices, and infrastructures of tomorrow and most of the machinery needed to run them—but also the size of products and currently unfathomable impacts in many other dimensions affecting our lives as individuals, organizations, businesses, and governance.

The reduction in size means saving trillions of tons of raw materials used for the production of the same products. It also impacts processes that, in turn, affect how everything is organized, the amount of physical space needed, energy consumption requirements, the business models, the final size of these products, enterprises and employment.

At the same time, one could venture to say that *the move toward miniaturization is probably one of the first concrete moves of humanity toward real sustainability*. Imagine how many things would not be possible today had we not reached this level of technological breakthrough and how many things might be possible tomorrow. Nanotechnology has as many benefits as it does shortcomings. Much work still needs to be done to make it safer, nonhazardous to human health, and controllable. But let us begin with some of the upsides.

In the field of medicine, for instance, things impossible only last year could become possible by working at molecular levels. Healing and combating viruses or tumors—at dimensions either equivalent to or infinitely smaller than the viruses—could involve becoming a virus's own virus or acting as a transportation vehicle for delivering medicine to specific cells. This would save the patient's healthy cells by putting them out of harm's way from the drastic side effects of many medicines or of invasive surgery.

To be impartial though, there are also several medical studies, which argue against some the declared benefits of these solutions and provide valuable insight with regards to problem areas that need to be considered. Imagine nano-robots that destroy a tumor, down to the last cell, and then apply only a finite level of chemo- or biotherapy to those cells that need it. Scientists will finally be able to study the inner workings of maladies that have plagued humankind in ways unfathomable until today and finally provide real answers to what today are incurable illnesses.

New performance material will emerge for new applications, affecting every sphere of our lives. Production processes might end up being cleaner (under stringent conditions, i.e., if, for example, they are done under vacuum or in sealed areas) and less damaging to the environment, providing new answers and solutions to previously irresolvable or economically nonviable investments and business enterprises, employment, etc.

On the other hand, new challenges will emerge: how to prevent nanostructures from being dispersed outside their needed space of operations and keeping them active only for the time necessary, preventing them from becoming airborne or waterborne hazards involuntarily entering ecosystems or sensitive membranes of the body, such as the lungs or the brain.

Let us now start examining some of the shortcomings, concerns, and challenges surrounding nanotechnology today.

Areas of Current Concerns, Risks, and Needed Improvement

According to a report produced by the US Government Accountability Office (GAO 2010), the following is a non-exhaustive list of findings of different research conducted to evaluate different aspects of nanotechnology:

1. Properties, surface, reactions, and interactions of nanomaterial. There is not enough information about unfamiliar properties/ types/interactions/reactions that can materialize at nano scales.[12] It would seem that at those atomic levels, properties, and interactions could "differ in important ways from the properties of conventionally scaled materials" (GAO 2010, 1). Studies would indicate that some nano-scale particles, for example, "may be potentially explosive and/or photoactive" (24)—meaning that sunlight might trigger chemical reactions in them.

   Additionally, because of their very small dimensions, nanomaterials can enter the human body through: inhalation, ingestion, and dermal (skin) penetration. As stated by the GAO's (2010) report, in some cases size "may pose a risk to human health because these materials may be able to penetrate cell walls, causing cell inflammation and potentially leading to certain diseases. . . ." (23–24). Moreover, humans, the environment may also be exposed to nanomaterials through releases into the water, air, and soil during the manufacture, use, or disposal of these materials with unknown effects on flora and fauna.

2. Shape. "The shape of nanomaterials may be connected to the type of health risks they may pose. For example, some carbon nanotubes resemble asbestos fibers known to cause mesothelioma" (GAO 2010, 24).

3. Militarized use. There are many applications where this technology can be a strategic advantage of unfathomable destructive capability. On the other hand, the problem is the

---

[12.] e.g., chemical, photoactive, electrical, magnetic, thermal, mechanical, optical

uncontrollability associated with size and shape—hence, unwanted dispersion affecting friendly forces.

Opportunities

According to the same report, "The world market for nanotechnology-related products is growing and is expected to total between $1 trillion and $2.6 trillion by 2015" (GAO 2010, 1). The report goes on to provide concrete examples of nanotechnology uses in different sectors:

Civilian and Aerospace and Defense Applications

Examples of areas of possible application of nanomaterials in both civil and aerospace and defense arenas are

- nano weapons, sensors, surveillance, and delivery systems/platforms;

- stronger and lighter material for aircraft bodies that also offer are better protection against lightning and fire;

- microbe-free interiors of aircraft and clean rooms; and

- clothing material that can change color or match mood or environment, or become rigid to protect injuries, or help block bullets and/or chemical and/or biological agents.

Advanced Electronics

In the electronics sector, apart from the known effects on size-reduction in circuitry, lead-free, conductive adhesives could eliminate tons of toxic and leaded solder used every year by some industries, leading to more efficient and longer-lasting data storage with an estimated storage capacity of one terabyte per square inch while micro-batteries may open the door to many new applications.

Robotics

Advanced robotics is used not only in manufacturing, mining, and other places where there are particularly dangerous working conditions, but also in hospitals and other industries where precision and time-related issues are key requirements. Robotics is used to perform ever-increasing numbers of tasks previously performed by humans that have undesired consequences on human health. Robotics is also used increasingly in advanced studies, outer space explorations, deep ocean surveys, maintenance, and salvage operations. A form of robotics is used in unmanned vehicles in the military and civilian fields.

For now, each of these is mission-specific. For example, some vehicles can only fly on intelligence-gathering missions over enemy territory. Alternatively, they can act as mini-helicopters that can hover. They can also be used to search for and destroy explosive devices. They can be waterborne, acting as fast-moving patrol boats, or they can do underwater maintenance work for oil companies. The possible application of nanotechnology to this area is vast and its implications astounding and noteworthy.

Medical

This particular area is the fulcrum of much debate and opposing views. Nanoscale sensors could be used to identify biomarkers, such as altered genes and early indicators of cancer and show presence, location, and contours of cardiovascular and neurological diseases and small tumors. They could track particles to the site of a tumor, resulting in earlier detection of tumors. Nano-instruments could allow continuous and detailed health monitoring while other applications could include the following:

- producing enhanced images from deep inside human tissue used to guide surgical procedures and monitor the effectiveness of nonsurgical therapies in reversing the disease or slowing its progression

- less invasive and painful drug delivery and accuracy, additionally turning a drug into a multifunctional tool or platform for diagnosis and treatment

- antimicrobial wound dressings, requiring fewer excruciating dressing changes for patients

- delivery platforms for targeted interventions such as "gold nanoshells . . . [to] image and destroy cancer cells using infrared light . . . kill[ing] tumor cells without disturbing neighboring healthy cells . . . [potentially reducing] the amount of chemotherapy" as suggested by the National Institutes of Health (GAO 2010, 21)

- healing burns, mesh scaffolds to treat bone, nerve, cartilage, and muscle injuries, improving, or stopping the flow of blood and other liquids

Mind-Activated Applications and Processes and Mind Capability Augmentation

Several researchers, universities, and institutions around the world are making the final tweaks to these applications, opening the way to currently unpredictable uses, such as allowing differently abled people to perform tasks, see, and hear—impossible only a few years ago. Its industrial and personal uses are theoretically endless and anyone's guess is good.

Many advanced studies have yielded concrete results also in the area of mind capability augmentation. Tests thus far have concluded that expert capability can be acquired artificially via electromagnetic stimulation to the brain through new applications. This stimulus seems to augment synapse generation or activity in specific areas of the brain, allowing people to acquire capabilities that would otherwise require years of training to develop.

The example here involved creating expert capability in intelligence analysts in evaluating aerial photographs and finding enemy targets in a very limited timeframe (weeks?) that would have otherwise required years of training and experience to develop.

The degree to which this might be achievable (net of yet to be understood undesired side effects) might imply an advancement in human learning unparalleled in history—completely altering many of our millennia-old dogmas, models, and convictions, not only in the area of education.

Environment

Applications here can range from cleaning up waste to substituting nonrenewable resources with renewable ones, to reducing pollution, to increasing the efficiency of solar power generation (GAO 2010, 15). Using nanoscale catalysts, hydrogen could be produced from water up to six times more efficiently. In addition, nanotechnology-enabled water desalination and filtration systems may offer affordable, scalable, and portable water filtration in the future. Filters have the potential to allow water molecules to pass through but screen out salt ions, bacteria, viruses, heavy metals, and organic material.

Energy Saving and Next-Generation Alternative Energy

Nanomaterials could improve the efficiency of energy transmission by increasing the capacity and durability of insulation for underground electrical cables. This would allow smaller cables to carry one hundred times more power than larger cables and to last longer whilst reducing transmission losses, saving billions of dollars in fuel consumption (equivalent to 24 million barrels of oil just in the United States, according to the study). Many new advances in this arena are making headlines each day. New technology is allowing, for instance, a substantial reduction in solar panel sizes and costs while increasing performance levels n-fold. In another example, the US Navy Research Laboratory believes it may be possible to make jet fuel derived from seawater (JP-5) on board ships (IHS Jane's International News Briefs n.d.).

Food Production and Agriculture

Applications in this sector range from strong oxygen and carbon dioxide barriers in plastic bottles and films for packaging food and beverages to "encapsulation."[13] to agriculture enhancement; monitor

---

[13.] Delivering material inside the human body to target nutrients release drugs on a controlled schedule, and mask tastes—for example, some vitamins are difficult to deliver in beverages because they degrade and may not be easily absorbed by the body.

food quality and freshness; track food products from point of origin to retail sale; and modify the taste, texture, and fat content of food. Nanomaterials will administer pesticides, herbicides, and fertilizers more efficiently and safely by controlling more precisely when and where they are released and in what quantities. Sensors can detect bacteria such as salmonella in water and liquid food and contamination of crops, such as spinach, lettuce, and tomatoes, potentially reducing the spread of food-borne illnesses. Nano radio–frequency identification tags could be integrated into packaging for food products, potentially resulting in improved food security and better inventory tracking and management.

Additive Manufacturing and 3D printing

Additive manufacturing, though still in its infancy, is already being put to use in real-world applications. The current manufacturing process usually starts with a slab of material (such as a sheet or a block of aluminum), which is then machined down and creates great levels of waste and raw material.

Additive manufacturing uses a revolutionary technique that flips the entire model around. It works at molecular levels, building objects that have been designed on a PC using advanced 3-D technology to create the object from a printer that, instead of spraying ink, sprays tiny particles of matter. As the particles settle, row after row, the "printer head" moves back and forth, stacking the rows of fused material one on top of the other until the object materializes in front of your eyes from the bottom up. The use of nanotechnology in this new area could have multiplicative effects.

Exoskeleton Applications

This technology is already in use and will have many possible applications in diverse fields. In the medical field, it could help injured individuals and veterans, paraplegics or other differently abled people to improve their freedom of movement and quality of life. In construction, mining, and labor-intensive industries it could reduce exposure of workers to injury, improving delivery timetables and making more types of task achievable.

In the fields of applied sciences, research, mining, marine applications, or anything requiring significant amounts of muscle (but not enough to require specific larger machinery), this application could provide new answers. Combining nanotechnology with exoskeleton applications could yield many more possibilities.

Other Nano Applications

Many other examples could be in the areas of personal care and cosmetics products; performance improvement and reinforcement of many day-to-day items such as bicycle frames, tennis rackets, baseball bats, hockey sticks, skis, and tennis balls; new water- and stain-resistant, power-generating clothing; stronger, smoother, more scratch, dust and stain resistant surfaces; more efficient and longer-lasting data storage; more energy-efficient, robust yet flexible, readjustable (assuming the original shape after being solicited) construction materials; alternative energy and reduced consumption.

Undeniably, new technology development and commercialization require a phased rollout. Their use or the timeframes involved are no longer in question. The questions rather are how these will impact our existing models? Which existing models are geared to address and leverage these new game-changing variables? How will we be able to exploit the opportunities they offer to create sustainable, long-term development, prosperity, and security whilst adequately addressing concerns, shortcomings, and risk areas associated with this new technology.

Important Considerations

Unless conspiracy theorists and doomsday catastrophists are right that there is no lasting solution in sight, there is a way out. Before we seek a solution, we need to review an important set of considerations:

- The Internet and mobility bring many opportunities but have their shortcomings.

- Web inclusivity is a reality, and it must be considered and addressed.

- Mobint and Web inclusivity continue to impact our lives dramatically in all spheres, from investments to business to employment to KES[A].

- The impact of nanotechnology on current models, process, and everyday life will be astonishing.

- Mobint and KES[A] are variables formed from a different/evolved DNA.;

- These variables constitute game- and paradigm-changing dichotomies and systemic blocks to our existing models.

- Our existing models have difficulty in appropriately addressing new variables and, in a growing number of cases, are not equipped to tackle the many new challenges posed by technological advancements.

- But in the same way that each coin has two faces, these variables and innovations also open the door to many opportunities.

The successful strategy lies in understanding how they operate and how they affect our lives. Once this is achieved, we can understand how to leverage their strengths, manage them, and exploit their true potential.

What could be defined as the law of Technological Innovation, Advancement, and Inclusivity or TIAI (which encapsulates Web

+ Mobint + Nano + Robotics and Nanotechnology and other advancements) contemplates the merging of new technology into something that might go beyond the tablets and smartphones we have become accustomed to over the last few years into *higher levels of inclusivity in different domains affecting every-single-area-and-facet of human activity and interaction.* Innovation in nanotechnology, for instance, might bring about media invisible to the naked eye in their standby state, which can be enlarged simply by hand motions and or *mind-activated* via *neuronal communication and data exchange.*

Media may become virtual screens of the size necessary for different uses—from watching TV in 3D (or more) on displays larger than the current sixty inches, which we can temporarily hang or place where we wish, to converting them into picture-in-picture screens where we can develop our thoughts without having to type them while watching the news, receiving an e-mail, etc.

It might allow us to reduce the size of the display to that of a handheld device to access any information we might need at any time in a private modality—for example, on a plane—or size it down to an object as small as a coin—or fit it into any medium such as eyeglasses or contact lenses. Such a display could become a phone on the move without the need to have a physically visible smartphone, TV, tablet, PC, movie and picture camera, wallet, ID, driver's license, document container, music/film/picture database, travel agent, personal assistant, trainer, medical advisor, idea manager, social network manager, calendar, apps list, stereo system, etc. It could be whatever we would like it to be.

Yet, all of these areas of advancement represent just the tip of greater number of icebergs. In fact, these innovations do not consider the wider possibilities deriving from other advancements in all other scientific fields, and the incalculable number of possible interconnections with biotechnology, medicine, physics, electronics, nature, the human body... and so on.

So how and where do we go from here? How many businesses, investments, and jobs will be lost or gained from these innovations? What impact will these innovations have on the economy at large, independent of geographical location? Will there be an economy, as we know it? What form will our economies take in the near future? Is this the end of the road? Or the beginning of a new era?

Without being ingenuous about things, it should now be clear why (in the medium- long-term) it does not really make a difference what emerging nations such as BRIC nations are up to today, if they are using the same reference model. Our destinies are interconnected on a planetary scale more than we might wish to think.

Once the current economic model peaks (in my modest opinion if not already there we are possibly very close), it will produce the same effects on the neo-economic giants as it did with developed ones—with an impact relative to their sizes or even worse, if unknown cumulative effects come into play. Entire echelons of society are disappearing on a global scale—the middle class being the first and most affected in the immediate term. Should things remain unchanged, are we sure that anyone might remain unaffected by it? To what degree?

Reactions, Implications, and Effects

There are several natural reactions to advancement, technology, and innovation: curiosity, opportunism, irony, contemplation, cynicism, extremism, conspiracy theories, and so forth. Although productive in healthy debates, each of these stances might—or might not—add anything to the equation of how to address a step-level evolutionary transformation that is already taking place.

It is necessary to understand how these innovations will continue to transform our lives, beyond what has been discussed thus far, i.e., investments, business models, employment, processes, etc. and their implications. We must understand how each of these innovations affects other elements making up the existing economic model.

Now that we have looked at a minute number of new technologies and some the challenges innovation, new game-changing variables pose (touching possibly only a very small fraction of the total new technological innovation being created today), in the remaining chapters of part 1, we will touch on some of the challenges these generate for business, stakeholders and the economy.

Business Challenges in the Twenty-first Century

This chapter wishes to go beyond the abundant literature available on the failures and shortcomings of globalization, and single/sector specific challenges businesses face. To-date, growth for a business, in economic terms, has come primarily through two means: non-organically through the acquisition of a competitor, technology... or organically by winning and taking more space in the market, be it in the form of more space on a supermarket shelf, a new customer, or an increased share in a territory. Any space left in a market will be filled by others, so long as there is a demand for it. A business is usually fueled by the future and the potential for growth.

However, this requires critical capabilities, such as riding successive waves of newly evolved products and services (P/S) and activating and maintaining an innovation loop. As sales for certain P/S in a portfolio begin to accelerate, the true entrepreneur is already ahead of the competition if he or she is already finding a replacement for it, as demonstrated in the following diagram.

Innovation Cycle Activation Capability for Products or Services (P/S):

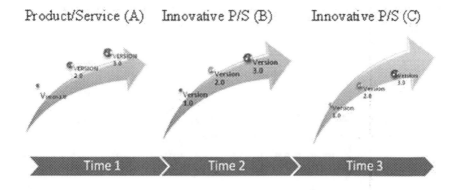

Success and long-term survivability need a fine balancing act in choosing the right moment to invest in innovation and selling off parts of the portfolio to those who business that have economies of scale and strategies best fit to take these forward in more meaningful and profitable ways. Should the timing be miscalculated, the future of a business is at risk. It is a continuum—a bicycle that needs to be pedaled continuously throughout each cycle. So long as it is done properly, it will increase the probability of a place among the first few in the introduction of a market-winning idea at each turn. For some executive teams, it is not hard sometimes to become self-indulgent. Provided it does not happen often, some can afford to lose a few contests. What we could call the *strategic success mix* is another element indispensable to survivability.

Non-organic growth (buying/selling businesses, technology...) presupposes the full awareness of a very important axiom: The intent of the seller might be straight-forward or not at all. The liquidity the seller achieves, drains vital resources from the buyer which can be used to destroy its competitor once and for all with a totally new evolved much less costly business model. The case of Rockefeller and J.P. Morgan is emblematic. This axiom however, is also valid for a nation and its government's strategic stance. It is essential to keep this axiom in mind before any strategic decision is made.

Similarly, poor leadership, misguided focus, dispersion, entropy, indecision, and lack of strategic vision can also contribute to the ultimate collapse of any organization. Many premonitory signs and indicators can show if a company is on the road to failure. One of these is simply recognizing that the minute a company becomes more internally oriented and cost-focused it has reached a pivotal point in its success cycle. If it fails to acknowledge this and jump onto a newly forming innovation wave, its surfing time will be over as fast as the wave on which it is currently riding loses energy and momentum, unless it is strategically focusing on the next wave.

One does not have to go too far to find real-life examples. The overused example of the Apple comeback is a perfect case in point. What needs to be emphasized is that this took place in today's economic environment, with the globalization factor, the credit crunch, and the many other challenges facing businesses in this unique recessive period. Samsung's surprising growth in areas previously dominated by others (smartphones, TV's, etc.) is another example.

To put things into context, one must also add that Apple and Samsung operate in one of the most competitive industries. Brand names that not long ago made headlines have subsided as companies have stood still instead of continuing to innovate. What made Apple and Samsung's successful was strategic vision and leadership, among other things.

Continuously creating a new factual or perceived level value and quality, that outweighs costs in a customers mind, through constant innovation, is the substance that separates winners from the rest in any industry or organization. So long as a business model is aligned with this axiom, it has better chances of success—and name, clout, image, size, brand, market share/reach cannot but be subservient to this. When economic concerns are shortsighted or miss strategic objectives, they start falling into an inevitable cost-centric vortex from which it is exceptionally difficult to rise. This vortex is usually preceded by a set of formal organizational communications that sound very much like mantras anticipating change-management projects. These mantras can be presented as "shared service centers," "streamlining," "rightsizing," "delocalization," "outsourcing," "redundancy," and "plant closures." In essence, these concepts are not new. Companies have always been focused on generating profits and returns on investments for their stakeholders, and they have always been looking for innovative ways to reduce costs and improve efficiency. What is different is the time variable.

A company's reaction time is becoming increasingly reduced also due to market-driven requirements, short mandates of key executives, short-sighted objectives not tied to any long-term strategy, unwillingness/inconvenience to tackle more challenging feats at the core, creating new value propositions.

Many expert articles published by authoritative media such as Harvard Business Review, McKinsey Quarterly, Deloitte and Pricewaterhousecoopers reports, all too often confirm that companies entering a cost-only focused trimming exercise, not having finished the first round of these programs, all too soon find themselves having to repeat the exercise—opening decade-long vicious self-consuming cycles of continued cuts. One of the underlying motives for failure of such activities that the above exercises exclude or do not necessarily properly convey a very important notion: growing the business and creating new value.

Were the primary pillars and scope of a going concern and a healthy business not also those of growth, profitability, returns on investment, market shares, competitiveness, etc.? Yet the process is a logical one, under the existing economic model. If data suggests that revenue outlooks are dim, the only other variable deemed to be left is cost—allegedly because it should (?) bring faster results. But even more unique is that this behavior was (and still is) activated across the board in every economic sector quite simultaneously.

So was this driven by madness? Some sort of collusion? Objectively and reasonably, probably not. More times than not the answer is more logical—not necessarily right. In the last two decades or so, increasing numbers of think tanks, economists, universities, and top-ranking strategy consulting firms have been engaged by industry and governments alike to analyze economic outlooks. After much analysis, most came back with similar scenarios:

- A paradigm of increasing market shares internationally could no longer be sustained.

- Emerging countries required more and more localized stakes, participation, and independence.

- More players from emerging countries entered the markets in the globalized world with economies of scale that could not be rivaled easily. In the case of China and India,[14] in numerous cases it would be nearly impossible to replicate their cost base or compete on costs unless this is not achieved via investments game-changing innovation.

- Market forecasts indicated saturation and stiffening competition.

- In many sectors, old paradigms centered around reaching double-digit growth and returns on investments above a certain percentage were deemed no longer possible.

- The invention of new technology projected a move away from intensive industrial and physical asset models toward newer ideas—christened by some as the new industrial revolution.

The need to change strategy rapidly was made evident to investors in developed countries. Since change does not happen overnight, finding a bridge strategy of disengagement was necessary. Many large businesses that had access to this wealth of information went and continue going into cost-centric mode, laying-off, delocalizing, and disposing of whole or

---

14. Recently even these countries are looking for cheaper labor bases outside their own respective countries.

parts of businesses. The focus: cashing in before sales, profits, and share prices started to be affected significantly. Were the think tanks wrong?

Though it is hard to predict the future, the projections are logical. But was the reaction correct? Though it is easy to understand how boardroom decisions were influenced by short-term logic and necessities and why no one might have wished to go against the flow, it is more difficult to understand how the overall impact on national economies of such parceled decision making failed to become a geopolitical issue, at least one that addressed this before allowing things to reach the stage they have reached.

While businesses need to be free to execute the strategy they deem best, from a macroeconomic perspective, it should be equally important to evaluate the overall impact on the general economies, assess how this affects geopolitical balances, and provide general direction to avoid or at least mitigate the occurrence of scenarios with extreme economic impact.

It is both credible and plausible that many steps were taken, however, it may be equally plausible that many voices were not heard. In an analogy, everyone jumping ship without necessarily needing to do so at the same time is a grave event. If everyone had jumped ship from all of the US Pacific Fleet on the days preceding the naval battle of Midway as US code-breakers caught the first glimpse of the monstrous disadvantage in forces they were going to be dealing with, that would have been a totally different affair, one with a devastating leadership failure, formidable consequences, and unknown historical repercussions.

Adopting a winning strategy, through a different reference model is what allowed the US Pacific Fleet to work against enormous odds. To be fair, to put things back on track is far more difficult for today's leadership if it does not start to think beyond the current reference models to find a winning strategy. A strategy than must start considering the compound effect on an economy and corporations if at each downward turn in the spiral, an ever-increasing number of investments, businesses, jobs, markets, and customers are lost.

Unfortunately, there are other effects on the economy holistically and in geopolitical terms. The following is a possible sample:

- loss of strategic competitiveness

- increased dependence on others

- loss of freedom of movement

- loss of momentum

- loss of rcsilicncc

- loss of credibility and gravitas

- loss of relative weight in international fora

- loss of representativeness

- loss of economic returns

- loss of leverage capability

- loss of critical decision-making possibilities

- decreasing levels of freedom, choice, and alternatives

And what might be least apparent is the potentially impact on the intrinsic devaluation of shareholder value and stock prices (different from their official market value), consequential exposure to economic loss, and initiation of another self-consuming loop. Unfortunately, so long as the reference economic models remain the same, paradoxically, decisions undertaken by boards, investors, executives, and businesspeople—in absence of new perspectives, reference models, and strategic vision may pass, or be considered as justified since they may perceive to have very little pragmatic maneuvering ground. But until when, and for how much longer?

Effects on Customers, Suppliers

In this section we try to understand the impact of the current crisis and cost-centric focus from the customers' and the suppliers' points of view, but also as it concerns the effectiveness of the roles individuals play (professionals, employees, management, senior executives, or shareholders). From the customers' point of view—be they businesses or individuals—cost-focus increasingly influences the following critical elements to the point of becoming *key failure factors* for many businesses (a few examples):

- Quality and uniqueness of an increasing number of brands, products, or services. Notwithstanding the enormous comparative means the web provides, ever more brands which were historically associated with different manufacturers, providers and quality levels are now being produced by the same manufacturer overseas and or joint/third party operated; hence, the true demarcation line between them is becoming very difficult to assess.

- Customer intimacy and the distancing of customers from businesses: what was once considered a fundamental pillar of success for a business; the invaluable interaction and human relationship with a customer is being increasingly reduced, de-humanized, transformed or jettisoned by businesses. Travel to meet customers, listening to their feedback, presenting new ideas, exchanging thoughts, addressing concerns and resolving issues, building and fostering rapports, networks, etc., are being increasingly relegated to a webpage, conference calls, call centers, or webinars. Increasingly, notwithstanding the breadth of additional resources technology provides, more and more business concerns and organizations are rubber-walling their interaction, reducing contact possibilities, automating customer feedback, automated call-centering without truly addressing customer requirements, or impeding interaction via no-reply e-mails and text messages—exasperating and frustrating customers and increasingly reducing contact references on all media. While opening Internet-based channels into organizations has in the past created many challenges (i.e., security, spam), adopting a *communication negation strategy* is not proving effective either.

Until new models evolve to improve human experience, customer intimacy and retention, most business face a real dilemma—real customer relations. While this is not about the real advantages of innovation that need to be levered, if left unaddressed, this silent killer virus can strike large organizations astonishingly quickly.

- Diminishing value added services are post-sales support (value, effectiveness, quality); warrantee, guarantees, product life.

- Exposing customers to financial loss, fraud, etc., deriving from a growing number of unrequested and unwanted pushed services, apps, e-mails, interruptive in-your-face-promotions / communications / video's, etc., that thrive due to a lack of common international and cross-border customer friendly accepted norms/modalities, legislation, enforceability and punishability of offenders and defrauders, etc.

In a cost-sensitive economic spiral, the destructive effects of this self-consuming paradigm appear even more evident in a business-to-business scenario. As parts of businesses are merged, sold, or outsourced, ever-larger numbers of economic concerns and organizations remain increasingly devoid of the products and services and the quality levels for which they once were renowned.

In this environment, from a supplier's point of view, one of the survival strategies is positioning the business in the crowded space known as the "prime contractor" or system integrator space (not necessarily the one making most of the money, but simply the one on top of the pyramid). Primes and integrators in turn become collectors and coordinators of layers of subcontractors below them, each of which in turn seeks to create a pyramid under it.

As increasingly improbable cost centered tenders are launched, requiring best-in-class products and best performance for lowest price, shifting the problem to the bidders/suppliers. Desperate to win, in a growing number of cases, suppliers revert to "*dumping*"[15] with the hope of recuperating costs somewhere down the line through more sales to the same customer or through future business deriving from after-sales services such as maintenance.

This practice leaves declining chunks of real in-house business for each company in the supply chain, virtualizing their added value and

---

[15]. Selling at the lowest possible price, sometimes below cost, to win.

forcing the same logic down the chain in order to remain in business. Ultimately this reactivates the cost-centric vortex of cuts. What is more, in today's economic scenario of lowering budgets, dumping with the hope of recuperating later with additional business might simply be a chimera in a growing number of cases.

This self-consuming cycle has increased in the last few years and has eroded the fundamental blocks of the real economy since the financial crisis began. Reduced access to financing, decreased demand as structural real unemployment rises, higher taxation, and cyclical stringent austerity measures only add to the problem and suffocate any leftover business. Even more importantly, after a cost-cutting spiral, the amount of money left to invest in research and development (R&D) and, in general, innovation is curtailed.

Programs on which millions have been spent are dumped, frozen, or halted as it simply becomes easier and less costly to put someone else's product in the bundle offering for the customer or, in a best-case scenario, buy the company that supplies the specific product or service. Programs, ideas, and licenses that once formed the lifeblood for future business growth become objects to sell off to the highest bidder. In many cases, this forces businesses to lose their competitive edge, which requires much time and cost just to recover.

Left with lesser chunks of business to capture, suppliers revert to mergers and acquisitions as a strategy of increasing survival possibilities. Competitors are bought, hopefully for their market share, so that the sum of the two companies will create enough synergy and complementarity to bring about the so-called $1 + 1 \geq 3$ result. According to this notion, the sum of the two should yield an organization that will produce, not twice the business volume, but something in the order of more than or equal to three times this.

Many mergers and acquisitions (M&A) analysts, investment banking firms, consulting firms, and executives, however, know all too well that although this particular objective is theoretically achievable or even logical on paper and has in some cases been achieved, in many cases, this does not materialize, especially in economically difficult times.

Any readily available website dealing with M&A will provide ample insight into the very low success rate of corporate marriages (sometimes in excess of 70 percent fail to integrate). The few successful examples are due to particular factors. One such factor is an acquiring company investing in a post-merger/acquisition program and sticking to it meticulously. This requires a lot of money, time, and resources, but mostly capable and confident leadership with a vision.

After consolidation be it as a result of a merger, acquisition, or simply an incorporation/fusion of owned companies into divisions of the holding, the resulting company is usually, physically, a much-bigger concern, theoretically with access to complementary products, services, markets, and a larger customer base. On the other tip of the scale, the new larger entity ends up dealing with at least a subset of the following challenges: redundancy, duplication/conflict of processes, and different methodologies, approaches to customers, procedures, systems, production facilities, offices, organizations, corporate cultures, strategies, etc.

What is least evident in most cases is that what is logical on paper, in many cases, is not so in reality, especially when it comes to acquisitions, mergers, or fusions—as important levers and key success factors—vital to each piece are lost in the processes. In many cases, the organization impedes itself from being effective in the marketplace while competitors fill the void that is created by the introspective focus, without proper consideration of the effect on the companies' prospects, customers, markets, etc.

Factually, senior management mandates are scope, time and or task limited—hence with hardly any room for delivering any other objective. The extent of damage this exercise creates is not known until it is too late, as valuable expertise, management capability, and established networks (all the results of costly experience) are lost, generating increasing levels of entropy, insecurity, disaffection, cynicism, loss of morale, and knowledge, which no current knowledge-sharing tool can replace, at least for now. Valuable employees jump ship as soon as they can in order to avoid being laid off or become redundant.

In any merger, the buyer in more cases than not will (whatever the contractual clauses stipulated to protect key high-level management figures from being fired for a certain timeframe) dispose of the bought-out executive team through different means. The new consolidated company soon finds itself with a gargantuan gap in understanding how the other half or bits of the company works and ticks. Offices that once acted as central locations lose importance and the new companies leave them on their own.

The inevitable results of these cyclical cuts are less populated organizations. Note that the term "lean" was not used since this suggests that an organization embodying this adjective is healthy. What is hidden from the official income statements and balance sheets are time bomb–like liabilities with long-lasting destructive effects. Organizations might be left with a mix of killer viruses detrimental to human establishments of any type: reduced resilience; reduced innovation and modernization capability; curtailed strategic focus; entropy; lack of clarity and direction, even in day-to-day activities; reduced confidence in strategy and management; immunity toward yet another round of costly change-management programs; indifference; and a reduced sense of belonging, usefulness, pride, and ownership.

Forced by an inward-looking logic, organizations nowadays dream of becoming flat or lean, as if dealing with obesity rather than becoming healthy and winners, the only difference being that reducing weight in an organization sometimes equates to losing parts of vital organs, such as brain tissue, eyes, kidneys, liver, and ears, rather than just fat. Finally, a cost-effective organization *per se* is not by any means synonymous with a healthy or winning organization and one with a future. Reduced human capital does not necessarily equate with success. An organization is like a body.

Repetitious crash diets reduce natural defenses and induce maladies. Sooner or later, the stakeholders in a company end up with an organization that will not be able to sustain itself for long. Each organ and cell plays a vital role in the health of an organizational body, and if the slimming cure inflicts damage on any of these, that organizational body will most likely not perform as it should. Eliminating successive groupings of synapses (e.g., expertise, coordination, and management) in different areas means affecting the brain of the organization permanently.

Losing entire levels of expertise based on years of experience is like expecting a patient to lose parts of his or her brain or vital organs and remain lucid and healthy. Inner focus over time brings loss of customers, business opportunities, and markets, taking the organization a further step down the self-consuming vortex.

Multiply this effect across an entire economy, and the result is a self-destructive economy. De facto, there seems to be a trend developing in major corporations, one that denotes an ever-increasing pressure on top-level management to resort to bringing results either for short-term market quotation objectives (note: that this expectancy in stock performance is done against a backdrop of impossible to reach returns achieved Internet-based paradigms) and or through extraordinary financial transactions— buying and selling assets or deriving profits from stock-market-related activities, acquisition, disposal, and/or sale of parts of the company, patents, shutting down otherwise profitable subsidiaries, and so on.

This cycle also forces many concerns to add fuel to the transfer of technology and production to more "cost-efficient" countries or regions of the world, leaving a greater void in the countries of origin—not only in the Western world. Even countries such as India and China are now moving their production facilities to regions such as the African continent.

It would be interesting to assess the real cost of these factors to an organization and determine the resilience of merged organizations, such as the *true net cost savings*, loss of opportunities of closures, and mass layoffs over a medium-term period, not only for existing shareholders, but also for future prospect buyers. This assessment should include the effects of these on new indicators, such as "*true net capabilities left*" (to understand if an organization is left with the capabilities it needs to survive), "*resilience ratio*" (an organization's capability to react), and "organizations' *post-cure survivability ratio*" (organizations' probability of survival).

Additionally, new indicators such as *propagation cost and ratios* that measure the extent of this damage on entire supply chains, local, state and national economies—allowing for a better cost benefit analysis of such decisions on wider scales—that, under a new model, can become a source of opportunities, rather generators of additional damage.

These are all new notions and will need to be elaborated in a separate study. In the meantime, the problem is that, given the market pressures to achieve numeric results in very short terms, the true net cost might never become visible or relevant to market analysts or investors, leaving a potential disaster waiting to happen out of sight.

All this brings us to a set of additional considerations that of accountability for the longer-term success and potential of companies (and organizations alike), their contribution to the well-being of an economy, but also social and environmental responsibility; that of adaptable new models fit for the challenges of the twenty-first century—many companies have already begun this long journey. To be even more effective though, these will require new models, key success factors, new strategies, new modalities, and levers. A growing number of these new models can be seen being developed in different parts of the world, these go from sharing and usage concepts (overriding legacy concepts of ownership) in automotive, and hospitality sectors, to use of app-based platforms/networks that no longer need to bring together different expertise for a given project in a single physical location. In the design of a car that can take years and millions of dollars to accomplish, for example, recent real-life paradigms have been able to drastically reduce cost and completion time frames.

In a nutshell, over and above what has been so far discussed, many legacy economic sectors (if not all) are on the verge of facing the greatest paradigm shift in their models, and processes since their inception. The speed of change and the level of disruption some companies might face could be virulent (affecting adjacent sectors), devastating, and more time sensitive than can be imagined today.

Emerging Nations—Fear or Opportunity

Equidistance and detachment are important. As mentioned this book is not about east or west but about providing an additional perspective inherent the paradox emerging nations might be facing in a not so distant future. Despite the brief moment of glory that emerging nations are currently enjoying, unless the model changes, exposed to the very same variables and challenges as developed nations exacerbated by many endemic problems unique to each, there is a possibility that emerging nations will end up sharing a similar fate, but one with greater challenges and consequences. Unless that there is a "coupe de théâtre"[16] in geopolitical balances—that as history all too often reminds should by no means be underestimated. Let us examine some of the more significant views.

While some of the hyped headlines every now and then might induce many to fear the seemingly unstoppable growth in BRIC countries or other emerging countries, the solidity of such affirmations is not as apparent if more data is analyzed in greater depth and positioned in the context of historical cycles. As best evidenced by many information sources basing judgments of a country's economic conditions, standing, or growth prospects based on a few single parameters, is extremely misleading.

Questions such as relativity and weight with respect to many other variables such per capita income, unemployment rate, poverty numbers, and so on make substantial difference in forming a more correct perception of reality that will still need to pass the test of a in-country verification. Many other factors need to be considered in evaluating vast quantities of data, and even then, given that source data, at the very least needs to be interpreted and rendered comparable; notwithstanding, the outcome is in many cases, the object of much-animated discussion and disagreement.

Having said this, one has to start somewhere and rely on the best data available. This is usually the result of much labor; elaboration,

---

16. Unexpected twist in theatrical plays

analysis and updating on behalf of those that painstakingly are given this responsibility. From the many reports provided by various authoritative information sources the following seem to emerge as reoccurring themes, conclusions and in general implications:[17]

- In China, c. 950 million people (more than the combined number of citizens in North America and the EU) are in the productive age bracket meaning access to a theoretically unlimited renewable basin of persons; an unprecedented local customer base and market size; but also possibilities for the devastating consequences of unemployment, social unrest, the unfathomable effects of virtualization of processes and business models, especially if accompanied by economic slow-down, bubble bursts, and or destructive climate, geological, or biological events.

- In India, c. 774 million people are in the same category.

- In China, c. 611 million people live in large cities (this rate is growing alarmingly), exerting unparalleled pressures on the most elementary life support services (e.g., food and water supply, sewage, waste management, pollution control, health and epidemic control).

- In India, c. 360 million people (more than the United States's total population in 2012) are in the same condition (while growing at an even faster rate).

- China and India account for 35.7 percent of the world's total population with a growing life expectancy, meaning a tsunami of people unprecedented in scale who will need pensions, growing medical assistance, jobs, housing, etc.

---

17. Constantly updated information available on institutional web sites of United Nations organizations, US government agencies, OECD, EU, and other sources. Numbers and percentages are time-dependent hence will most likely vary.

Implications: This also means a gargantuan stress on the backbone structures of these countries. Should everything else remain the same in the near future, this demographic pressure will most likely exert the same burdens on the respective economic systems as those faced in developed countries—but at exponentially greater levels, with the scale of the remedies titanic compared to the ones currently faced by developed countries.

These economies of scales are unprecedented in human history; therefore, it is difficult for anyone to foresee systemic breaking points, due to the population numbers involved. We do not know, for instance, if there might be health considerations once a certain human concentration is reached. Some studies estimate the number of persons living is cities in China will reach a staggering one billion people by 2020.

The population of the municipality of Chongqing in southwestern China (one of its technological centers of excellence) has reached a phenomenal number of c. 33 million individuals. We do not know if there are critical mass issues that emanate from waste management, the distribution of electrical power, an inundation of lethal concentrations of electromagnetic waves emitted by wideband and cellphone broadcasters, or human carbon dioxide production.

If we factor-in the possible devastating effects of ever more frequent natural disasters and extreme weather-related phenomena the picture we get assumes additional connotations. This excludes any fall-out from increasing numbers of near-failed states, mass-migration movements, and geopolitical volatility in a growing number of regions.

Adding labor force to the equation, data suggests that, with approximately 800 million people, China has by far the largest available working force in the world, followed in second place by India, with 487 million, the EU, with approximately 228 million, and the United States, with 153 million. Indonesia and Brazil follow with approximately 100 million souls each.

The data might also suggest the following: China's workforce is nearly equivalent to the sum of the combined workforces of India, the EU, and the United States! This implies that it theoretically has access to an unlimited source of continuously replaceable cheap labor, theoretically willing to work at ever lesser wages and lower working conditions, rendering the model impossible to replicate, but also that consequently it has the biggest potential for social disaster in case of economic slowdown, requests for social rights, etc. Yet another element to consider is the fact that already many emerging nations are delocalizing production to cheaper labor countries. Some recent studies in fact disclose that the African continent, potentially holds the greatest basin of available work force globally. Correspondingly, an equally noteworthy phenomenon (as provided by UN data) is how specific geographical areas such as Europe, the US, and Australia for example, are becoming targets of an unnatural, and historically unprecedented, incredibly well-organized, and financed set of mass-migratory movements.

While the definition of poverty line is subjective and each country uses its own definition, adding poverty levels into the equation leads to the following information, as declared by each country (CIA 2011; World Bank n.d.):

- *Twenty-five percent of the Indian population, or 300 million people, lives below the poverty line. Among other implications, this could denote a rising potential for ideologically fueled revolts, as differences in wealth, and access to primary services widen.*

- In China, 13.4 percent of the population lives under the poverty line. This is a new level set by the government in 2011. *Hence, under this definition, there are approximately 128 million people (circa half of the US population) living under the country's self-defined official poverty line.*

- Twenty-six percent of all Brazilians live below that country's defined poverty line.

The absence of a universal definition of the poverty line is problematic. However, the crude reality is that the number of poor people is likely to be different from and probably much higher than the official data, however defined.

Differences in perceptions derive from cultural origins and upbringing. Nonetheless, it is hard to think that the vast majority of people living in unhealthy slums or shantytowns, work in sweat-shops, in all honesty, can be considered well off by any human standard. Otherwise, it is not clear why as soon as the mere chance of moving out of such places arises, most residents flee from these horrendous situations.

To be balanced, please note however, that poverty numbers should not be equated to, or confused with, backwardness of a society. A growing number of citizens in China for example, benefit from, enjoy, and have access to levels in technological advancements in their cities that are comparable to and in some cases even more advanced than their counterparts, much beyond generalized perceptions.

A report by Serge Hoffmann and Bruno Lannes of Bain & Co. estimate that "2013 will be remembered as the one in which China surpassed the US as the world's largest digital retail market . . . a sum that has grown more than 70% annually since 2009 and is expected to continue on its amazing trajectory, reaching RMB 3.3 trillion by 2015.

Digital retailing has profoundly transformed shopping and purchasing habits, opening up vast opportunities for retailers and brands that pay attention to the nuances of massively changing consumer behavior." We must remember that BRICS are enjoying a period of economic vigour.

On the other hand, it is a well-documented fact that globalization, access to the Internet, mobile technology, satellite television, international travel and immigration, growing interaction with foreigners, and even the mere possibility of seeing different lifestyles produce an increased desire to experiment with new ideas, freedoms, and ways of life (positive or negative), especially in younger generations in less developed countries.

Many sociologists and economists agree that recent Arab Spring revolts, events such as those that spurred the Tiananmen Square and Hong Kong movements and growing momentum in politically conscious movements in India and many southwestern Asian countries are all indications of heat being generated in the social magma chamber of these countries.

The greater the perceived social disparity, the greater the pressures accumulating. Social inequality and reduced individual freedoms have well-confirmed sociological interconnections. Although democracy and political liberties can diminish the chances of explosive, implosive, or runaway social revolts, there is a natural breaking point for everything. If the exemplary high growth rates experienced in some developing countries still yield impressive unemployment both in absolute terms and in terms of the number of people living under the poverty line, what will happen the minute internal bubbles[18] burst, especially for those segments of society that have tasted new freedoms and living standards and those on the opposite end of the scale?

Considering the high growth rates reported by countries such as China, India, and Brazil, the unemployment and poverty rates are substantial indications of potential viruses brewing within these economic realities. *As far as unemployment goes, data suggest that some 84 million people in China are officially unemployed and that 117 million individuals are unemployed in India according to those countries' official data. And this excludes the staggering number of underemployed or unofficially unemployed people.*

Whatever the method used, the information available denotes the overwhelming difference between income per capita among developed and emerging countries. The other important information this might suggest is that there is no pragmatic or realistic way for developed countries to match the cost of labor of emerging countries unless it is through the adoption of a different model and a better strategy.

The subjective use, opinion-ability and volatility of data, and the importance we give it can affect the way we perceive opportunities and threats, organize our lives and economic models. Additional insight on how much can be done in coming up with new definitions, models, perspectives, and ways of accounting for things comes from a document produced by the UN in the Inclusive Wealth Report 2012 (IWR), a joint initiative launched at Rio+20 by the United Nations University's International Human Dimensions Programme on Global Environmental Change (UNU-IHDP) and the United Nations Environment Programme (UNEP). The full document is publicly available on the UN website[19.] Below is a small summary excerpt.

The world's fixation on economic growth ignores a rapid and mostly irreversible depletion of natural resources that will seriously harm future generations. The report unveiled a new indicator aimed at encouraging sustainability—the Inclusive Wealth Index (IWI).

The IWI, which looks beyond the traditional economic and development yardsticks of GDP and the Human

---

[18.]   i.e., housing, stock market, etc.

[19.]   UN University and UNEP 2012

Development Index (HDI) to include a full range of assets such as manufactured, human and natural capital, shows governments the true state of their nation's wealth and the sustainability of its growth. . . .

"Gross Domestic Product (GDP) . . . is far too silent on major measures of human well-being namely many social issues and the state of a nation's natural resources," said UN Under-Secretary General and UNEP Executive Director Achim Steiner. . . .

"The IWR stands for a crucial first step in changing the global economic paradigm by forcing us to reassess our needs and goals as a society," said Professor Anantha Duraiappah, Report Director of the IWR and Executive Director at UNU-IHDP. (1–2)

Governments and international organizations should establish research programs to value key components of natural capital, in particular ecosystems. Many other indexes, such as "wellbeing" are being introduced and establish extremely positive trends. The question however, is how these indexes concretely translate into, impact, and or create tangible, real returns to citizens, businesses, organizations, and so on.

The Next Neopowers?

The focus of the previous section was on internal issues that contribute to the paradox effects within growing economies. Yet not losing track of outwardly looking facets is as important, as they could heavily contribute to increasing the contradictions for these countries.

In providing an additional perspective, many analysts suggest that some emerging countries such as China and India for example, are growing their presence and influence internationally. The argument is that it is not only about markets but also about access to vital resources and projection of political influence in two distinctly different ways. They suggest that China and India, for example, on the face of it, differ substantially in their apparent approach to international presence.

Because of the incredible growth in the economic power of China, many theories are developing to explain how China is projecting its power internationally. Each of these produces a wealth of information and different perspectives. The purpose here is not to promote or demote any of these ideas but to go beyond them. For example, China has grown its GDP *tenfold* since 1978 (CIA 2011). It has become the second-largest economy in terms of GDP. It is increasing its presence on a worldwide scale and growing economically. Hence, for all practical purposes some of these counties might already be "neopowers."

Projections are very important, some analysts are at odds over the when these might happen—whereas we might need to focus on addressing important, impelling geostrategic issues now, appropriately. China is said to operate in the international arena with a model for its projection of power. One of these is called the Beijing Consensus. The Beijing Consensus seems to build its foundations on the Chinese model of development, which might be summarized in three strategic priorities (Cooper Ramo 2004):

- Focus on infrastructure development.

- Produce economic reform.

- Evaluate implementation of civic reform. In other words, instead of pressuring others to create reforms, provide economic possibilities and let the people adhere to and adapt to the existing system. This substantially frees China from many external pressures deriving from international organizations and nations, allowing it to write its own book—in a we-can-do-it-using-our-own-model context.

The Beijing Consensus seems to encapsulate the essence of the approach used by China in developing international relations and trade. According to these sources, the cornerstones of the Beijing Consensus seem to be centered primarily on the following elements:

- Use of the Chinese model of development.

- Structural development: China can provide both the means and workforce at unparalleled costs to roll out large-scale infrastructure projects that can improve productivity. The reasoning here is that if you do not have dams, electricity, roads, ports, etc., you cannot produce anything effectively and efficiently.

- Noninterference: China is interested in trade with no strings attached. If the two nations find a common ground, no concern is given to other factors, such as respect for human rights and democratic rule.

- Friendship and respect: China respects standing rulers and their followers and sees reciprocal respect as a long-term key success factor.

The same sources have expressed increasing concern over Chinese presence, power projection, and influence in the context of a much broader global and geopolitical picture and are trying to appreciate its consequences fully. The growing presence of the neoeconomic giants might not be limited to supermarket shelves, jobs, and local economies, but about a strong strategic stance and the implications of things such as island-building, and the envisioned, but yet to be confirmed, construction of Nicaragua's 278 km long, $50 billion Interoceanic Grand Canal, expected to rival the Panama Canal not only in length, width, and depth, as reported by Reuters and other sources, but more importantly its location, hundreds of miles northwest of it, meaning an enormous saving in fuel and time most transportation concerns.

This projection is highly visible in the Caribbean, South America, Africa, and Asia. The void created by budget cuts that led to the substantial withdrawal of developed countries is being naturally filled in many parts of the world by the BRIC countries.

An OECD paper by Martin Davies on "How China Is Influencing Africa's Development" (2010), citing other studies by *Deloitte*, *PriceWaterhouseCoopers*, and *McKinsey Quarterly* on state capitalism suggests that since the first half of 2009 while the developed world was at grips with the financial crisis, China's investments in the African continent "had increased an impressive 81 percent . . . compared to the same period the previous year" (5). Davies also states that at the 2007 World Economic Forum, Mr. Li Ruogu, EXIM Bank's CEO, said that "as much as 40 percent of the Bank's loan book is now held in Africa" (Davies 2010, 12).

The same source states that at the FOCAC meeting held in Sharm El Sheik on November 9, 2009 Premier Wen Jiabao stated that "China would provide 10 billion US dollars" (11n15) of investments in this continent in the next years.

The following is a brief sample some of the major projects financed by China in Africa and nearby island states in the Indian Ocean (CIA 2011; IMF 2012; World Bank n.d.):

- Sudan: CNPC acquisition of 40 percent of the Greater Nile Petroleum Operating Company; China owns most of the oil fields in South Darfur; pipeline to Port Sudan; 60 percent of Sudan's oil production goes to China.

- Nigeria: CNPC bought an oil block (six by 2005) in exchange for hydroelectric power; Lagos Kano Railway.

- Angola: $5 billion loan for oil and national infrastructure-related products to be paid back in oil.

- Tanzania and Zambia: railroad

- Zambia: copper-related industry

- Mauritius: manufacturing, trade, tourism, hospitals, and stadiums

- Ethiopia: electrical machinery, construction material, and steel industries

- Egypt: petroleum equipment, electrical appliances, textiles, and automotive industry

- Algeria: highway project

- Guinea: Souapiti Dam, bauxite, and aluminum mining

- Congo: Congo River Dam for oil

- Ghana: Bui Dam and cocoa

- Gabon: key infrastructure for iron ore

- Madagascar: nickel mining

- Zimbabwe: coal mines and thermal power plant for chrome

- Mozambique: coal

- Democratic Rep of Congo: roads, rail, copper, and cobalt

- Others: timber, gold, diamonds, and minerals

Currently, unparalleled sums are also being invested by China in the middle-east (e.g., a billion-dollar joint petroleum project in Iran). They are investing in the majority of the countries in this region, including Iraq, the United Arab Emirates, Syria, Yemen, Saudi Arabia, Jordan, and Lebanon.

Moving over to Asia, notwithstanding cultural issues dating back centuries, the economies of entire states in Southeast Asia are heavily influenced by large investments to the point that they have created a counterbalance of "real" influence and power with respect to the indigenous populations, which still represent the majority in terms of population. This can be witnessed in countries such as Mauritius, Indonesia, and Malaysia.

Indian and Pacific Ocean islands are ever more (willingly or not) pulled into the sphere of influence of China and India. Most of the countries in these regions have the same characteristics. They are either rich in mineral resources or strategically positioned, denoting a factual need for projection of power.

Davies (2010) suggests that state capitalism allows state-owned firms through state-owned bank financing to permit these companies, which would otherwise not be able to invest in these times, to fill the void by riding economic growth countercyclically with respect to the rest of the world "[manipulating] market outcomes for political purposes" (Bremmer 2009, para. 6).

Additionally aiding such a policy is a different capital risk model used by Chinese state-owned banks that, as some analysts suggest, might not need to be as accountable to private stakeholders as to political interests. This creates a totally different set of premises and operational platforms—rendering what is considered risky and not viable for the developed world as possible for China. Some might see in this the possibility of playing with an additional and/or different set of cards.

Moreover, soft loans and preferential financing conditions go not only to governments, but also to state-owned enterprises that act as the key implementers of the large infrastructure projects. *Many more analysts, instead are starting to pose concerns over the overexposure of distressing magnitude of some of the banks involved—postulating the likelihood of a bubble of massive scales in the making.*

Furthermore, the reports suggest that the China uses these economic zones, such as the one in Egypt's Suez region, to penetrate adjacent markets—in this case, the Middle East and North African countries with "Made in Egypt" products to avoid the growing psychological effect sometimes associated with the "Made in China" branding. Market development is one of the key objectives here. Other objectives, as discussed by Davies (2010), include access to resources and political influence.

Aid is another tool used to help China's localized consolidation—in symbolic gestures that generate acquiescence in the masses. *To sum up the geographical extension of China's activities around the world, the above areas cover circa 50 percent of the world's emerged lands and have a real presence in over 75 percent of the world in absolute terms, including seas and oceans.*

This is becoming a matter of concern for many analysts, policymakers, and businesses. However, to maintain equidistance, we need to bring in other points of view that state that though it can be seen as an unprecedented level of potential global reach in human history, it is not. To add some perspective, the United States has already reached a significantly higher level.

If one factors in historical timeframes and the strategic importance other nations have played, Britain came close to this in its period of maximum expansion. This, however, should by no means suggests it is unnecessary to be aware of the full geopolitical implications and ramifications of this phenomenon given the unprecedented level of reach in global presence within the context of Chinese history, the numbers involved, and the short time frames in which this has materialized.

Assessing whether or not there is a neopower projection strategy, its parameters, the accuracy of the viewpoints presented, and to what extent—these are not the objectives of this book. Rather, it conveys that many variables are at play here, exerting additional pressure and that induced imbalances add considerable complexity to existing models.

One needs constantly to be reminded that, with all their shortcomings, the civilization, prosperity, freedoms, and fundamental rights we so much take for granted in the developed world are, in many cases, not fully available to the billions who wish for them in their own countries.

Ultimately, BRICs will probably do what they deem best for them and try to reduce competitors' superiority as a natural strategy. This can lead to different types of strategic reaction; succumb, defend, follow, or lead. The first three strategies denote weakness, lack of resilience and confidence. Leadership instead denotes the adoption of a winning strategy. The current state of affairs seems to be led by and fuelled by an ongoing positive economic exchange between nations. Ideally, the objective should remain exactly that—creating the conditions for collaboration, trade, and the free movement of people and ideas. The development and protection of free societies, a healthy geopolitical balance and strategy, well-balanced polarity, and stability are key to future prosperity, development, and peace internationally.

Seen from a different prospective and using a different model and strategy, as will be self-evident later, BRICs can be an opportunity for a much more win-win remunerating multilateral economic growth. The wealth of a society or a nation is linked to its ability to leverage and enhance uniqueness and diversity successfully. These have provided and will continue providing one of the most successful survival strategies and the base of development, knowledge, trade, and the advancement of nations. Building this wealth on the foundations of fundamental rights and freedoms while respecting others has and will continue to allow an ascent toward ever-greater levels of civilization—constituting the cornerstones for prolonged economic development and prosperity.

Ultimately, one of the key levers for lasting peace is economic development, as much as possible, locally/globally, and not limited to only certain parts of the world, fostering an environment in which business and people can prosper and focus on wellbeing in a geopolitically, continuously balanced context.

Intellectual Capability

Two to three decades ago or so, some companies started giving away production that was deemed unwanted or costly, at increasing rates, to less developed countries. At the time, there was limited indigenous know-how and capability. Most of the concern was about reverse engineering and, in some cases, the illicit copying and replication of products and processes by local businesses. In the meantime, many things have mutated. One of these is the number of native engineers that are being educated and absorbed by these economies.

There is much discussion about everything from the number of graduates to the quality of their education, their qualifications, etc., in newly developing countries. According to Geoff Colvin (2010), the number of engineering PhD students graduating from top universities in China exceeds the number of US graduates, most of whom are non-US citizens.

According to Duke University professor Vivek Wadhwa, in testimony before the House Committee about the competitiveness of US engineering colleges, the number of engineering students in 2004 in each country follows (Brunette 2006):

- United States: 137,437

- India: 112,000

- China: 351,537

Citing the same source, David Epstein (2006) produced substantially different numbers:

- United States: 222,335

- India: 215,000

- China: 644,106

The point here is not about the precision of the numbers, as both articles correctly state that Wadhwa's findings and testimony to the House Committee clearly pointed out the flaws of such numbers, which did not factor in important variables, such as the difference in classifications of graduates in the different academic systems and the quality of education. However, the fundamental point might neither be about when emerging nations might catch up technologically with the developed ones, nor about forecasting the specific time when this event could take place.

It is about acknowledging the reality that many nations are moving rapidly from reproducing technology to developing new technology. In addition it is about being cognizant that different sources estimate the number of university degree holders in China alone, to reach 200 million laureates by the year 2020. Accurate or not, a wealth of potential and knowledge with no precedence in history.

Similar debates took place in Britain from the late 1800s to the 1930s. The United States—then still a young country with hardly anything comparable to the global presence, might, resources, know-how, technological and research base, investment capabilities, etc., of the British Empire during the period of its maximum splendor and power—advanced at such a pace that it surpassed the giant by leaps and bounds without Britain ever being able to recover.

Given the new technological enablers and the hunger for knowledge and prosperity, it would be highly unrealistic to think that developing countries might wish to stop or slow down. In response, there are many options from which to choose: wait and see, watch and learn, flank, and so on, or being cognizant of an evolutionary process and a need for a step-level transformation to develop and implement a new wining paradigm.

Moreover, a country's competitive advantage is intrinsically derived from the sum of many additional variables (e.g., infrastructure, capabilities, social advancement, civil liberties, education, legislative and judiciary systems, rights, healthcare, and the general organization of society).

The most important aspects, though, seem to be the ability to keep at the forefront of development and to have the opportunity to realize dreams—things that have grown hand in hand with the advancement in developed countries, not things that can be replicated easily.

Furthermore, using only few parameters such as the number of engineers, doctors, and college graduates only makes sense when you factor in crucial elements such as a country's/market's capability to effectively utilize, absorb, and leverage this unique intellectual capability in challenging and well-paying jobs. It is not only demotivating and degrading for thousands of engineers, doctors, lawyers, biologists, astronomers, and laureates in all fields who work precariously in low-paying nonintellectually stimulating jobs for an extended period of time, but it is also a shameful waste of extremely valuable resources. *A systemic failure—but one that increasingly is becoming a reality also for developed countries.*

A key to long-term development and prosperity depends on these capabilities, but also on a healthy economy, and other parameters such as, motivating, incentivizing, career development, leveraging expertise, respecting fundamental rights, experience and seniority are as equally important.

Conflict: Economic Paradigm of Last Resort?

In an effort to consider the most important variables concerning the current model, unfortunately, we must also discuss strategies or thought processes that might consider conflict as a solution. History confirms a use of conflict as an economic revival strategy of last resort (and sometimes even earlier). It is one of the major shortcomings of the existing economic model and its predecessors. These are unquestionably very peculiar times, and we *cannot* allow ourselves the luxury of not considering alternatives to conflict, especially if the adopted solutions do not produce results.

To start with, there is no guarantee of who might win an eventual war—even a proxy war,[20] secondly the devastating effects of war will not be just limited to the period of physical conflict but the overwhelming repercussions on the debts generated and their repayment to the winner. Germany was able to finish its repayment only recently, some sixty years after the war involving generations that had for the most part nothing to do with the war.

Last but not least, entering a war means being cognizant that in the event of the loss of a conflict the citizens of succumbing nations will have to face unforeseeable consequences in their independence, freedoms, creeds, wealth, housing and properties, and sometimes even life and relations with their family members and loved ones.

UN data suggest that an increasing number of countries are facing wars, social revolts, civil wars and ideologically driven genocides, creating among other things a displacement of persons and families of biblical proportions.

This list must include the destructive effects of the recent wars and conflicts on the citizens and families of the many nations making up international coalition forces and UN led intiatives, be they American, British, Canadian, German, Italian, Israeli, Nigerian or otherwise, just to name a few, who sacrificed love ones to each of these as well as peacekeeping missions also needs to be pondered. It is a global dilemma with global consequences independent of ones nationality.

[20.] Engaging in conflict on someone else's territory and/or through third parties.

Until World War II, for millennia the model could rely on a simple axiom: that full-scale war and destruction brings with it a period of production prior to and during a war and a period of reconstruction and economic revitalization after it. The distinction is that the world needed much economic development after the Second World War, which is by no means intended to convey that war is a solution. Quite the contrary, as the four recent wars in Kosovo, Gulf I and II, and Afghanistan would suggest.

Factually, wars in the last fifty years instead have increasingly failed to produce the expected outcome—widespread lasting economic reactivation. *We need an alternative to make sustainable long-term development possible.* Additionally, paradoxically, in today's interconnected world, defensive might in military power does not necessarily equate to invulnerability. In reality, historically, it probably never has. Correspondingly, it is important to never underestimate geopolitical scenario's, there are substantial examples of scenarios where sizably smaller adversaries were able to cause considerable threat, damage, and in some cases defeat to previously "undefeatable" opponents. *Historical precedence confirms that prolonged survivability of any successful society is directly linked to its capability in leveraging winning strategies, fostering economic development internationally, spearheading the promotion and protection of liberties and rights, whilst maintaining a high level of defensive deterrence.*

Implications on Defense Policy & Intelligence

Today's exorbitant public debts render a new arms race impracticable, but then again Germany and Russia were heavily indebted before the rise of Nazism and during the birth of the Soviet Union. Military doctrine is split between the need to maintain high-impact visible power projection capability and asymmetric strategy (both physically and virtually/ digitally).

The reality is that you might need both, but more importantly the ability to win a conflict before it ever begins through a solid economy and viable and dynamically updated deterrents. Asymmetry is not a new concept; it dates back several thousand years, and it may have always been used as far back as the first conflicts between two contenders with considerably different forces and resources. In essence, it is the use of weakness as a strength that can sometimes determine, at the very least, psychological setback.

Today the use of technologically asymmetric strategy is also inherent to cyberspace and nanotechnology. The news is full of examples of "real" virtual wars taking place in cyberspace today, inflicting real damage on the military, intelligence, critical infrastructure, business, economy, and individuals.

Increasing budgets are being dedicated to what could be called the *fifth dimension of warfare* after land, sea, air (and space), and unmanned combat. It is fundamentally different from other dimensions in at least two primary areas:

- It does not need proximity to inflict damage (physical distance to the battle-space and/or enemies' assets).

- It has "one-to-many" damage-inflicting capabilities. Theoretically, with a single algorithm, cyber-warfare could debilitate multiple assets simultaneously, far more numerous than the others.

Fifth-dimension asymmetric strategy can be a debilitating first move and might require, at least initially, the involvement of only a handful of individuals, probably unaware of one another, who are simply sitting in many different parts of the world, operating from a laptop to start their assignments. They do not necessarily need to be military personnel. Each might act in his or her official capacity as journalist, system administrator, investor, etc., to initiate the engagement.

For all practical purposes, they might not even be aware of the repercussions of their actions, or they might even not be the enemy, but simply unwary individuals whose only fault has been purchasing a PC, smartphone, or any other device with access to Internet, belonging to a very particular batch.

Cyber deterrence or offensive capability is achieved through substantial investments in very strong cyber strategies, resources, applications, etc., both of offensive and defensive natures that in many countries might not even show up in publicly declared budgets. These domains could include:

Offensive cyber warfare (examples):

- access inhibition/denial, application destruction, data loss, etc.;

- economic cyber warfare through deliberate coordinated economic transactions;

- intelligence (i.e., sniffing, phishing, intelligence gathering, decryption, information/data distortion, manipulation, propaganda, etc.).

Defensive cyber warfare (examples):

- cyber protection, firewalls, system/data protection, etc.

- counterintelligence

An even subtler strategy might reside in what could be called adding *end-user product prefitted destructive, manipulative, and inhibitive logic* (or PDMI-Log) onto ordinary electronic circuitry. This refers to the incubation or infestation of simple logic that could include implanting hard-to-detect, deeply embedded logic or applications in firmware of innocuous-looking circuits or chipsets of any nature (at different points of their manufacturing processes) that self-destruct, inhibit, or manipulate a system, its data and or connectivity, or its way of operating.

As an example, imagine a chipset or miniature circuit embedded in a seemingly innocuous day-to-day appliance, such as a washing machine, that could be deactivated or activated to operate differently at a distance by an innocuous electric pulse, a particular yet simple radio wave, or other means. Now imagine a theoretical, purposely exaggerated scenario of a washing machine being prompted from a distance to open its door as it is running, dumping the water it contains on the floor of one's home. Now multiply this effect on a neighborhood, town, city . . .

Theoretically, this sort of embedded logic might go in not only a washing machine, but also more vital equipment used for drug dosage in hospitals of various ingredients in common medicines, smartphones, or truck braking or fuel systems (70 percent of US goods are moved on trucks).

It could sabotage emergency center control rooms', sprinkler systems, hazardous material handling rooms in research centers; temperature control indicators of reactors; signaling systems; ventilation systems on ships or submarines; fuses in military machinery, aircraft, and platforms; elevator command modules, aircraft fuel engine valve controllers, rudder controls, or landing systems; or dams' electrical generation unit circuit breaker subsystems, a city's sewage or water distribution systems, mass transportation, elevators, ordinary spark plugs, control indicators and switches on defense systems aboard military ships, aircraft, submarines, and vehicles. It could operate HVAC system shut-off circuits in server farms around the world on which clouds and terabytes of websites' information and data reside, including those of financial institutions.

It could activate via a simple keyboard key which until that specific moment only represented a simple letter but which instead activates a software routine affecting market decisions. It could affect factory conveyer belt speed control units, the handsets of emergency responders,[21] it could also be downloaded and remain dormant in music and movies we like to hear and watch until the specific moment, etc. The potential use of similar strategies is within the capabilities of not only developed nations and emerging economies, but even those with the least amount of

---

[21.] e.g., police, ambulances, firefighters

technological capability. Seen from this additional perspective, questions that might be posed by geopolitical strategists include as follows: Will dependence, "cost only-focused" economic logic, wild-delocalization, or relinquishment of knowledge and strategic sector sell-off still be as intelligent and or economically viable as they have sounded thus far?

Independently of what has been discussed in this chapter, we must remember that unlike other historical moments, in the unwanted event of a future conflict of substantial proportions, after a brief reconstruction period, the survivors will be confronted by the same dilemmas and challenges we face today. They will have to deal with the numerous game-changing paradigms and systemic paradoxes that inhibit the proper functioning and prolonged success of the current economic model—unless, of course, Albert Einstein's predicament is correct that whoever survives the next war will revert to a technologically more primitive society.

While it might not be hard to foresee with what balance of forces a conflict might be commenced among two contenders, there are two things that are not foreseeable: the outcome and the price at which this comes both prior, during and after the conflict. Theoretically, for the first time in human history, changing the economic paradigm might help add a protective layer or cushion between the economic motivation for war (deriving from a conflict-based economic axiom/paradigm) and the need for conflict itself. The need to maintain strategically strong deterrence in different domains is a totally different story—and requires serious reflection, and effective dynamically evolving strategies.

Winning Strategies

After all the argumentations we must remind ourselves that it is those whose economies prosper that will have leverage and leadership potential. Additionally, in any head-to-head confrontation, everyone loses something. A better alternative, might simply be a better strategy that promotes long-term economic prosperity, fosters hope, and one that turns the tables or at least provides other possibilities. This must include seeking solutions to sustainably address and tackle the many challenges societies face in different parts of the world. Although some signs might indicate differently, the fate of nations with very large ambitions that enact fast expansionary policies is historically well documented.

From Alexander the Great to Napoleon, to Hitler—they all failed—all colonization attempts futile. All ideologically driven internationalizations botched. Even the greatest of empires succumbed due to their inability to create and maintain continuous economic traction and the relentless chipping away of their power and energy on the outermost outskirts of their perimeters of influence by revengeful groups through the use of asymmetrical warfare.

Yet some might argue that their epitaph were the mere frames of entire films. Some might be more than glad to live out parts of the movie and jump ship before the film ends. Nevertheless, although in the short run there might be wins, some of the challenges the neoeconomic giants may face include some of the following factors that have failed past expansionary policies:

- sustainability of complex models

- overextension beyond control

- limits of resources and capability

- congestion of priorities

- overlooking small fires that can become uncontrollable

- inexorably arriving at one-size-fits-all policies that backfire

- energy-draining governance loops (controlling the controllers)

- long-term inefficacy of satrapy control (appointed leaders to regions on the outskirts who do as they please and fuel dissidence among locals, absorbing greater levels of energy)

- overlapping powers and conflicts of interests

- internal conflicts

- power hunger of emerging rich and middle classes

- energy-absorbing cultural aspects

- unsustainable economies of scale

- inability to sustain win-win scenarios across the board, creating waves of growing dissatisfaction

- failure rate factor (as news of failure of initiatives spread)

- too many compromises, many creating sharp contrasts

Additionally, internally the neoeconomic giants might have to deal with social divaricators; civil liberties; property rights; poverty; corruption; infrastructure, resource, and energy deficiencies; unemployment; thirst for freedoms; inflation; bubble burst potential in local markets; and control of richer and influential groups (e.g., religious, sectarian, political dissident, minority) similar in many ways, to the ones developed nations had (and in some cases continue) to confront in their evolutionary paths with differing levels of success and failure.

Additionally other not so obvious and apparently innocuous variables need to be considered. For example an article in *The Economist*[22] pointed to growing concerns over India's trade deficit with China. India imports

---

[22.] "Friend, enemy, rival, investor" 2012

nearly three times more than it exports to China. In June 2012, this equated to circa $40 billion, representing nearly half of India's overall trade deficit with the world if oil imports are excluded. This has translated into a devaluation of the rupee by a fifth during that period.

On the other hand, other articles on China and India state that economic growth in these countries is not affected by the economic crisis enveloping the developed world, as the population forming their respective economies is big enough to sustain such growth for some time.

Though there is room for debate on every issue, there are at least a few certainties: It is hard to foresee the future; historical data tends to convey that extremely generous growth periods are, at best, cyclical events. Globalization and the economic crisis in developed countries will affect demand from developing nations; exposure to bubbles in different market sectors increases during rapid growth periods.

Unless structural remedies are implemented, the current economic virus might only linger longer, and once it hits, produce more damage, for an even longer time, and affect larger numbers of people, families, businesses, governments, nations and union of nations. *Fundamentally, if the model does not work any longer, this affects everyone, including BRIC and developing countries.* Furthermore, this argumentation excludes the effects of paradigm-changing variables, such as Mobint, advancement, disruptive models, innovation, and Web inclusivity. Historic evidence suggests that structural reforms that undermine rights and liberties of a society be they relative to employment, business, taxation; protection from fraud or embezzlement; regard security and privacy, only translate in additional layers of complexity, induce systemic weakness, and corruption, and erode the vital foundations of a society.

Seeking a winning strategy means be willing to substantially evolve the underlying policy toward: achieving the right balance, creating the preambles to revive economies from grassroots. In reality, the number of possibilities and opportunities has never been so vast. Adopting a winning strategy is at the base of prolonged economic development—globally; it has taken humanity out of the darkest scenarios and allowed it to prosper and achieve what no other known species has been able to accomplish.

Implications on the Evolution of States, Nations, and Union of Nations

In order to provide a comprehensive approach, it is necessary to introduce the longer-term considerations about the possible evolution of today's notions of state, nation, and union of nations. This is not to state that such an eventuality will happen, but a matter that might need reflection. It is a very delicate subject, and hence equally difficult to address.

Let us then begin with, and stick to facts. Historical data register the evolution of human agglomerations from tribes, to city-states, feudalism, and nationalism, to the current concept of union of states. With the exclusion of a very limited number of examples, the post World War Two geographical boundaries of many nations, at best, is the result of political compromise that encase previously separate, often conflicting ethnic groups, religions, cultures…and viewpoints that from time to time, kindle the cyclical resurgence of separatist movements.

Adding several elements of complexity to this scenario is the fact that, with the exclusion of the EU that for some analysts constitutes an example, the world went from the concept of independent nations to globalization, practically overnight in historical terms, without intermediate milestones.

Today's and tomorrow's epochal challenges, recent evolution of new concepts such as open boundaries and the free movement of people and goods, and so on, pose new feats while providing new opportunities. On one hand, political analysts record, for example, the shortcomings of union of nations such as the EU in addressing specific needs of its citizens, their true political representation, and its effectiveness in addressing issues such as mass-migration, debt, taxation…while on the other, it is hard not to recognize and appreciate some of the benefits and advantages it brings. A border-less union which allows freedom movement and of doing business in each of the nations comprising it, constitute but a couple of examples.

Hence, a fundamental question looms. How might the need to address epochal challenges, and game-changing innovation influence current national or cross national aggregations? It is a good question and one that needs serious consideration. The answer though is not simple. We must eventually come to grips with the undeniable fact that the world is becoming ever more interconnected, and its societies interdependent. A decision taken in one geographical area of the world, more than ever before, might affect societies and citizens of countries on the other side of the planet. Epochal challenges such as mass migration, climate changes, and dangerous failed state and ideologically fueled geopolitical phenomena, for example, are no longer the problem of those immediately affected by it. Moreover, blaming, underestimating, or procrastinating can no longer represent viable solutions.

The evolution of the economic paradigm towards a value-generating model can facilitate and remove some of the current inhibitors and make available resources to begin addressing these critical challenges.

What the third millennium has in store for the evolving notions of states and union of nations is difficult to foretell. However, if one were allowed to freely venture beyond known models, consider different possibilities, and for example, extrapolate the unfolding of current events into the future, some of the hypothetical scenarios that could emerge might be:

- A movement towards greater aggregation that fosters increased sensitivity to regional representation and autonomy, i.e. new "super-leagues (i.e. North America and EU; Pan Asia; African Union) of adhering independent regions and nations". The citizens of such super-leagues might have equal, factual political representation through for example, direct voting of political leaders and representatives, but also, for the value programs they propose (substantially different from today's EU model)—and who's regions/states are guaranteed political, and administrative autonomy—while critical aspects such defense, and foreign policy could become common to adhering regions/states. Theoretically, the only thing limiting the growth of such scenario to include growing numbers of regions, and states, realistically in the long-term timeframe, enough to mature these eventualities, is our will, imagination, and or, even a matter of political convenience.

- A movement towards greater fragmentation with separation and constitution of smaller political entities that might or might not adhere to larger political unions.

- An improved evolution of the existing United Nations concepts.

- A new value-based concept of adhering federations (a subject too complex to be covered in this book). Other.

Which scenario is the best, and in which direction evolution will eventually take us, is purely subjective, and based on personal preference, and might ultimately need the test of time. What is becoming evident though, is that the world we know today might evolve in many ways we might not be able to imagine. A focus on generating value though, might be able to create the preamble for a better, more fruitful, and stable international geopolitical scenario. At least much more so that the current model.

What Governments Are Doing

To ensure a balanced view, this chapter sheds light on some of the most important measures governments and policymakers are trying to implement around the world to address the global impasse.[23] A few of these are mentioned below. For brevity, some of the more emblematic have been selected.

The Washington Consensus

Though this strategy is said to have been set aside amidst very animated debate by a growing number of economists, it is one that, leading up to the 2008 crisis, was initially envisaged and implemented around the world with varying degrees of accomplishment by G-20 countries. First embraced by many G-7 and G-20 nations (in full or in part) and then abandoned to varying degrees, the so-called Washington Consensus entailed embracing the following ten broad sets of relatively specific policy recommendations (Williamson 2003):

1. public debt reduction and fiscal policy discipline

2. redirection of public spending from subsidies toward primary education, primary health care, and infrastructure investment

3. tax reform, broadening the tax base, and adopting moderate marginal tax rates

4. interest rates being market-determined and positive (but moderate) to promote investments and reduce government debt

5. competitive exchange rates

[23.] This information is available in the public domain: in order not to distort the real intentions or meanings, excerpts of some these policies are made available here.

6. trade policy: import liberalization, in particular elimination of quantitative restrictions (licensing, etc.)—any trade protection to be provided by low and relatively uniform tariffs

7. liberalization in favor of foreign direct investments

8. privatization of state enterprises

9. deregulation: abolition of regulations that impede market entry or restrict competition, except for those justified on safety, environmental, and consumer protection grounds and prudential oversight of financial institutions

10. legal security for property rights

The following are a small sample of polices being currently undertaken in the United States and internationally among the G-20. This data has been gathered from US Department of the Treasury, the White House, the Federal Reserve, and international organization websites.[24]

Wall Street Reform

The Dodd-Frank Wall Street Reform and Consumer Protection Act addresses key deficits and flaws in the system to reduce the probability of future financial shocks and their consequences, essential to investor confidence and the safety, stability, and integrity of the financial system, allowing for capital to finance businesses and innovation that hopefully produces jobs. Its objectives are as follows:

- promoting a safer, more stable financial system focused on sustainable growth and job creation

- putting in place a dedicated watchdog for consumers

[24.] Such as the World Bank and IMF

- bringing the derivatives market out of the darkness and into the light of day

- providing new tools for winding down failing firms without putting the economy in jeopardy

Housing Finance Reform

Reforms to address important flaws in the mortgage market through stronger/improved consumer protection, transparency, underwriting standards, and other critical measures, providing targeted and transparent support to creditworthy but underserved families that want to own their own home and affordable rental options.

Recovery Act

This was an effort to jump-start the economy, create or save jobs, and put a down payment on addressing long-neglected challenges. The act is an extraordinary response. It includes measures to modernize US infrastructure, enhance energy independence, expand educational opportunities, preserve and improve affordable health care, provide tax relief, and protect those in greatest need.

G-20: Sustainable External Imbalances and Orderly Global Adjustment

President Obama made the following proposals to G-20 countries (White House 2010):

1. Bolster . . . cooperation to achieve sustainable current account balances. . . . Reduce external imbalances across the global economy, treating surplus and deficit economies symmetrically.

2. Assess persistently large imbalances against indicative guidelines to evaluate the root causes of impediments to global adjustment (para. 5).

3. Move toward more market-determined exchange rate systems, enhance exchange rate flexibility, and refrain from competitive devaluations of currencies.

4. Pursue structural reforms to boost and sustain global demand and deliver on commitment to medium-term fiscal responsibility.

5. Undertake further financial regulatory reforms to safeguard and strengthen financial systems and economies.

6. Keep global markets open and resist trade and financial protectionism given the serious risk that proliferation of protectionist measures could derail the recovery (para. 7). The combination of commitments to pursue balanced demand growth, flexible exchange rates, financial and structural reforms, and sustainable public finances will lead to a stronger and more sustainable growth path globally and in the United States and to the good jobs that our citizens need (paras. 8–9).

Financial Reform in the G-20 Agenda

Subsequent to the Dodd-Frank Wall Street Reform and Consumer Protection Act, the United States has promoted a race to the top so that all international financial firms face the same tough standards everywhere on a level playing field. The main points declared in the G-20 agenda (White House 2010) are:

1. End too big to fail (para. 2).

2. More capital and better quality capital: discourage excessive leverage . . . [R]educe banks' incentive to take excessive risks, lower the likelihood and severity of future crises, and enable banks to withstand—without extraordinary government

support—stresses of a magnitude associated with the recent financial crisis (para. 3).

3. [A] safer, more transparent derivatives market to help Main Street businesses: *The Dodd-Frank Act will benefit those businesses that use derivatives to manage their commercial risks. That is good for every farmer and every manufacturer that uses derivatives the way they were meant to be used* (para. 4, emphasis added).

4. [Close] loophole in regulation of major financial firms: [create] accountable regulation for all firms that pose the most risk to the financial system (para. 5).

5. Bring transparency to hedge funds (para. 6).

6. Constrain the size and risks of the largest firms: The largest and most interconnected firms should be subject to mandatory international recovery and resolution planning. In the United States, the Dodd-Frank Act prevented financial firms from growing by acquisition to more than 10 percent of the liabilities in the financial system (para. 7).

7. Reform pay practices at financial firms: "Excessive compensation . . . encouraged excessive risk taking" . . . implementation standards [are] aimed at aligning compensation with long-term value creation, not with excessive risk taking (para. 8).

8. Separate banking and speculative trading: Reform[s] . . . "to mitigate excessive risk-taking practices" . . . make clear that banking entities must focus on their customers, and not on proprietary trading or hedge fund or private equity investments (para. 9).

9. Strong consumer protection . . . through disclosure, education, and protection from fraud and abuse. . . . There will be one agency instead of seven, dedicated to establishing and enforcing

clear rules for banks, mortgage companies, payday lenders, and credit card lenders (para. 10).

10. Crack down on the abuses in mortgage markets: [This] requires, for example, that mortgage brokers and banks consider a family's ability to repay when making a loan. [It] requires lenders and Wall Street securitizers to keep skin in the game. Reforms of credit rating agencies will help make sure that investors do not rely unwisely on their ratings on these packages (para. 11).

11. Support long-term job growth by helping prevent future crises: The Dodd-Frank Act will ensure that businesses have a more stable and predictable source of credit throughout the business cycle and will reduce the risk of a sharp and sudden cut-off because of financial panic (para. 12).

IMF and Other International Organizations

The IMF and other international organizations (e.g., UN, FAO) are also involved in realizing different initiatives around the world.

Conclusions

This is all a testament that things are being done and that efforts and energies are being spent. If implemented properly, they might help to address some of the many challenges posed thus far. A question remains: Are the above measures translating into a prolonged structural and *systemic* recovery for economies, investors, businesses, and citizens of these countries? Or is it a temporary short duration revival?

Many periodic institutional reports, articles, studies, and papers from different authoritative sources provide ample evidence of the effectiveness of the measures undertaken and the economic scenario that the global economy will be facing in the immediate future (Federal Reserve System 2012b; IMF 2012; US Department of the Treasury 2012). According to these reports, there seems to be a consensus among organizations and government agencies around the world[25] that much work remains to be done.

The impressive amounts of "Financial Facilities," *Rescue Facilities*, the *European Financial Stability Facility* and its successor(s), the *European Stability Mechanism* (ESM); bank recapitalizations; "financing" pledges by IMF, Bank of Japan, and Bank of England; *asset purchases,* European Central Bank *refinancing,* UK Treasury *new funding*; and other forms of grants, loans, liquidity, etc.,[26] have produced some results in a few sectors and specific geographical areas—*but there is an objective recognition that we are substantially far away from a systemic and structural recovery*.

The reader is invited to visit these institutional, continuously updated sources and websites—it is important to rely on the most recent versions of these reports (or new ones) to augment one's understanding of the depth, breadth, extension, and growing ramifications of the global economic, societal, and political scenario.

Geopolitical tensions around the world, the continued financial risks associated with the Eurozone, and now even some BRIC countries such as China, the frailty of the recovery, and the public debt levels and fiscal issues of many countries only add layers of complexity to the already delicate scenario.

---

25. i.e., World Bank, OECD, Bank of England, IMF, European Central Bank, Federal Reserve, US Treasury, Bank of Japan, etc.
26. Federal Reserve System: Monetary Policy Report to Congress (Federal Reserve System 2012b).

These efforts undertaken by governments are very important, and many might become part of the long-term solution. Incredibly, they might be even more effective within the framework of an equally modernized and up-to-date model.

Some of these have produced some benefits and others might start to yield some positive results and signs of recovery. Yet taking into account the number of new variables incapable of being elaborated by our models (e.g., virtualization of activities, processes, Web inclusivity, etc., numerous systemic blocks, and important dichotomies) that overwhelm almost all economic sectors, for how long can current models be overstretched and overexerted before something gives? In short, is the current model geared to withstand accumulating strains from new era variables for long? How long? As with all preceding models is it bound to fail at some point?

Should there be the slightest doubt that the measures might not be able to address these structural and systemic challenges, might it be worthwhile to start considering the possibility of looking at these important issues from a different perspective or even an evolved modality? According to the US Department of the Treasury in 2012, the cost of the crisis, just in the United States, has been as follows (US Department of the Treasury 2012):

- 19 trillion lost in household wealth (Q2 2007–Q1 2009)

- 8.7 million lost jobs (December 2007–February 2010)

- 6.3 million more Americans in poverty (2007–2009) (13)

Yet these only represent a partial rieality limited only to one nation. If and when there will be other short cycles of mini recoveries as business and jobs are shed and new lower levels of economic plateaus are reached, and for example, key indicators, such as unemployment, redefined to exclude ever growing real numbers of jobless, business closures, and so on from official numbers, would these though provide structural remedies and address the growing number of very real concerns that indubitably affect independence and leadership.

Surrendering Leadership

The inefficacy of our search for appropriate solutions within existing models, some are starting to reason that they might be content passing on leadership, reaching illusionary secondary, or tertiary places in the global economic scenario with respect to other economies that might seem to benefit temporarily from an ephemeral positive growth rate. This reasoning would suggest the following (non-exhaustive list):

- the acceptance that little or nothing can be done (loss of resilience)

- relinquishing a theoretically dominant position

- the cognizance of not having answers

- conscientious acknowledgment of lack of independence and acceptance of dependence

- the acceptance of a new polarization rather than a multipolar one

Other views contend that there might be nothing more wrong than this seemingly logical conclusion, stating that if the scales tip toward economic leadership by others, one thing that might need to be considered is, that succumbing societies will need to adhere to the rules, living standards, ways of thinking, social structures, political and individual liberties, and levels of freedom dictated by these others. Additionally we must remind ourselves they might be in similar boats, facing analogous fate, in a not so distant future. What sense would it make to arrive second and become subject to someone who is in the same dire position, if not worse?

Whether these considerations are right or wrong, one aspect is of tantamount importance—civil liberties, freedoms, and advancements in all fields, matured through centuries of evolution and wars on behalf of many civilizations are exposed more than ever before in shorter timeframes than one could ever imagine. Recent revolutions have set perfect precedents. Moreover, what sense would it make to move toward archaic models if the citizens of many developing countries are increasingly seeking freedom and more evolved forms of democracy or, in some extreme cases, at least different shades of it, to the point of risking their lives and those of their loved ones? It is easy to jump to the first logical conclusion and think that this dispute could be between East and West or North and South. In reality, in today's volatile scenario, sparks can ignite in any geographical context vis-a-vis any other. Contests could involve regions such as Africa, Southeast Asia, the Caucasus, or Australasia. Small, apparently insignificant, examples of such disputes seem to be emerging in the news all around the globe.[27] To this list we must add a growing number of near-failed states, disaggregation of entire societies, civil and territorial wars, mass-migratory movements they generate, the possible diffusion of deadly viruses, rebirth of evolving forms of terrorism, boundary-independent insurgence, piracy, slavery . . . occurring around the world.

Although there is room for debate, there are two certainties. Historically, moments of extreme frailty lead to voids and voids are filled at faster rates than we might wish to accept. Once filled, balances change, especially those of leadership. Once independence is relinquished, if ever regained it is only at an excessive cost.

With uncertain stock markets, enormous sums are still being placed into speculative higher-yield or flight-for-safety investments. This has generated pressures on some governments to implement arguably quasi-authoritarian-style austerity measures on their citizens (e.g., PIGSI Portugal, Italy, Greece, Spain, Ireland), only fueling social unrest, dangerous rekindling of historical sentiments, and discriminatory thoughts of preoccupying proportions for the first time since World War II. The point in case might no longer just be a pro- or contra- regional unions such as the EU or the so much needed peace in the middle east but one of increasing geopolitical complexity.

The reality is that the US, EU, and a growing list of other economies are not by any stretch of the imagination where they could or should be; furthermore, no economy in the developed world is where its citizens might like it to be. For that matter, this might be true for the majority of citizens of BRIC and emerging countries as well. Without gaining an appreciation for the acceptance of new ideas that can bring sustained recovery and real growth,

---

27. e.g., litigation between countries previously under the sphere of influence of the ex-soviet union; disputes over islands around Japan, the Philippines, and China; resparking of separatist movements in many regions and countries

continuing on the current path is likely to expose our models and economies to more volatility and vacillation.

The welfare of a society affects everything, including its organization and freedoms. Freedom is a concept that has seen its birth and resurgence in several countries across the globe. It has been enriched by evolution through the contributions of many across the world. It is the result of numerous people who fought and died against slavery, racism, totalitarian rule, and the many different ideologies and countries that adopted them against those who committed genocides, those who suffocated liberty of thought, choice, of creed, of assembly; against those who prohibited free trade and free movement of persons; against all those who oppressed and segregated; and against those who used hate and fear to dominate others. It owes its existence to the cumulative sacrifice of people from all across the planet—from Greece to Britain, from the United States to Iraq and Afghanistan, from North/South Africa to South America, from China to India, from the Australia to southeast Asia, from South Korea to Israel, from Canada, and the Scandinavian countries to all the nations making up the former Soviet Union—in any place the quintessential nature of humanity desires its reaffirmation.

Freedom does not belong to a country or physical place; rather, it is implemented and exercised by those who desire it. It does not need to be exported or imported. It is an idea that lives a feeble existence and walks on a thin line between two daunting and damning extremes. It has provided humankind with its biggest leaps in advancement and its explosion of ideas individually, as a society, and spiritually.

The democratic process today is far from perfect and in need for much modernization, but it is the freest governance system humankind has been able to produce. It is up to us to face the challenge of improving it and evolving it toward new, higher, and better levels of rights, freedoms, democracy, governance, and civilization. The new model proposed herein promotes and provides some of the most significant building blocks for such progress.

Hence, a more salutary strategy might be maintaining a healthy and balanced innovative leadership in evolving the economic model and policy, to the next level of sustainability and long-term prosperity, paving the way for a new area of opportunity, well-being, and progression of civilization.

Is the Current Model Reaching its Point of Failure?

As seen in earlier parts, increasing numbers of new model-changing variables are being introduced at growing rates, and they will continue to be introduced probably at even greater rates. As the number of endemic systemic blocks grows, destabilizing the economic model, it no longer responds overwhelmed by new variables with which it was not meant to deal.

Given where we stand today and the outlook for the foreseeable future, notwithstanding all the titanic efforts put in place by many, there is substantial evidence that existing models might not be fully equipped to provide concrete answers to the challenges posed by the multitude of new paradigms and variables.

Each of the foundations of the existing economic models is possibly already overstretched in addressing the existing complexity of the impasse. Multidimensional dichotomies introduced by sustainability, new variables, and disruptive paradigms, only add more complexity and exacerbate the situation even further increasing the exposure to possible virulent systemic events as these fail to elaborate and or process them adequately.

An analogy could be an older-type PC connected to an elementary network with other old PCs, running on prior-generation operating systems, extremely limited CPU capacities, and dated circuitry and logic. They use earlier programming languages with interfaces that are no longer geared to work with today's programs, interfaces, connections, data volumes, processing capability, and transfer rates.

What has happened is that we have connected this rudimentary network to the Internet via a high-speed connection with applications running in a cloud environment. For now, we are managing to maintain frail connections and minimal processing capability with many patches.

The more the existing models are exposed to and challenged with new variables and paradigms, the greater the number of multidimensional dichotomies created, generating additional challenges and substantially escalating the possibilities for systemic failures and unwanted effects. The interaction between the primary pillars of the existing economic models is becoming growingly nonresponsive. Current policies are struggling in yielding concrete results in the recovery process, let alone lasting solutions. Nonetheless, the worst might be yet to come in terms of the necessity in addressing game-changing variables. Considering the last couple of market bubble bursts, the effects of the self-consuming systemic vortex might be depicted as an implosive/explosive cycle (similar to the cycle of a dying star).

Effects of the Self-Consuming Systemic Vortex/Paradox and Its Implosive/Explosive Cycle in the Last Two Market Bubble Bursts and Financial Systems Near Meltdown

From Implosive　　　　　　**Toward Explosive**

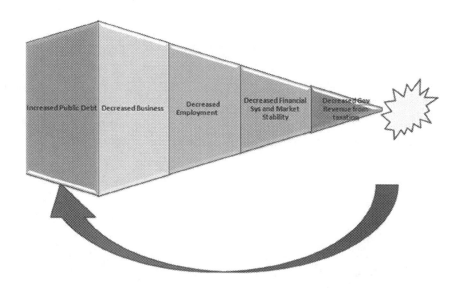

Due to the complexity of the current scenario, all the above considerations might only be of purely academic relevance and may be subject matter of curiosity for future historians.

Model Fixation: A Syndrome to Fret

Each ideologically formed "ism" seems to have come about in a specific historical moment in answer to the stimuli, needs, and requirements of its time. It thrived for a while and then entered a downward spiral until a very distinct moment—when models start to become acknowledged as "untouchable" or unquestionable "sacred monsters"—giving rise to a phenomenon that could be called *model fixation*. After a while, as more and more start voicing objective concerns about the real nature of these dated, archaic, and counterproductive models—a final—in most cases, previously inconceivable, very rapid series of events replace these.

To provide a parallel on model fixation, a documentary centered on psychological experiments, carried out in the late 1950s, asked a diverse group of volunteers to ask a set of true-or-false questions to a person in an adjacent room who they could hear, but not see, via a speaker.

For the experiment to be successful each time they received a false answer to the list of questions with which they were provided, participants were to push a button without hesitation, knowing that it would inflict increasingly severe electric shocks and pain to the person in the adjacent room. Each time the person behind the wall provided a wrong answer, the volunteers pushed the button and could hear the lamentation from the person behind the wall. The volunteers believed they were consciously inducing this pain.

The volunteers did not know that the entire experiment was staged. The person behind the wall was not tied to any electrical circuit and, thus, was not being shocked. The person was just acting. Only a couple of the participants refused to complete the experiment while the rest continued consciously inducing greater levels of pain for the full length of the long experiment.

The study suggested that if you provide a context, a seemingly valid purpose, a set of rules, a set of objectives, and a professional-looking ambiance, only a few people will question the experiment to the point of deciding to stop it and, in this case, refusing to be taken over by sheer madness. This is evident to everyone outside that context.

This tendency is called model fixation. The previous analogy, of course, was an extreme example, but given the drastic nature of the current world scenario, whatever we do in life and the role each of us plays in society, are we sure we collectively want to leave our destinies and those of our children to the workings of a set of accepted norms, even those developed out of goodwill? They worked for a time but are now only inflicting greater amounts of unnecessary hardships on the vast majority for an indefinite period.

We cannot allow things to get out of hand for too long out of complacency and/or fear of judgment from those who staunchly remain attached to a model. Complacency and blind reverence toward a model was at the base of scenarios where millions lost their priceless lives in wars, gulags, and concentration camps in Europe, the Soviet Union, and mass exterminations in Africa and Southeast Asia not very long ago. With the benefit of hindsight, it took the willpower of very few men and women in key roles and the incredible sacrifice of entire generations to end these horrendous genocides.

Model fixation is the central theme of many advanced studies and is conducive to many real-life problems that can cause varying degrees of harmful damage to individuals, organizations, businesses, governments, and nations. It is so harmful that a growing number of large corporations and key government organizations are evaluating the possibility of introducing what we could call the "nth man counter-proposer, advisor, or decision maker"[28] in their key decision-making and governance teams sometimes conferring them with considerable veto power.

It seems we are currently suffering from an advanced forms of model fixation in a growing number of areas of human activity. The prolonged deadlock and other feats testify that our current models have not been devised, geared, or equipped to recognize, identify, elaborate on, and address a growing number of new variables properly and effectively. They substantially fail to address the challenges they pose and provide the necessary answers.

Additionally, the properties and characteristics of new or evolved versions of these new variables are so different that our models simply fail to keep up, distinguish them, and inhibiting their effectiveness. Looking around it is not hard to see that there is a mounting need for answers to the increasing new challenges.

It is difficult to assess if there has been a time similar to today, where the fate of so many (individuals, business, investors, governments) across the globe is interlinked. With few exceptions, essential questions

---

[28]. A person among every n members of the same team chosen to counter validate key decisions based on accepted norms or assumptions.

and needs seem to coincide on a planetary scale. It is now time to pose the very tough questions and to seek valid workable answers that can withstand the test of time.

Factual data suggests that the frequency of catastrophic economic events[29] has increased with diminishing intervals between them; both the events and their effects seem to last longer and the scale and magnitude of the damage in absolute terms seem to be greater each time. The challenges we face seem to grow, each time requiring a new set of tools and frameworks on distinctly different planes. We have been dealing with the same type of malady for many years now.

The cures adopted so far, however, only seem to have given temporary relief from some of the symptoms. The underlying metastasis might, in reality, be growing faster than we would wish. Are existing models to blame or faulty then?

To be balanced and objective, existing models seem to have brought humanity probably the longest and most prosperous period in its history, allowing an unprecedented distribution of wealth and security among the vast majority of people living in the countries using these models at least until a decade or so ago. However, the models, whatever their innate flaws and shortcomings were simply products of human intellect and valid for the timeframe and conditions for which they were developed.

What if we choose to look at the problem from a new and different perspective, stepping away from blaming the model and concentrating on the overall picture? On the large scale, two primary variables in the equation become evident—namely, the model and the context in which it was applied and worked adequately. So if the model was not at fault, where does that leave us?

It is clear that the world around us, and our way of doing things has dramatically changed and continue to change at increasing rates. It is not reasonably possible, hence, to expect the existing model to address increasing new challenges developing at exponentially higher rates.

In addition, there are other variables—for example, the interaction between the model and the context—that are also not working properly.

---

29.   e.g., Internet bubbles, real estate bubbles, and the 2008 financial meltdown.

Emerging from the Fog

Today's economic model is based on the interaction between a set of well-defined dimensions, elements, and components, such as public debt, fiscal policy, different economic sectors, employment, the banking system, and pensions. Imagine each forming a box that is interconnected with the other boxes, which in turn produce a reference model. Any reference model allows for the use of a finite set of tools. In theory, everything fares well as long as the underlying premises that gave birth to such needs remain unchanged.

Over an extended period, the relative success of a reference model provides the basis not only for its acceptance, but also for its consolidation as a principle. The longer this axiom holds true, the greater the chance for it to become an unquestionable reality. Once the context starts changing due to new, external forces, the natural tendency is to patch the boxes, interactions, and frameworks.

This, however, can only be done up to a certain critical point. Beyond this point, the external forces substantially change the underlying paradigms on which the boxes originally relied. Accordingly, not only is the effectiveness of such a strategy reduced, but due to the interconnection with other boxes, the fallout from these stimuli may produce worse effects or highly unpopular and controversial domino consequences.[30]

Another strategy is the adoption of policies that push the problems beyond the political horizon of new legislatures for a few more years. These strategies only lead to the accumulation of destructive forces that increase the potential impact on the overall economy. In the absence of real answers, yet another strategy is to force solutions by dismantling and demonizing single elements of the existing reference model without truly considering the medium to long-term knock on effects. Employment, retirement, pensions, and health care policies are but a few of these examples.

Decade-long mantras are devised to shape and convince public opinion that what used to be perfectly congenial and necessary elements have become vices and need to be curbed, reduced, or annulled—allegedly, in the general interest of the majority.

---

[30]   e.g., austerity measures, increased taxes

100

These strategies also hide unwanted avalanche effect of a myriad of other areas and usually create, among other things, many inequalities among living generations that have benefited from them and those that are called to contribute to them amidst other hardships without being able to benefit from them.

It is not clear that policies that have tried to change public views have produced tangible results and resolved the issues. *The increase in retirement age, for example, does not appear to have produced any tangible positive outcome regarding net costs or benefits for the majority of people, companies, businesses, investors, and pension funds* or addressed real-life issues that real people live every day.

They, instead, seemed to have produced an additional layer of complexity in things such as: the natural generational turnover, freeing up space for younger generations in the marketplace, and creating the professional growth and career-development possibilities that are the lifeblood of any enterprise and economy.

Addressing the legitimate needs of generations (young, middle-aged, and old) that are left in the limbo of a proper and deserving form of retirement, pension, etc. (public or private). Or is the truth of the matter simply that these issues have become even more multifaceted?

These very serious and tough issues touch every single person sooner or later independent of generation. How realistic is it to think that the large majority of a growing number of people who are impacted by these policies will find employment or business opportunities in normal economic conditions before reaching current retirement-age ceilings, let alone in an era filled with new game-changing variables. Or be able to continue their professional aspirations in the current economic scenario? Pension funds exposed to volatile markets be able to assure and address the needs of growing numbers that seek proper returns or at the least assured and secured pensions.

The issue is not about public versus private pension funds or either of these being a vice. *To the contrary, since they deal with people's pensions, private pension funds can positively contribute to the healthy running of economies. In achieving just this though, a few challenges need to be addressed to make them produce even more benefits sustainably with greater business potential to all stakeholders over the long term.*

Seen from this new perspective then, are we sure that pensions, for instance, are truly the real demons (i.e., one of the major threats to national economies and debts)? *Might we be looking at the problem only through the prism of the currently boxed model and seeing a problem, wherein reality there could be a series of opportunities?*

And what to say, for instance, about the validity, effectiveness or objectivity, and reasonableness of growingly unsustainable fiscal pressures that individuals, businesses, and organizations are subjected to? We have reached a stage whereby in some countries it is gone beyond constitutionality while in others the fiscal levy outweighs the value/price of a product or service (e.g., airline tickets). To be balanced, some would argue that if you look at the issues from the prism of the current model, it all makes perfect sense—under the current paradigm, the mantra makes sense because the underlying reasons are linked to the theoretical effect it has on elements within the same boxes. But is it right or what it should be—especially if some of these concepts such as retirement was one of the major achievements of human advancement? *If analyzed from a totally different perspective, we might discover that current models are actually hindering or hiding opportunities.*

And yet, so far we have touched-on only one of a myriad of other variables that constitute our current model. *Remedies, reforms that do not produce desired outcomes and value to the majority of stakeholders, or produce more problems than benefits, cannot be called solutions.* We must ask ourselves if we are not following models just because they have been valid references in the past and, as such, have become the only reality.

The blind acceptance of brutal current events is not only unmaintainable but also unjustifiable and nonacceptable. For example, news headlines suggest that increasing number of families (in different nations), out of desperation, are leaving a growing number of children in orphanages, while in others more and more persons struggling in making ends meet face the incredible dilemma of having to take on loans to pay taxes. Is this sacrifice warranted? Without being idealistic or rhetorical, are these the levels of civilization twenty-first-century humans (we) wish to pursue? Is this the legacy we wish to leave as living generations? Is this what we are all about?

The centrality of the human element and the ecosystem in the current paradigm is increasingly jeopardized and sacrificed. This is not an ideological or an business/market/economic unfriendly issue. Quite the opposite.

Historically, every time these fundamental elements of an economy have become a hindrance, the existing reference model has ultimately been superseded by a more evolved one. The underlying fundamental values behind the nascence of the United States of America and a market-based economy set a perfect example. In today's global crisis, the number of elements that no longer find answers, such as retirement, public debt, markets, unemployment, business closures, investments, etc., is growing and will continue to do so *ceteris paribus*.[31]

The current scenario has truly economy-wide and planetary dimensions. Apart from exceptional and singular cases, which nation, government, or individual might be exempt from or unaffected by the current impasse? As paradoxical as it might sound, the level of exposure to risks grows with the level of wealth.

The risk of remaining fixated on current models and not being prepared to adopt an alternative winning strategy, even when it is apparent the current models might bring about defeat at exorbitant costs, is real. History books are full of examples of catastrophic consequences deriving from model fixation. Consider the following examples:

- As paradigm-changing machine guns appeared on the battlefield, entire armies still used old-style maneuvers, assembling entire battalions of soldiers in perfect company or platoon-sized units that would literally walk in militaristic fashion toward the enemy in a suicidal manner.

- The famous Maginot Line, built after World War I by the French to defend their northern border from Germany at exorbitant costs to its citizenry, was completely in vain, as a new German Blitzkrieg strategy flanked the entire French defensive line, attacking France through the Belgian border.

- The introduction of PCs in a world dominated by large mainframes and manual processes produced a revolution—those business models that failed to adapt quickly were exposed to considerable consequences.

[31.] Everything else remains the same.

Contemplate the impact the invention and concept of a needle, a simple fishing hook, or a nail had on the creation of a plethora of industries from its prehistoric origins until today—from fishing, to its many uses in medicine, to leather-made products and textiles, to armaments (a firing pin), to the predigital recording industry, to its use in skin care and orthodontics, to its use in furniture manufacturing, to its use in the automotive industry, or to its use in construction.

What can we say about the invention of glass and its geometric resonance and impact on vision, building and construction, medicine, science, vehicles, aerospace and defense, shipping, appliances, kitchenware, etc.? These examples, deliberately of relatively small significance, demonstrate how seemingly meaningless variables, innovations, etc., can have the most impressive and/or gravest consequences with effects much larger than might be expected.

If this is true for a small, game-changing innovation, what might the combined impact of many advancements already here or available in the near future, be on entire economies, nationally and on a global scale. Are we sure our current models provide the tools to address these challenges appropriately?

PART 2

VIRTUS—a Possible Solution

Introduction

In a world where all productive human activity is being virtualized, how is it possible to think of continuing to resolve issues with unfit/dated/increasingly unresponsive models—our existing models? With the potentially unknown number of new variables and paradigms we face and will continue to face, we will need equally modernized and evolved models to address these.

To succeed at this feat, we will need to step outside the existing framework and distance ourselves enough to see the true extent of the wider picture. It is unreasonable to believe that this evolution will happen overnight—but not even one that requires unrealistic timeframes. Transition toward a new plateau must be planned and migration will need to include soft switchovers to new models and modalities, facilitating the step-level evolution toward a new plateau of long-term development, prosperity, and civilization.

The following chapters explore the wider picture, appreciate where our models stand, and evaluate the options at hand. Next, a possible solution is introduced. New concepts, models, and protocols are defined and explained, providing a sample high-level road map together with possible migration and transition tools. Finally, a diversified set of concrete examples follows as indication for the real-life applicability of the model and concepts to a set of different economic sectors and economic dimensions, such as public debt and employment. The reforms henceforth discussed are structural and systemic in nature and aimed at achieving economic recovery in realistic yet short timeframes with long-term, prolonged impacts on national economies and prosperity.

This treatise does not provide the solution to all dilemmas or a magic-wand approach. Rather, it provides a possible alternative perspective from which the solution can be developed. The proposed solution introduced here is presented as an open, baseline framework, one that is modular and scalable, actively seeking to, and leave ample room for the contribution, continuous improvement, and completion of many people and experts from different fields.

Evolution: Life's Quintessential Strategy

Why touch on the subject of evolution? Evolution is said to be one of the constants in the universe. From the smallest particles of matter to the unknown number of galaxies that comprise the universe(s), everything is subject to constant evolution. Nature and the relatively tiny planet on which we live evolve geologically, chemically, and biologically. The lives of cells, plants, animals, and humans are affected by it; our lives evolve. Our bodies and our thoughts undergo continuous evolution on a daily basis, and anything in nature or made by humans evolves, including the level of civilization we enjoy. Evolution is everywhere and touches everything.

Evolution, adaptation, and choosing the appropriate strategies make the difference between success and failure. Anthropologists seem to agree that humanity is among the weakest species physically. Yet this evident impediment that exposed humankind to a very real extinction risk for thousands of years forced it to devise stratagems that allowed it not only to survive through many cataclysmic events, including an ice age or two, but also to dominate over the rest of the natural kingdom, leveraging human intelligence.

Current archeological knowledge suggests that early humans probably migrated from Africa and the Middle East to the four corners of the world. Humankind's initial survival, growth, and success were tied to three fundamental strategies: (1) improve survival and security by keeping in groups, (2) consume what is readily available in nature, and (3) move on to new ground as resources deplete.

In time, some separated or remained behind and settled. This may have been tied to economies of scale, the impossibility of satisfying the needs of ever-growing group members, frustration and exasperation from wandering around, a decreasing need for further migration as a better appreciation for the cyclical events in nature that lead to the invention of farming, and herding or a mix of these. Whatever the real reason(s), settlement became the new survival strategy, the new paradigm, the game changer—a precursor in evolution.

One thing seems apparent: the migratory strategy that led humankind to the next hunting ground reached its climax when humans reached the four corners of the earth advancing over allegedly, then-existing intercontinental crossings and there were few other viable spaces into which to venture.[32]

At this point, venturing back probably entailed entering the vital space occupied by those who had decided to remain behind and settle. And this, perhaps more frequently than not, entailed bloodshed. It is not important if events evolved in exactly this way. What is important is that humankind, at a certain point in time, faced the challenge of changing its survival strategy. Evolution could no longer be postponed and had to come about in a relatively short time through a *step-level evolutionary change*. The migratory strategy that once seemed to be the only reference model had simply ceased to be a viable strategy for the majority.

These moments of evolutionary change were driven by the cost of continuing with an existing strategy. Those who found new ways of survival were those who progressed and found new ways to thrive, grow, and succeed as individuals, families, villages, city-states, countries, empires, and republics.

Those who staunchly stuck to old paradigms, strategies, models, and ways slowly fell behind and, in most cases, either vanished over time or survived in very small groups at the fringes of new societies. Simply put, humanity is the master of its own success or demise. New survival strategies have continuously replaced existing ones that were believed to be the only possibilities in a series of iterations.

Fall of Empires:

When visiting places once occupied by great civilizations, a few questions immediately come to mind to many travelers. What happened to these civilizations? Why have they not continued building pyramids, ziggurats, or temples? Why is there no evidence of continuation? Why and how could the people who built these magnificent monuments simply vanish? Where did they go? What happened to the Egyptians, Persians, Greeks, and Romans? What happened to the British Empire? As societies developed, those that evolved became the new game changers of their

---

32. Some scientists suggest some of these intercontinental crossings (e.g., Asia-America, Asia-Australia) were made possible or facilitated by the lowering of ocean levels and glacial bridging (Asia-America) deriving from cyclical ice ages.

times. Disputes or wars sometimes ensued, as the new entrants instilled a natural fear in societies surrounding them that held onto dated strategies. Ultimately, most of the societies that feared the loss of their previously dominant positions lost these disputes or wars. The new societies that emerged as the winners immediately filled the void created by their predecessors in the evolutionary process.

The new entrants and the places they inhabited, most likely, became the center of attraction for all those who mastered a trade and, among these, the best and brightest. Most came from the defeated city or empire. Thousands, if not millions, migrated to the next new land of opportunity, leaving Egypt, Persia, Greece, Rome, etc., devoid of much of their know-how and the possibility of any substantial further progress. Then dust settled on these once great civilizations over time, until that is, the next cycle of evolutionary leadership.

That is why those lands did not continue creating Ur, Sumer, Babylon, Karnak, the Pyramids, Persepolis, the Parthenon, the Collosseum, and Westminster Abbey, which once stood as emblems of where the centers of civilization of their own time resided. This is even more evident when you visit museums such as the Louvre in Paris and follow the suggested chronological path. It literally takes you across a history of evolution, from the first human settlements and civilizations onward, showing how everything seems to fit the pattern of human progress.

One witnesses how everything—from useful objects in day-to-day life, such as pottery, to complex strategies of warfare, to engineering and construction methods, to the arts in the general administration of a state, to writing and record keeping, to channeling water across hundreds of kilometers—evolved over the centuries, as each new civilization added something more to the preceding model. It allowed new ideas to come into being and exploited them.

For example, one notices how the art of building columns progressed from Babylonia, Assyria, and Egypt, to Persia, to Doria, to Corinth, to Athens, and to Rome. Underground irrigation methods, such as the "Qanat," used to transport water under hundreds of kilometers of deserts across the Middle East, gave way to the fundamental science behind the building of spectacular aqueducts in Rome and throughout its empire.

Trade across sea and terrestrial routes, such as the Silk Road, brought evolution in textiles, food, tapestry, art, and musical instruments.

Each new perspective brought new ideas and new uses—from noodles to spaghetti and from gunpowder only being used for fireworks to its multiple uses in from warfare and mining to space exploration.

Throughout history, the new land of opportunity (the America of its time) would quickly attract the best artisans, architects, teachers, scientists, doctors, engineers, workers, and managers—the best of the best in each area of human activity.

Growing masses of people were fueled by the passion and desire to improve their lives for themselves and their children, leaving the old state of affairs to the dust of time.

All these men and women had one fundamental trait in common. They were eager to bring about an evolutionary change in their life. They believed that this move would bring them prosperity, especially for their future generations. As time went by, this growth and the search for a new paradigm went hand in hand with a growing need for individual freedom, rights, and more civilized societies.

Every time humanity approached a new dead end, it faced a new evolutionary need for change. Today, all signs indicate that we have reached a similar step-level evolutionary episode. If we are not there yet, we are very close. Pragmatically, does it really matter or make a difference knowing where the exact demarcation point is located?

Is It Time to Evolve?

We only notice evolution in the brief moments we look back at what no longer exists. Evolution is made up of many small steps. They seem insignificant when looked at individually on a daily basis, yet they are impressive when we notice the sheer distance covered. Yet if one does not begin the journey, nothing will ever happen, no one will ever go anywhere, and time will consume everything.

The time to change might be of secondary importance for those who begin to sense a need for change is imminent. Some just get stuck in a loop, wondering about evolution, while others are fearful to take the first step. A successful few will spearhead it, making history, inspiring many more to choose the road to continuance, survival, well-being, and progression for themselves and their loved ones.

Humanity has had to face many evolutionary changes and so far, each has been successful. Most of these changes occur linearly (e.g. the new version of a certain software) whereas others require or induce a step-level (no longer linear) move to a higher dimension(s). Such is the case of today's game-changing / disruptive technology, and so on. The invention and use of fire, agriculture, steel and other metals, and barter were all unquestionably game changers. Ultimately, money allowed trade in ways that bartering could never have achieved.

Even religions in many ways faced change in enriching humanity with an evolved appreciation for the world, spirituality, conscientiousness, awareness, and its rapport with life and other fellow humans. In recent decades, the inventions of flight, space exploration, computers, the Internet, mobile communications, nanotechnology, etc., have impacted our lives in numerous and incredible ways.

These changes have substantially influenced all of us and will continue to effect and inspire us in unforeseeable ways. Couple these gigantic technological advancements with the incredible challenges humanity faces with sustainability, natural calamities, and the current global economic crisis and all the elements for a new, step-level evolutionary need for change are in place.

Never has humanity been able to produce so much (e.g., products, services, ideas, processes) as it has done in the past three or four generations. According to *The Economist,* the combined economic output from the first century onward does not match that of the twentieth century, let alone that which might be produced in this century (Maddison 2012).

Even so, there is still potential for more advancement. It is necessary to find evolved ways of tapping into it. Today's generations have become so accustomed to seeing innovative solutions (that were science fiction literally only a few years back) pop up nearly on a daily basis that we might not appreciate the impact they have on our lives, at least in the short term.

To understand the extent of the impact of recent inventions on our lives, consider how many simple day-to-day activities are no longer necessary—for example, searching for and entering a telephone booth, dialing a phone number on a circular dial, cranking up a window in a car, inserting or rewinding a music cassette or VHS tape, manually loading garbage trucks, carrying heavy objects in our arms, forcing a typewriter carriage to the next line, licking a stamp, and manually washing dishes or clothes. Think of how many objects that were useful and necessary only a few years back have dramatically changed shape and are no longer in use.

Reasonably, it is no longer necessary to buy the following items separately: photographic camera, movie camera, stereo, agenda, telephone, writing pad, magnetic compass, pen, eraser, calculator, map, clock, game cards, board game, navigational system, TV, remote control, CD, DVD, book, newspaper, encyclopedia, stopwatch, speakers, voice recorder, a step counter, blood pressure indicator, a key and more. They can all be found in a smartphone or tablet.

Reflect on how many things have influenced our daily behavior and rapport with others only in the last generation: the disproportionate amount of time spent using a smartphone or the Internet, fixating one's thoughts and time on an a screen for an abnormal number of hours each day, 365 days a year, cell-phone anxiety, the different approach to human interaction moving from the physical to the virtual, the change in our languages and the way we communicate, and the endless search for information on search engines.

Yet, the impact of each of these on business, the economy, and the individual is astounding. Only three decades ago, entire stories of buildings pertaining to the same business were filled with people performing then useful jobs. It is absurd to think of going back. Our world is changing by the millisecond in and yet we try to address our problems with the same reference models of the past. This also seems to touch our very survival strategy.

Epochal Challenges and Mounting Feats

Net of possible mini-recoveries as lower equilibrium levels are reached after each cycle of business closures, and unemployment; Growing evidence all around us suggests that all levels of the economy (local, national, international) face mounting, increasingly irresolvable challenges that contribute to complexity and generate potentially virulent systemic blocks and dichotomies—the following is a non-exhaustive summary:

- Loss of "economic traction": Traction, we could say, is created and led by demand, availability of income, propensity to spend, etc. The more an economy fails in this, the greater the loss of traction and the challenges of restoring it. An analogy here could be a bicycle's eroded, dented sprocket wheel that fails to hook the chain properly, allowing the energy applied to the pedals to be transferred to the rear wheel for drive. Continued erosion and misngagement of the chain initially creates short, dangerous slippages of the chain that, in turn, erode the sprockets even further. Ultimately and beyond a certain point, any energy applied to the pedals will yield lesser advancement and any additional energy applied simply adds cost.

- Debt, tax, and structural problems: excessive public debt, its implications (e.g., fiscal cliffs).

National debt by country is more vividly depicted on *The Economist* website (Economist Intelligence Unit n.d.), which plots past and predicted debt levels. As dates in the future are chosen, the number of countries predicted to reach alarming levels of debt, and hence portrayed in red or shades of it, increases—practically covering most of the world's primary, secondary, and tertiary economies including countries those that today seem to be less affected by such phenomena such China and India, Canada, Australia, and many affluent middle-eastern countries.

According to the GAO (n.d.a), with this rate of increase in debt, sometime between now and 2040, mandatory spending will exceed government revenues, leading the United States toward a fiscally unsustainable path. Might this hold true also for many other developed countries, much before that date? States in this condition seem to be exposed instrumentally to large market forces and investors to conform and adopt certain measures. Should the total debt figure ($45 trillion) for the world be true (Economist Intelligence Unit n.d.) or close to it, US debt represents 33 percent of the total (c. $15 trillion). Whatever the real total number for the planet, it is of overwhelming proportions. What will the real additional impact of growing population age and growing pension and healthcare costs be on government debt?

- Persistent high (real) unemployment. According to the CBO, the last years of the recent recession were "the longest stretch of high unemployment in this country since the Great Depression" (CBO 2012c, para. 1); moreover, the CBO states that *the official unemployment rate excludes those individuals who would like to work but have not searched for a job in the past four weeks, as well as those who are working part-time but would prefer full-time work; if those people were counted among the unemployed, the unemployment rate in January 2012 would have been about 15 percent.* Compounding the problem of high unemployment, *the share of unemployed looking for work for more than six months* "topped 40 percent in December 2009 for the first time since 1948 when such data began to be collected; it has remained above that level ever since" (CBO 2012b, 9; emphasis added);

- Investment focus shifting away from real economy to financial markets. As the CBO put it, with business ventures becoming less attractive investments vis-à-vis investing in government securities, theoretically less and less funds could be available to produce real products and services, further impacting the economy.

- Structural impacts reducing further reducing growth potential and capability (e.g., mismatched skill needs and locations, erosion of management capability as a result of mass layoffs);

- Erosion of adequate or competitive technology due to limited investment.

- Effects of the volatile availability of credit on business, investments, innovation, closures, and resulting job losses that add to reduced tax intakes.

- Induced negative effect produced by the reduced funding, consequent wreaking, and deterioration of vital services necessary for an economy, its businesses, and citizenry, such as maintenance of key infrastructure, education, emergency and first responder services, natural disaster mitigation and reconstruction, defense, judicial and law enforcement services, public transportation, public health and so on, and the dichotomies these generate.[33]

- Liquidity quicksand: continued massive injections of liquidity that do not permeate into the wider economy, as intended to help recovery.

- Systemic failure of industrial life support: government support to industry has had short-lived effects under current models—in most cases the support has failed to produce long-term *systemic* traction or to regenerate lasting development, business growth, increased stakeholder value, and long-term employment.;

- Increased exposure to risks: particularly of financial institutions irrespective of numerous reforms and policy measures.

- Increased endemic volatility of markets deriving from:

  o   uncertainty (e.g., Eurozone, growth of BRIC's);

  o   objective success / enforceability of reforms;

  o   excessive over- or under-valuation of equity (share) prices; and

---

33.   The White House blog referred to the president Obama's speech on the US national debt: "(see addendum chart 1). . . . to make matters worse, the recession meant that there was less money coming in, and it required us to spend even more—on tax cuts for middle-class families to spur the economy, on unemployment insurance; on aid to states so we could prevent more teacher and firefighters and police officers from being laid off" (White House n.d.).

o   prolonged adverse economic conditions and exposures

- Growing exposure to (real) inflationary, deflationary, or stagnation phenomena in a growing number of countries—beyond formally recognized and official key indicators.

- Income/spending dichotomy paradox: This is produced when sources of income are reduced or disappear while real inflation, austerity measures, and tax pressure increase at the same time, producing a systemic exacerbation.

- Critically increasing polarization of economic activity toward regions with economies of scale and disproportionate cost structure advantages that cannot be reproduced elsewhere and are achieved through exploitation of a practically endless supply of very cheap labor.

- Increased endemic and systemic loss of competitiveness as a result of

    o   capability and know-how migration;

    o   loss of resilience (e.g., as companies become inwardly focused, fixated on "cost-only" paradigms);

    o   decreased positive economic environment;

    o   excessive taxation;

    o   loss of motivation (e.g., as a consequence of continuous restructuring, change in leadership, prolonged periods of uncertainty, organizational confusion, lack of visibility, change-management overdose, growing precariousness, and the resulting sense of uselessness of efforts);

    o   loss of independence (e.g., relocation and delocalization of processes, business segments, and/or units; increasing dependence on external factors; loss of vital entrepreneurial independence and decision-making capacity);

o reduced value-generation capability (e.g., emptying the business of value through the sell-off of a growing number of its pieces); and

o strategy (e.g., reduced strategy development capability as companies lose important assets).

- Disproportionately different standards and applications of sustainability, health and safety, and eco-environmental protection: disrespect for such important aspects, exert incalculable negative effects on both societies that are directly impacted by them and those that become indirect recipients of these effects.

- Effects in one area impact other areas—in the closed loop scenario of ecosystems disregard of environmental issues in one region/nation is of direct concern to other regions/nations. *There is currently no conclusive scientific evidence for the link between increase in frequency and destructive forces of natural climatic events and the concentration of productive activity in Asia for example—yet it is curious how these commence and increase quite simultaneously with the concentration and growth of manufacturing activity in Asia in the last two decades*; what is sure, however, is that the combination of such effects with that of global climatic change produces only added complexity and harm.

- Increased fiscal/taxation pressures on individuals, businesses, organizations, and investments. We might need to introduce new indicators such as *total tax imposition* (definable as the sum total of all direct and indirect taxes individuals, business or organizations are subjected to over a determined period e.g., month, year) in order to fully appreciate the true effect on spending, and investment potential that is being curtailed or lost not only individually, but also by sector and in an economy (*lost spending and investment potential*).

- Increased level of exposure to risks associated with deterioration and aging of critical national infrastructure.

- Risks from and repercussions of new/extreme forms of speculation (not investments).

- Saturation of credibility (economic, political, etc.), perceived leadership, and the shift of real and perceived geopolitical and economic power balances.

- A general environment of growing social unrest and a potential breeding ground for ideologically fueled extremism and regional wars with high probability of spill-over.

- In general a vacillating and highly unstable economic framework, market, and business environment.;

- Population growth—with a total world population of 7 billion allegedly reached on October 31, 2011, according to data from the UN Population Division, the world population has grown by 1 billion since the start of this century, while another billion were added between 1987 and 1999 (see addendum 2). According to the same official sources and an article by Eric McLamb, today our planet's population is "twice what it used to be in 1968" (McLamb 2011, para. 2).

The projections for the near future are even more telling. The World Bank (n.d.) estimated that the world population grew by 30 percent in just a decade (1990–2010) and that the largest growth occurred in India with 351 million (greater than the US population) and 196 million in China in just ten years (two thirds of the US population or nearly half of the population of the EU). [34]

[34.] During the same decade, growth in terms of percentages tells a totally different story: the highest increase in population in percentage terms occurred in the United Arab Emirates (315 percent), Qatar (271 percent), India (40.2 percent), China (17.1) percent and the United States by 22.5 percent (UN Department of Economic and Social Affairs, Population Division n.d.).

According to the same source, our planet's population should stabilize around the 9 to 10 billion mark by the end of this century. *This however, is only a projection, and unfortunately this information alone does not convey whether or not a ten billion population can be sustainable or when the tipping point might be reached.* Can our current models cope with this added challenge? Logically, some of the alternative scenarios we might face include the following:

- Population pressure cannot be managed and can lead to increasing risk of exposure to unwanted risks (e.g., poverty, environmental pressures, sustainability and resources, disease, famine, extremism, war, or new factors such as an increase in oxidized nitrogen and other toxic gases (Galloway, Levy, and Kasibhatla 1994).

- Human-friendly population growth strategies are developed and implemented to some degree and commitment on behalf of governments is achieved by reducing or stabilizing the growth rate within sustainable parameters.

To this scenario we must add that short-duration mini-recovery cycles induced by downward vortexes of further business closures, job cuts, and/or artificial means only shift/postpone latent effects and accumulate potentially destructive energy.

Furthermore, the cost-focused paradigm will naturally force delocalization of greater economic activity to geographic locations with cost bases impossible to match or replicate, creating *terra bruciata*[35] not only in the economies they abandon—but in the medium term also in the emerging regions they move into every time a new cheaper source is found.

Note that in all the above we have not even considered the impact of new technology, disruptive models, paradigm- and game-changing variables, Mobint, Web inclusivity, etc., which, as we saw in earlier chapters, are and will continue to be incremental challenges that cannot be addressed through the current models.

[35.] Scorched earth

The matter here is grave. It no longer can be addressed with patchwork solutions, postponement, slogan-based, or dilution strategies. The world economy and geopolitical stability is approaching unknown levels of exposure to risks with potentially devastating effects. All actions/reforms thus far undertaken should have produced tangible results. Pragmatism and realism call for evaluating or at least considering viable alternatives. Unfortunately, we need to seek answers soon.

Signs, both formal and informal, are preoccupying. In some countries, for example, the economic impasse is leading to riots that are increasingly involving the silent majority and the middle class and are becoming more common, while in others it fuels devastating civil or ideologically fuelled wars that generate hazardous spill-overs and mass migratory movements.

In other geographical areas, we are increasingly witnessing the dangerous commencement of power-flexing exercises on behalf of neo-economic giants, or geopolitically strategic nations, in this phase only limited to seemingly small contexts but that in reality hide long-term effects of strategic significance in the balance of geopolitical scenarios.

Desperate strikers are becoming more resolute. Unsolvable dichotomies are deepening. Adoption of constitutionally and democratically dubious policies such as severe austerity measures, citizen tax spying,[36] and citizen/business spending investigations are becoming ever more frequent and demanding.

In some cases, recent headlines suggest that we might have stepped over a demarcation line of what is reasonable in terms of both what is being asked and the methods chosen.

The matter is so serious that a growing number of articles and research papers have even suggested that some of these measures are reminiscent of very dark periods in recent history. Whether this is true or not and, if so, to what degree it is true is a matter of debate. The real question is how far down this line do we wish to go before something gives?

---

36. Spying on one's neighbors' lifestyles and pending habits and reporting anything that can justify verification and investigation.

Who's Job, Business, Investment, Wealth . . . Will Not Be Affected?

As brutal as this might sound, disruptive technology, innovation, inclusivity, miniaturization, virtualization, together with the many other challenges we need to face (geological mutations and climate change, mass migration, growing ideologically-fuelled instability, the negative effects of globalization, environmental destruction, neo-slavery, purely cost-based logics, population growth pressure, etc.) will affect every single job, business, investment, organization, model, means, and modus operandi. So far, the Internet has created some jobs while transforming or replacing others. To date, the net effect of the Internet on job creation and loss is a subject of much debate. However, the crude reality poses a series of genuine questions. How many net job losses or increases is the new model really generating? Will *Web inclusivity* produce a natural extinction of previously crucial human expertise and added value?

Will Web inclusivity, for example, only consume lower levels of KES[A]? Or will it also devour its own flesh and blood, additional Internet businesses, and jobs?

What happens to all those sites and related jobs that fall out of the new economic loop, where higher levels of *Web inclusivity* become the winning paradigm? What happened, for example, to the millions of people who worked in the travel agency business or other brick-and-mortar enterprises and sectors? Further, what will happen to all those working behind the scenes of the websites that might vanish simply because they lose out to more Web-inclusive sites?

Just considering our smart phones, how many industries has this device affected and how many jobs, processes, business models, and revenue streams might this virtualize? To name a few, those who build cameras and video cameras, photo printers and album makers, and filing media like binders; the publishing industry; editorial services; those who build compasses, produce maps, navigators, flash lights, clocks, encyclopedias, computers, television sets, musical instruments, and music. In addition, the postal systems of entire countries; logistics related industries; translators; those who teach languages; entire sectors that provide information, banking, payment systems, credit card transactions, and reporting systems; those who produce garage-door openers and hotel keys; travel agents; airline boarding card producers; Taxi-cab call-centers, cash register and parking meter manufacturers; private investigators; radio, CD, and music recorders; those who produce measurement systems, calculators, bank-note authenticity verifiers, address-books, paper-related products, and voice recorders; telecommunication service providers, those who provide news services and stock brokers, those who deal with providing information on menus and cultural and historical venues; tour guides; brochures and the many other products and services currently offered will be affected by new apps.

What does this situation imply in terms of jobs, entire businesses, investments, and wealth? Do these queries hold true for people in all walks of life? Is anyone or anything—investor, business, enterprise, profession, executive, manager, employee, worker, tradesman, representative, politician, or even a billionaire—exempt?

Is it possible that expert apps that rely on enormous databases—for example, in the medical field—built to requirements of professional doctors by software engineers might be able to perform diagnostic tests faster, more efficiently, and effectively, even in the comfort of the patient's home? Might these innovations completely affect the medical world? What effect would such systems have on thousands of jobs in the medical field? Would it leave a decreasing number of physicians simply to manage processes, data, and robotics (*probotics*)? Technology is programmed with increasingly more knowledge and becomes more intelligent, even able to performing surgery with minimal supervision, especially those types requiring very long hours and precision. How far away are we from such a reality? Factually, some operations are already performed through the aid of robotics.

Is there a single reason similar databases, applications and processes with diverse forms of expertise—to date the sole dominion of humanity—are not replicable in other fields (e.g., civil, mechanical, electrical, aeronautical, astrophysical, molecular, biological, mineral, or geophysical engineering)? What about the forensic professions (i.e., lawyers, solicitors, judges, prosecutors, etc.)? How far away are we from automated Web-based processes that run on databases of laws and verdicts? Could simple lawsuits, such as neighborhood and consumer litigation, which currently represent a large amount of the judicial backlog, exert incredible weight on the judiciary system and cause large fiscal costs to citizens to be resolved by automated judgments/settlements? Such systems could include the oversight of an automatically assigned judge and lawyers who might not need to be located in a courthouse. How far away are we from a stage where the average citizen can file a legal dispute using legally intelligent forms online? The legal application performs instantaneous checks against the updated laws or judgments, providing a first verdict that can be contested later by a professional who adds his or her contribution.

What about notaries public who, as strange as it might sound, in many countries are still delegated by law to a limited number of families that, for generations, have held these posts, passing down their profession to their sons and daughters and performing their duties at reasonably high costs, which are, in many cases, determined by law? What effect could the Internet and automation of processes have on these professions? For how much longer could these models survive in the forms we know them today? Will they ultimately be pushed to conform to new modalities?

Is the issue truly about how much time these processes might take to become reality? Or is it about being able to acknowledge that we are facing change to a degree unprecedented in human history? Is there anything stopping banks and supermarkets or other businesses from becoming even more automated? Yesterday's next-generation e-supermarkets and e-banking are already part of reality today, are they not?

While there may be a return to models that require real persons in some industries, such as call centers (because talking to a machine has become an unacceptable customer experience), these jobs are not able to compensate for the increasing number of job losses. In many cases, these jobs are the first to be delocalized in faraway cheap-labor heavens. Is there any job you might think of that will not be affected by technological advancement?

What about a pilot? As much as I love the art of flying, in the commercial aviation sector, there are advanced plans that will substantially change a pilot's contribution in a cockpit. As for pilots in the military, the new reality has already affected the lives of many professionals who have dedicated a lifetime to this profession. There are currently huge investments in unmanned airborne vehicles (UAVs).

Pilots sitting at game-like consoles are flying a growing number of sorties over dangerous, hostile territory today. They are doing so in rooms sometimes thousands of kilometers away from the physical locations they patrol. They supervise and, at times, steer these UAVs once they reach the vicinity of the target areas—with simple joystick movements. These platforms theoretically could perform the entire mission (for now, only some types of missions) with decreasing levels of human intervention. The only real reason why there could still be a need for human intervention, is to mitigate the eventual risks deriving from hacking, intrusion, unauthorized control, or manipulation. These vehicles are not limited to use in the air; many prototypes and deployed unmanned assets are being used for naval, terrestrial, and undersea operations. Consider that similar vehicles have been deployed on planets such as Mars in the past two decades.

What effect will this technology have on the thousands of jobs in the armed forces, the aviation sector, and the advanced sciences? And what about the companies in their supply chains, in adjacent sectors, or in seemingly unconnected far-away sectors, such as camera operators who make a living covering breaking-news events from helicopters? What about maintenance crews, airport flight and ground operations crews, and air traffic controllers? What about all the other sectors that, in turn, form their supply chains?

What about a mechanic's job? Already, being a mechanic is no longer a profession associated with people who have grease all over themselves. Rather, a mechanic works in a clean environment, usually interacting with a computer. Could the future of automation transform this job even further? In the not-so-distant future, your car might communicate the chance of failure directly to a manufacturing site in a distant location, prompting you to accept the replacement offer. Should this automotive problem be resolvable by simple upload of a software update, it will automatically upload the fix; otherwise, it will prompt a maintenance engineer to visit your address at a time of your choosing and perform the intervention.

What about a garbage collection crew? We have already witnessed the evolution of this profession in many cities. Until not long ago, it was a job requiring at least three individuals. At a growing rate, in many instances, crews have been reduced to just one person managing a truck that performs these duties automatically. How will technological evolution transform this job even further? How far are we from a completely automated garbage collection scenario, with minimal remote human supervision?

What about a specialized subsea oil and gas maintenance crew? Was the last mega oil spill in the Gulf of Mexico an example of how this job has been transformed?

How far are we from voice-activated smart-phone apps that can provide a walk-through animation of a supermarket designed to your fantasy that is also cognizant of your home-supply levels—your health conditions, your allergies, your weight objectives, or simply your household's shopping list? Once purchased, the order would be processed by remote intelligent warehouses and delivered to your doorstep automatically or by a smiling clerk.

Would this model not be replicable in many other retail stores? What happens to investors or businesses that have large retail facilities? What about those who used to work in supermarkets and their supply chains? What of real estate agents and agencies when visits become virtually led through a house on sale and home plans and documentation are printed on demand or downloaded directly to your smart phone and banking, loan enquiries, and bids/offers are elaborated instantly online? What about a profession as seemingly "technologically unaffected" as that of a policy maker (e.g., a politician)? The question here is not whether we will end up with automated leadership, but how technological progress affects a policy maker's mode of operations, choices, challenges, accountability, relationship with constituents, law-making capacity, independence or dependence on new factors, lobbying effectiveness, relations with other government agencies, mandates, responsibilities, remuneration criteria, and so on.

Already the number of increasing variables heavily affects the day-to-day life of a head of government, both during his or her election phase and after taking office (e.g., Twitter, YouTube, online news, blogs). Technological advancements also pose new challenges in the way policy is formed and affected or terminated, as in the case of growing numbers of tweeted public sentiment evaluations, campaigns, rallies, and uprisings. Won't technology also affect policymakers' jobs substantially? And what about the management and execution of policy and policy making? The greater the government structure, the greater the potential exposure.

Many are fixated on the fate of the wealthy—billionaires and tycoons—who might be perceived as having barely a chance of being affected by any of these changes. Incredibly and paradoxically, the level of exposure to increasingly numerous risks that extremely wealthy individuals, estates, trusts, or concerns face through Web inclusivity and, in general, innovation and the cumulative effect of new variables is more than might be apparent at first glance, potentially more devastating than can be imagined, and more time-sensitive than can be appreciated. Though it is hard to establish a priori to what degree such changes will affect these people, because it depends on each case, it would not be unreasonable to guesstimate that the individual level of exposure might be somewhat proportionate to the individual's wealth.

The inclusive nature of wealth, as demonstrated many times in history, dictates that, as economic scenarios vacillate and deteriorate, ever larger nuclei of wealth or those that enact game-changing strategies, pull relatively smaller sized wealth towards larger concentrations, leaving growing numbers of organizations, entities, businesses, and individuals devoid of sizable portions of their capital. Statistical evidence indicates many foreseeable, unpredictable, and even seemingly banal variables can influence and contribute to the curtailment of wealth.

Finally, what can we say about software engineers, programmers, or general experts in information technology? At this rate of technological advancement, the "innate intelligence" of code (currently written by software engineers) and next-generation languages may gradually auto-replace a growing number of currently needed experts in these fields, at the very least starting with the most basic or most commonly used subroutines. It is highly likely that programming and software development as we know it today might be gradually replaced by thought-, movement-, or voice-activated requests for a computer to automatically develop and correct code. Following the same logic, it is not hard to think that, sometime in the near future, the concept might develop further towards self-programming. Confined within the walls of our current models, how many more business and job losses will such developments cause in the information technology world, which is currently thought to be one of the most important sources of business and jobs? Finally, what about the awareness concept as defined in the first chapters of this book, the risks it conveys, and its impact on future models?

In general, whose job will not be affected directly or indirectly? Whose business model will not be transformed? Whose investments might not be touched? Does the question of when this will happen become of secondary importance?

However, to this point, we have addressed only the effect of inclusivity, just one of the many variables that influence processes, human interaction, societies, individuals, and everything that concerns our way of life. The brutal reality is that it is very likely jobs as we are accustomed to today may gradually, transform or cease to exist. Similarly, a growing number of currently valid, useful, profitable processes and business models will not be such any longer. Are we all doomed to sit at home then? How is the economy to provide sustenance and business? How are policy makers going to provide a basis for jobs for the growing numbers of unemployed? How will policy (economic or otherwise), business strategy and models, etc. address business leaders, entrepreneurs, investors, owners, executives, and employees who lose their sources of income? How will they stop business closures? Should we turn back technology? Stop advancement? Go back to twenty years ago?

Fortunately, we might not have to, should we wish to open our horizons beyond the models that lock us into a world—and context that is no longer consistent with current and future reality, challenges, and opportunities. In the next chapters, we will explore what is needed and how.

What Might a Solution Need to Address?

Any solution geared to resolving the challenges that have been discussed thus far in essence needs *at least* to be able to do the following (the following represent just a subset):

- address *real needs* of the majority of stakeholders (e.g., job seekers, families, business, investors) independent of sector.

- Address new (foreseeable and beyond the horizon) paradigm-, game-changing variables such as innovations, Web inclusivity, etc., in a continuous manner as they emerge.

- Create new cycles of long-lasting, virtuous economic traction, regeneration, development, and prosperity on a continuous basis.

- Address epochal challenges such as global warming, climate change, mass migration and their impact; geopolitical stability... and so on.

- Rewarding and promoting positive corporate/governance conduct: things such as achievement of longer term results made up of the sum total of shorter-term objectives that cannot just be limited to currently know merely financial KPI's.

- Create an environment for continued incentives to grow business ventures and provide new opportunities and investments.

- Be able to build balanced economies locally (not just based on current delocalization criteria/requirements) and also promote international trade.

- Realign competitiveness nationally and internationally—playing with the same deck of cards and rules.

- Remain independent of current cost-focused paradigms.

- Free to redefine concepts such as cost and create new elements and perspectives.

- Find an appropriate replacement for other self-consuming paradigms that also impede proper leveraging of new variables, advancements, and vital elements such as value and sustainability.

- Unblock/resolve the current systemic blocks and dichotomies discussed earlier and unleash hidden potential.

- Finally provide a pragmatic/realistic framework to start addressing difficult issues such as famine, neo-slavery; water cycle management; flora and fauna regeneration, population growth, local economic development in a viable way.

- Be realizable in reasonable timeframes; be evolvable to address ever new challenges; and open to the contribution of experts from as many fields as necessary.

A model anchored in deeply rooted systemic reforms made to address new paradigms creates possibilities for new, virtuous, and lasting economic renewals based on new evolved concepts such as "value creation" and what can be called "value balance" (as elaborated later). Last but not least a model that will allow achievement of new levels of civilization.

Birth of a New Economic Model

If we look carefully, we may perceive the actual formation of a new economic model. The difficulty is that the evolved economic model uses a totally new set of definitions, requirements, modalities, logic, and underlying truths and premises—on a new and totally different, higher plane (plateau(s)) explained in the next section. Paradoxically, it is of our own making.

The sooner we grasp this reality, the faster we might be able to leverage this opportunity and evolve, increasing our chances of achieving economic recovery in the short run. But even more importantly, maybe we will begin a new phase in human evolution by using an evolved model to exploit new potential for long-term sustained development and prosperity.

This requires spearheading calculated decision making and action to achieve a step-level transition toward an economy made by humans for humans, protective of ecosystems—one that is sustainable and one that can develop continuously to new levels, keeping pace with our evolving needs, requirements, advancement (technological, economic, and otherwise).

The following sections introduce the following concepts:

- New plateau(s) of long-term development and prosperity

- Virtus: The newly forming Value-Based Baseline Evolutionary Economic (Prosperity) Model (BEM^{HESD})

- The Alpha-e transition and migration Protocol:

  o its definition and framework

  o its set of tools (samples)

  - Evolutionary Conversion Process

  - eVolve Migration Process

- o   key phases and milestones

- o   ideas about possible organization models

- o   implementation and transition strategy to immediately address successive levels of Business models, Work, Jobs, and Employment Virtualization

- the evolved "value creation" and "value balance" concepts

- an evolved governance and equilibrium framework

Let us now look at the bigger picture, assess where we are, decide where we wish to go, and only then establish what we need to do to get there. To accomplish this, first we need to introduce the notion of the next economic plateau(s).

New Economic Plateau(s)

*Should we look at matters from a more relevant perspective,
we might notice that we are in the presence of a step-level
evolutionary event and a newly forming economic model that
works on a totally different plateau(s) with evolved characteristics,
requiring evolved tools, frameworks, and reference models.*

To explain the concept of a different plateau(s), we must refer to the preceding and existing ones. The following image better conveys this concept:

Step-Level Changes in Economic Plateau(s)

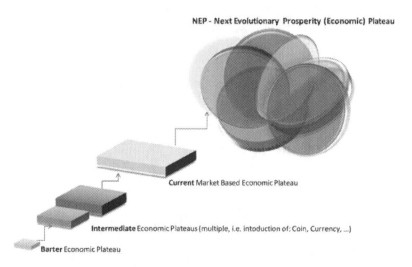

NEP - Next Evolutionary Prosperity (Economic) Plateau

Current Market Based Economic Plateau

Intermediate Economic Plateaus (multiple, i.e. intoduction of: Coin, Currency, ...)

Barter Economic Plateau

The focus here should not be how these plateaus are physically depicted, unnecessarily delving into the size, dimensions, and shapes as the objective here is to provide an initial notion of a concept in an understandable way. In essence, the above image tries to explain that our economic models have evolved through a number of economic stages creating new plateaus of economic activity and possibilities (not just the above).

As innovation provided new plateaus of perception, awareness, technologies, and capabilities, the limits of preceding plateaus were overcome, forcing a step-level movement toward a higher level with characteristics that could address and leverage new ideas and requirements, creating further development. The barter economic plateau was miniscule and limited compared to its successors. The common feature in each economic plateau, including the current one (depicted as the fourth for simplicity), is that borders and limitations bound each.

Driven by new disruptive models, game-changing innovation and new variables that take us beyond the physical dimensions, a new evolved plateau is forming as a result of our activities. We could call this the newly forming or next evolutionary economic/prosperity plateau(s) (NEP).[37] Though a shape has been given to the NEP to make the point in a simple way, in reality the next economic plateau(s) is shapeless (amorphous), dynamically evolving and multidimensional.

The reason for this is that innovations and requirements have evolved to such degree that any future plateau(s) will need to accommodate levels of possibilities, awareness, and perception that are unprecedented in human history.

Any new plateau must allow us not only to find new possibilities to address the numerous paradigm-and-game-changing variables, dichotomies, and blocks we are faced with today, but also allow us to exploit currently unperceivable opportunities as we migrate to and use different, dynamically mutating, coexisting planes (hence plateaus). It must contain evolved reference models that are able to identify new variables and to address each, finding equally evolved solutions to paradigm-changing innovations, needs, requirements, advancement, etc., that the future might have in store.

To describe this notion better let us investigate where we stand today and how the current model works.

[37.] Each letter, *N, E, P* in the NEP acronym represents words that begin with the same letter ("Next, New," "Evolutionary, Economic," and "Prosperity, Plateau"). The same technique is used for successive acronyms to avoid excessively long ones.

Where We Stand

Basic Legacy Model

The basic legacy model, which lies on the current economic plateau, is based on the following basic concepts and generic cycle:

The idea here is to present the concept in generic terms, because what matters is not the fiscal accuracy or level of detail of the model, but the way it flows overall.

Basic Legacy Model

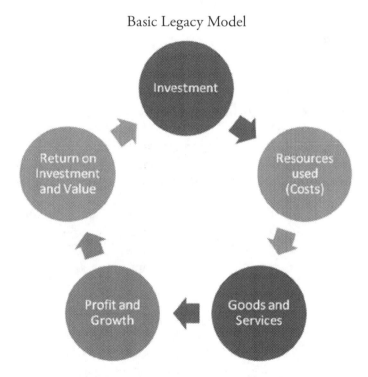

To describe the flow of the current model, we could say the following:

- Capital is pooled and invested in business enterprises (e.g., production, services, retail).

- These enterprises bring together, organize, and utilize resources to produce goods and services.

- Goods and services are sold to markets to grow a company's sales, increasing profits, and producing a return on investment and stakeholder value.

- The remuneration from these activities forms the basic incentive to provide additional investment from different sources, such as shareholders, banks, and individuals, reactivating the loop again.

In essence, there is a sequence in the cycle where each element follows the preceding one. This model has worked more or less in the same way since the inception of a money-based economy. With the advent of new variables and technology, this model, however, has already evolved, creating a new intermediate or hybrid legacy model.

Intermediate or Hybrid Legacy Model

The *intermediate or hybrid model* is a small but significant evolutionary step away from the previous basic legacy model. It represents the current model in use, and the intermediate stage where we stand today. Conceptually, it is the *basic legacy model* plus the added layers of complexity currently known new variables add to it. If one could use an analogy, from an evolutionary point of view, the current hybrid model resides in a no-man's land. No longer a purely basic legacy model, the current *hybrid legacy models* is far from being a new and comprehensive model able to address increasing complexity, and structural blocks third millennium, disruptive, game-changing challenges produce.

Furthermore, the current *hybrid legacy model* also lacks equally evolved levers, tools, paradigms…to allow effective exploitation of new possibilities, opportunities, and delivery of desired outcomes such as: prolonged sustainable development; structural solutions to unemployment, debt, retirement, taxation; climate change and mass migration mitigation; biosphere preservation…and so on. Similarly, the current *Hybrid legacy* model does not provide the proper terrain for the formation of many possible new perspectives, and consequentially the development of equally evolved new solutions.

The differences from the original basic legacy model might seem subtle. In reality, their impact is both structural and systemic; and significant and extensive. The *hybrid legacy model* is also critically impacted by new short-circuits that reduce or inhibit the natural flow of capital that has fueled the economy for centuries, affecting the survivability of the rest of the elements within the model.

The following diagram depicts the general flow of the intermediate *hybrid legacy model*.

Intermediate or Hybrid Legacy Model

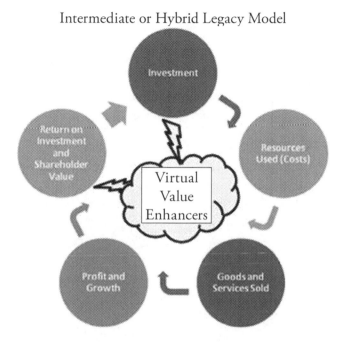

What we are witnessing more and more today is that the hybrid model and the search for immediate, higher reward, (apparent/relative) less risky returns, and/or simply flight to safety leaves out some of the fundamental elements of the legacy model, leaving ever fewer resources to fuel them and substantially modifying the paradigm.

The following paragraphs describe the general flow of the intermediate hybrid model.

- With the introduction of new paradigms and elements, such as innovation, technology, and Web inclusivity, the economic returns from historic activities based on the current models' cost focus are becoming less remunerative, less attractive, and, in some cases, riskier than they used to be with respect to more virtual forms;

- remuneration possibilities offered by more virtual means, which we can call "*virtual value enhancers*" (e.g., innovative financial instruments, speculation, Web inclusivity, intangibles), form the basic incentive to lure increasing amounts of investment from increasing numbers of actors and sources (e.g., investors, markets, shareholders, banks, individuals) toward them, short-circuiting and reactivating the loop without necessarily fueling the other elements/domains within it—*de facto* bypassing them and depriving them of vital resources (e.g., investments, liquidity);

- to compete for investments, legacy model-based enterprises (e.g., industry, manufacturing, retail, services, paradoxically including banks, financial institutions) must increasingly find new ways to survive in both form and substance.

The following diagram provides another depiction of the consequences and the systemic imbalance generated when more and more financial resources are diverted toward virtual value enhancers and away from real business in today's models.

Diversion of Investments toward Virtual Value
Enhancers rather than Real Business

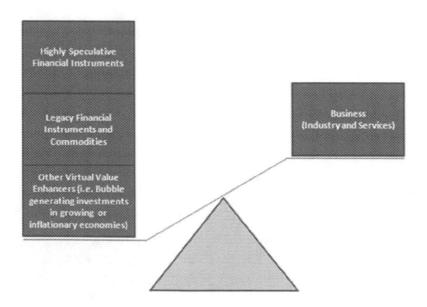

As more financial resources and potential investments go toward *virtual value enhancers* for remuneration, rather than being invested in business ventures, the hybrid scenario we live in today will most likely leave a growing number of businesses, enterprises, professionals, and people from all walks of life out of the economic model, which will continue to drain resources and energy.

Money will continue going where it finds growth possibility, preferring the shortest and easiest route and the path of least resistance and complexity.

These very important transformations are in addition to the cracks and systemic dichotomies forming in the fundamental pillars and cornerstones (e.g., public debt, unemployment, monetary policy) of the current hybrid models. These additional transformations only exacerbate the problems with the current models' sustainability capabilities.

But this is not all. Today's economy unequivocally relies on trust in the system, together with its fundamental governance frameworks (e.g., policies, laws, norms, rules), more than it has probably ever needed. Imagine the basic legacy economy as any object delimited by a set of dimensions—a square, rectangle, octagon, etc.—anything with a length, width, and height, set within a definable shape (as with the following diagram).

Legacy Economy

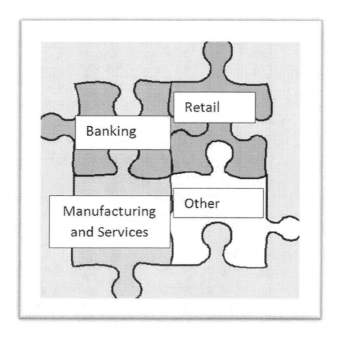

Then imagine that the rules governing this area have been tailored to a similar length, width, etc., covering the underlying legacy economy. Each time a new area was formed in the economy, a patch was added to it (see the following diagram).

Legacy Economy with Overlay of Legacy Governance Framework

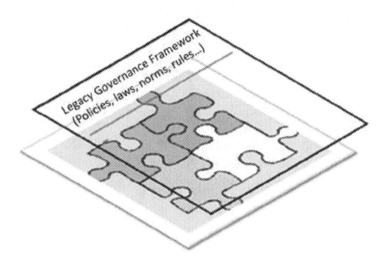

As time progressed, adjustments were made to the rules (governance framework) to fit the growing size and complexity of the underlying legacy economy (the square). The two dimensions grew mostly hand in hand. Now imagine the increasing number of changes (paradigm-changing variables) that the world has experienced just in the last two decades, adding new dimensions to this model and its needed governance framework.

The invention of computers and wireless and digital communications, network-centric interactions, delocalization, the streamlining of processes and human organizations, the growth in concerns over sustainability, the exponential growth in population and mass-migrations, the inclusive nature of the Web and technology, the fusion of the Internet with mobility, nanotechnology, and all the other recent technological advancements are already substantially modifying the way we live, communicate, work, interact, and do business.

Now imagine each of these paradigm-changing variables is a non-geometrically definable multidimensional form, not only on the horizontal axis, but also in depth, width, and height, occupying new amorphous areas all around, below, inside, above, and at tangents to the original square.

Intermediate Hybrid Economic Model with the Effect of Overlay of New Paradigms, Variables, etc.

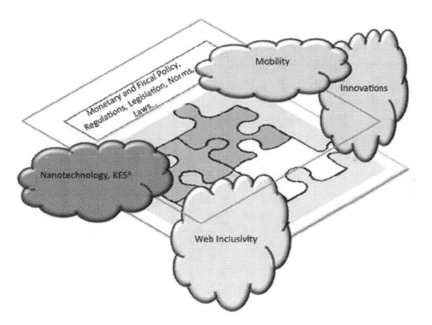

By the introduction of a plethora of new variables to the legacy model, what we get is a totally different picture, one that denotes the impossibility of the current model continuing its existence for long. Furthermore, in order to complete this picture we have to add the many endemic, systemic and structural blocks and dichotomies we have discussed previously. Once this is accomplished we have *de facto* a depiction of what could generically be the reference model—today's hybrid economic model. To be fair, it is easy not to see it without connecting all the dots together. Whatever the reasons why it has not been easily visible, this scenario provides a new perspective from which to develop a starting point.

Taking a step back, it becomes clear how the growing number of systemic dichotomies being created as time goes by, will only increase the level of complexity and the challenges we need to confront. Evolution comes about when the limits posed by a model are no longer sustainable. They act as impediments to growth, and spur the need for new solutions, which in turn give way to the adoption of new models.

In reality, as these lines are being written, as mentioned previously, there is a new economic model developing—Virtus (or BEM^{HESD}), evolving from the hybrid legacy model, but on a higher, distinctly different plateau(s) (NEP). The same forces that form and fuel the emergence of new disruptive and game-changing variables, together with the need to find new solutions to real and virulent blocks, and third millennium, no longer postponable challenges such as prolonged structural economic recovery, sustainability, mass migration, and climate change create the foundations for the formation of the new economic model.

So far we can only witness non-homogeneous, and disconnect, fragments of it emerging here and there. In reality, we can witness examples of it in all new game-changing innovation; new or evolved business concepts such as "sharing" initiatives and non-physical-asset based paradigms; carbon and foot-print reduction efforts; new financial instruments and so on. But all these lack a comprehensive, all-encompassing framework, and an equally evolved model. Among other things, this situation potentially provides a unique opportunity. For decades, scientists have been trying to fathom the mechanics of the big bang, trying to go back in time to reach the moment of the primordial explosion and the nanoseconds that followed the explosion that gave birth to our universe. In much similar fashion, economists and historians tried to assess the exact moment of switchover between the barter and currency-based economy.

In economic terms, it is as if we had the opportunity to witness the occurrence of this renaissance of something similar to a big bang in an economic evolution, occurring right in front of our eyes. We might, in fact, be in the presence of the nascence of "Evolutionary Development and Prosperity Genomics" as a new economic science for the new evolutionary economic model that is being generated. The reasons for this particular subject name will become evident further on.

Primary Differences

If we could synthesize what the fulcrum or essence of the new Virtus model is in very few words, we could say that it is a natural evolution of the current market-based economy, focused on generating value holistically (not just financially, but paradoxically one with economic ramifications, and potential, exponentially higher than today's model) and prospects well beyond what is currently perceptible and achievable opening new dimensions, levels of awareness of possibilities, levers, and opportunities.

To illustrate this concept, the following analogy might be useful: by operating changes to the fruit or leaf of a tree, one modifies the fruit or leaf only; doing so to a branch will affect the branch and possibly the fruit and the leaf. However, working at the level of the lowest common denominator, that is, the DNA of the tree, allows for incalculable possibilities.

In many ways, today's closed-loop economy and economic model restricted by its comparatively rigid boundaries will increasingly fail in producing and maintaining jobs and business. So far, these models have only allowed us to see, theoretically contemplate, design, and operate business models and possibilities that represent only the tip of an iceberg hiding 90 percent of the bulk of a potential ice continents in the making—below the surface—realistically and pragmatically beyond our visual or perceptive capability. As with similar times in history, we have possibly reached another unique, decisive, and critical moment—an irreversible systemic and structural point of impasse/failure. A moment requiring a step-level transition to a new level (plateau), paradigm, and equally evolved model (in continuous evolution) aligned with current and future requirements.

Undeniably, current models were tailored for the needs of the previous century, a different economic paradigm, and a fundamentally different context while everything else is evolving at astounding speed. The current model is increasingly an archaic system, primarily built around aged concepts of cost-focus, debt generation and no longer sustainable fiscal policies and impositions. It is a system that has increasingly become dependent on different forms of liquidity injections, grants, aid, incentives, tax credits and rebates, facilities, quantitative easing, and so on, but that no longer yields desired outcomes and incapable of truly addressing the challenges we face. Finally, the model is based on a self-consuming cost logic that destroys value, putting at risk our habitats, our planet, and our very survival.

As noted, these are but a few of the many elements that impede the current model from being effective and incapable of addressing a growing number of no longer postponable challenges. However, this discourse must not be a judgmental one, but one that presents a realistic snapshot of where we stand and a reflection of new options. After all, this very model has provided more than half a century of unprecedented development.

Under Virtus change will be the result of a planned and modular transition process. This means that existing legacy notions and concepts will not disappear overnight, but rather gradually evolve into new forms (as de facto already happening i.e., new instruments, processes . . .), and become a subset of many other new elements needed to address new challenges.

We are at an important crossroad: If nothing is done, employment, business, investments, wealth, human rights and freedoms, and our way of life are at risk. This time though, this axiom is valid, independent of one's nationality, culture, or geographic location. Our new era calls for a new economic paradigm—one that befits the pace of current developments and allows for new levers and models to enable structural long-lasting and continuous economic traction and development.

Virtus has been designed and conceptualized in terms of the need to address the challenges and requirements we face including a consequent natural evolution of relations between citizens and their governing bodies and governments. New economic paradigms have always brought with them new governance systems. Executed and implemented correctly, a new model based on the creation of value might allow and help democracy to evolve to new, higher levels of equilibriums between rights, freedoms, accountability, and responsibility, along with, it is hoped, new levels of civilization.

What is Value?

Before the introduction of the new model, the concept of value must be defined. It is easy to confuse the definition of value with its strictly financial attributes. In fact, many dictionaries and most economic or business literature published in the last decades focus their primary attention on the economic attributes of this noun. In most cases, it is defined as a "fair return or equivalent in goods, services, or money for something exchanged"; "the monetary worth of something"; or "market price." In the corporate world, value is commonly associated with stakeholder or shareholder value. However, the Oxford Dictionary provides a broader view of this term: "the regard that something is held to deserve; the importance, worth, or usefulness of something."

In light of this broader definition, is there something that we are not considering in current economic models? Yes, the economic value of what is being missed, not considered, or not potentially leveraged is astonishing by any standard. Theoretically, it is more than what the current economic model can develop through its extremely limited perception of value.

Value is generated, for example, in the work necessary to protect a city against the growing devastating effects of geological and climate change; to improve and augment the safety of highways, roads, and railways and processing and distribution of our drinking water and food-production cycle; to promote the development and growth of enterprises locally; and to reduce the damaging collateral effect of pharmaceuticals. It also exists in initiatives that improve educational systems and schools and first responder emergency technology, efficiency, and efficacy. In essence, it includes all those initiatives considered non-viable or economically unattractive in today's models.

We could say that "value" is the antitheses of purely cost-based paradigms, human or environmentally unfriendly practices, damaging practices, neo-slave-based business models, and so on. Similar to other historical moments requiring step-level changes in economic paradigms, it might be that, as time progresses value generation might gradually render many current models no longer viable or economically attractive unprofitable and unsustainable. Transitioning/transforming these same business models into value generating ones, paradoxically might potentially render them more profitable. Among many other issues to be disclosed, value is achieved by rewarding virtuous outcomes through a model that, of itself, generates value. A system capable of dynamic regeneration and responsive and adaptive to evolving challenges to guarantee a continuous revision of checks and balances, safeguards, and use of the most effective and appropriate levers is needed to address shortcomings, exposure to risks, undesired effects (e.g., inflation, deflation, etc.), and possible misuse, abuse, fraud, and so on.

How new perceptions of value can be translated into concrete opportunities and the activation of a more virtuous economic paradigm will be addressed in the subsequent chapters. From the feedback thus far received from readers; a recurring theme seems to be a new, more articulated perception of reality; the ability to see new possibilities, dimensions, and a better appreciation for how each individual, business, and organization can contribute in creating real value in all areas of specific interest and, thus, benefit from such participation.

However, even more rewarding is how each can make a difference in creating a new reality. Many readers indicated they cannot stop thinking about value generation during the day in everything they do and witness. The sincere wish is that all get as much as possible from this new awareness and be able to use it to fulfill specific aspirations, improving their worlds, those of their loved ones, and even of others a bit more. More than an exercise in changing the world, value generation has probably more to do with changing oneself, one's processes, business models, and so forth working that is, at the lowest common denominator.

VIRTUS

The word, concept, model, theory "Virtus" in this book - is not to be confused with, or assimilated to any other, eventual, equally respectable concept, theory, model, description, organization, and so on, which might use this same word. Virtus,[38] represents the evolutionary next phase of the economy and economics that will reside on the next evolutionary plateau (NEP) as described earlier. It substantially differs from the current model in that it is a holistic value-generating model, i.e., not solely focused on financial outcomes/benefits as existing models, but one that will also allow visibility over new revenue streams, possibilities, and opportunities that cannot otherwise be seen, leveraged and/or implemented from the filters, restrictions and prisms of our existing model(s). Technically it could be called the newly forming, Value-Based (Generating) Baseline Evolutionary Economic (Prosperity) model (BEM^{HESD})[39] or for simplicity Virtus. The general definition of the new model is as follows:

- It is newly forming because it is at the beginning of its development, evolving away from the hybrid model on a higher, distinctly different plateau(s).

- It is value-based because it transitions away from the legacy notions such as the cost-focused paradigm of existing models. The primary objective of the new model is to create value continuously, be it in the form of investments, business, employment, sustainability, biosphere preservation, etc. able to continuously lever new variables and redefine existing elements to achieve greater levels of value generation potential; Value forms

---

38. The concept of "virtus" derives its roots from the Greek word "arete," which in its basic sense means "excellence of any kind," that is, in addition to what we usually associate it with, moral virtue.

39. The same acronym-reduction technique adopted previously in defining NEP is used here. This technique will be used henceforth for all new acronyms.

the DNA, the quintessential traits of the evolved model and it is expressed within the superscript letters ^{HESD} (introduced below).[40]

- It is baseline because it provides an underlying open, modular, and scalable framework for future models.

- It is evolutionary because it cannot be static. It will continually evolve dynamically. Any model henceforth must be able to leverage new opportunities and to face, address, and master new variables, paradigms, and challenges.

- It will use concepts such as "prosperity" to denote an evolved notion of economy and economics. Later on we will notice that we may wish to change the name of "Economic Model" to fit a more appropriate definition, one that could be connotative of long-term development, well-being, and prosperity, a new level of civilization (i.e., *prosperity model*).

- The superscript letters ^{HESD} enclose the model's (initial) fundamental characteristics or DNA properties/traits—value. The acronym is made up of the letters representing the initial DNA, fundamental characteristics, traits, and properties of the Virtus model. All elements inserted into the new model must be able to generate the same DNA (i.e., *create value* to guarantee long-term development and prosperity).

In other words, in order to find answers to existing endemic blocks, new variables and challenges, to come out of the impasse, create long-term economic traction, and be able to step up to a new plateau(s) of development, the model must create value (e.g., not only financial, but investment, business, and employment opportunities). This means that each globule, component, sub-component and element of BEM will need to produce/yield value (HESD), i.e., be:[41]

---

40. Please note that the superscript letters are not to be taken as a mathematical formula or expression but merely to denote the makeup of the new model.

41. The letters forming ^{HESD} are not limited to the few descriptions or traits thus far outlined: these provide only examples.

- **H**uman centric (put humankind and ecosystems at the center), **H**olistic (not focused on just single aspects or dimensions, begin addressing hard issues such as employment and jobs, business potential, healthy business environment, but also humanitarian, hunger, slavery, poverty, conflicts at their root in countries of origin), **H**ealth and well-being focused (e.g., addressing ever frequent outbreaks of new infectious diseases and viral strains) etc.

- **E**volutionary (being able to evolve continuously in a positive way), **E**nterprising (promoting and creating a premise for generation of new business, enterprise models, advancement, ideas, technologies, definitions, processes, modalities, means, levers, etc.), **E**conomy generating (fostering initiatives that keep it producing positive results, value, equilibrium, competition, etc.), **E**ducational (e.g.: long-term knowledge enhancement); **E**nvironment focused, **E**nhancing and **E**nriching things such as the *quality of life, motivation, positiveness*, health affecting *stress reduction*, at all levels (e.g., individual, family and work), attention to value of family quality time, and relationships, addressing the requirements and needs of the different phases of growth, etc. quality of child upbringing and experience in its different phases, porper attention to adolcence and positively channeling ernergies, capabilities, and individual steghths, providng enriching responsbaility and social experiences augmenting such things as selfesteem, sence of belonging, acceptability etc.

- **S**ustainable (finding viable solutions to the limitations set by our planet), provide **S**ecurity, **S**tability, **S**urvivability of ecosystems, **S**trategic inclusive **S**urvivability (i.e., eye toward the future, natural disaster protection, space exploration and exploitation), **S**uccess oriented and win **S**trategy based, etc.

- **D**ynamic, focused on the **D**evelopment of opportunities, long-term prosperity, and (such as virtuous cycles of innovation, investment, and business opportunities, paradigm-changing strategic mega projects), **D**elivery of value results, etc.

In its initial state, the traits composing the acronym ^{HESD} (value) establishes a starting point, the foundations upon which the concept can be developed further. As is probably becoming obvious and evidenced later, the letters/traits forming ^{HESD} are not limited to the few descriptions or value traits thus far outlined: these provide only examples. They also include other traits omitted for brevity and traits that may need to be added by experts from different fields.[42]

---

[42] i.e., those that might form the evolutionary "transition task force" or any other organization that might be elected to perform an eventual transition, all new concepts that will be elaborated in the following chapters.

What Might the New Virtus Model Look Like?

In order to provide the best possible visual depiction of what Virtus might look like, the following depiction could provide a glimpse even though it is not and cannot be fully representative of the form Virtus (BEM[HESD]) might take. Firstly, it is impossible to portray all the globules, components, elements, dimensions and synapses of the evolved model on a two-dimensional page.

Virtus (BEM[HESD])

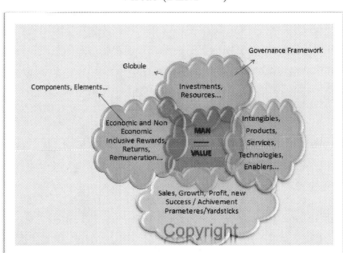

Accordingly, a depiction of it would also be impossible, because, as in a movie, the emphasis is not on a single frame.

Key Characteristics of the Newly Forming Virtus

Taking into account the many challenges discussed thus far, an evolved model must be dynamic if it is to remain successful. Given this particular feature, what is important is that everything in the evolved model has innate dynamism—it is non-static. Each variable entering the evolved model must (ideally) have the same DNA (be able to create value). Nothing impedes the addition of other globules or their intersection, interaction, convergence, separation, deletion, reductions, additions, and transformations. These will occur, be included, or be shaped, as necessary, within equally adaptive legal and governance frameworks.

Because of its dynamic nature, one should not become obsessed on the titles or localization of components and elements of the model or those depicted for simplicity in the previous diagram (these are neither exhaustive nor complete, for example, though central; the ecosystem is not indicated because it underlies the model, etc.). The fundamental components of each globule will change and may position themselves freely in different areas within the model, forming new globules, deleting others, etc.

A *globule* refers to a temporary aggregation of *elements* and *components* (temporary aggregation of single elements) that join for a time and that can be connected via a virtual network of synapses. Globules can be activated or deactivated, increased or reduced, forming new network connections with other globules or elements and components in other globules dynamically.

Being multidimensional, the relations, interactions, and positioning of each element contained within each globule will also be prone to constant evolution, transformation, and change, moving progressively away from the sequential nature of the current models.

The globules forming the model could be imagined as permeable. Their elements can easily mix with others and create new components, networks, and synapses related to other globules, components or elements as things evolve, creating the base for an incalculable number of new perspectives, possibilities, and opportunities in all sectors and professional spheres. If applied correctly, the domino effect on the economy could be geometric.

For example, a globule could bring all elements used in providing measuring tools and performance yardsticks for the initial Virtus or its future versions, under the same umbrella. These components could include return on investment, net income, return on sales, and other key performance indicators. Each of these, in turn, could create synapses with other globules, components, elements, etc., as required.

The previous example (the globule of measurement yardsticks) could create interconnections with other globules, components, and elements such as jobs, creating new, currently unimaginable remuneration criteria. Any element can also be simultaneously part of different virtual globules.

A globule's length of existence depends on its utility and value creation capability.

All in all, the only constants of the newly forming Virtus are value creation, versatility, transformability, and evolutionary capability. In essence, they are all focused on the centrality of humanity, sustainability, well-being, prosperity, prolonged economic traction, and the preservation of ecosystems and habitats. This means that each element making up Virtus in the future must provide the above characteristics. They are vital to the continued success of the economy, our lasting security, lasting prosperity, and the survivability of evolving civilizations/societies/ecosystems with a time horizon to cover at least the short term, ideally the life-span of living generations, and possibly the immediately successive one each time it is revised.

The evolutionary step between our legacy or hybrid model and the Virtus is so marked that it is highly probable that once the terminology of the word "economy" has been changed to reflect something that is holistic and more linked to prolonged/lasting prosperity, well-being, and advancing our societies and civilization to new levels. This acronym might evolve into EPM (*evolutionary prosperity model rather than evolutionary economic model*).

The word economy, in fact, in many languages still denotes an ancestral legacy to the concept of scarcity. This is in no way meant to imply that we should lose sight of sustainability or depletion of resources, or similar, equally important arguments. The exact opposite. It will be ever more important to assure the respect of variables and manage these ever more efficiently and effectively going forward in producing greater prosperity.

As time progresses, there may be a need to include other DNA characteristics to HESD that at this moment cannot be known, currently non-necessary, and or premature, hence the model should contemplate the possibility of additional traits as necessary.

To accomplish this we need to contemplate the addition of these through the addition of an open variable X (i.e., EPM^{HESDX} or simply $EPM^{X\,ver\,n}$ in the longer-term)[43] becomes important as the model evolves toward new versions. The reason why we need to start-off with BEM^{HESD} is that it forms the initial baseline version.

---

[43]   Where ver. n refers to the version number the evolved model has reached in any given moment in time.

The models in use today (legacy or hybrid) cannot match the dynamically changing shape or nature of Virtus, especially as it continues to evolve in unpredictable ways. Current remedies or stimuli that work along dated or totally different assumptions, configured around a completely different set of paradigms, applied to the current models, cannot be effective in providing lasting solutions. This situation leaves us with a very limited set of alternatives. Let us examine some of these.

Options

How will we be able to address the new form the global economy has taken and the form into which it will continue to evolve? In this scenario, we are possibly left with the following set of primary alternatives:

- Ignore the existence of a newly forming reference model. Continue as is.

- Acknowledge the existence of a newly forming holistic Virtus model, but continue addressing issues with current (i.e., legacy/ hybrid) policies, tools, reforms, and remedies (e.g., austerity, indebtedness, increased taxes, cuts in fundamental services, projects, grants, etc.).

- Take drastic action. Force the Virtus model to conform to the previous framework, using a set of radical approaches to shape the multidimensional amorphous evolutionary model back into its primordial legacy form (i.e., the square), potentially increasing exposure to drastic, extreme, or unwanted outcomes. In many ways this is what is currently happening through some of our current remedies and reforms.

- Alternatively, acknowledge that we are in front an *evolutionary step-level event*, requiring a need for change, possibility of tackling issues from new and different perspectives, mastering a new dynamic model, leveraging potential and new possibilities which novel frontiers could provide us.

Should the first three options not bring the desired results, choosing the last alternative (i.e., taking the issue from a different perspective) implies first having answered the set of very important questions:

- Can we do away with the current advancements (in all fields)?

- Can we afford to, be able, or wish to, go back?

- Are current remedies providing solutions?

- Can legacy and hybrid reference models apt to address the plethora of challenges we face today and in the future?

- Does it make sense to force existing models to achieve what they can no longer reasonably accomplish?

The winning alternative might reside in choosing a different strategy, one with a greater potential for success in the long run. Viewing the challenges we face from an evolved perspective allows us to drive Virtus, harnessing the potential for new perspectives that are invisible to us today because they currently reside on a higher plateau. This is the real shift in the paradigm, potentially one similar to the one witnessed by humankind when transitioning from the barter system to the currency-based system.

However, this approach is not sufficient, because if we fail to provide this strategy with an inbuilt equally dynamic and evolving governance framework as human needs, environment and ecosystems, technology and innovation, and the economy evolve, we quickly will lose control over the outcomes—we will be in a similar position, if not worst position to the one we are today.

If left alone, Virtus will be driven by unknown forces rather than being governed (this word has nothing to do with the free-market concept or its inverse). Moreover, *if we do not do it, someone else will be filling that void.* Evolution is the real vehicle and opportunity. This is what we are truly up against. We must master an evolved model if we want to find solutions.

Just as we have a framework of policies, laws, rules, regulations, and norms that govern the current (legacy or hybrid) market-based models, we need an analogous framework for the newly forming evolutionary model, one that has the same DNA as the evolved model. An evolutionary governance framework that can address the holistic Virtus is one that addresses the constantly changing variables.

If handled correctly, this situation might turn out to be a chance for this and future generations to undertake the next evolutionary step—allowing us to focus on the aspects of our lives, values and objectives that really matter to us both as individuals and as societies and providing new unfathomable possibilities both in terms of business, investments, and material achievements, and as well as personal, professional, non-material aspirations and societal goals realizing personal *life projects*, opening new possibilities unforeseeable until today.

Performance/achievement metrics that made sense until recently, such as growth or profitability, might no longer be the sole measure of success or failure of human initiatives. They might be augmented by a myriad of other more valuable dynamically changing metrics.

To assure effectiveness, each new variable that becomes part of Virtus (BEM^{HESD}) and its successive versions (EPM^X: evolutionary prosperity model) must be tested for its DNA traits. Those traits that add value can easily enhance the model. Traits that do not provide immediate value to the model can be considered for transformation, frozen until they become of value, or become new DNA traits. This will be elaborated further on. Let's see how this might work in practice.

As new variables are introduced (e.g.: through new technological advancements), these must be tested to verify their contribution to the following areas:

Business and investment opportunities: if we are to find long-term opportunities, we must adopt those that (for example):

- put humankind at the core; address issues holistically (H);

- allow room for evolution to promote an environment that increases opportunities for investments (E);

- are sustainable; contribute stability, security, and growth of markets (not just financial) and have a positive effect on inclusive survivability of ecosystems that become a source of business possibilities that until recently were not economically attractive in a virtuous cycle (S); and

- allow dynamics and focus on the long-term development of new opportunities, prosperity, and security, fostering innovation (D).

<u>Employment</u>: if we are to find long-term solutions to this issue, the answer lies in adopting those options that (for example):

- put humankind at the core (H);

- allow room for evolution to be able to provide new forms of opportunity and remunerated continuous knowledge enhancement (E);

- are sustainable and contribute stability and security (S); and

- allow dynamics and focus on the long-term development of new opportunities, prosperity, and well-being (D).

And so on for public debt, monetary and fiscal policy, immigration, etc. If done properly, it is not hard to see the multiplier effect this will have in the prolonged and long-term development, prosperity, and health of the model (economy).

As new elements enter the holistic Virtus model and start forming new previously unthinkable synapses with other elements, components and globules new business models and opportunities will become visible and emerge; these in turn will introduce new requirements and needs that will be addressed.

So what does this mean to anyone? How will this affect our lives? In reality, the questions should be posed the other way around, as the model is already here and evolving. The real question becomes, how can we best leverage the naturally forming evolutionary model to improve our lives, businesses, employment, investments, remuneration, opportunities, and possibilities sustainably?

Now that we have a notion of the newly forming, value-based Virtus, we can probably perceive its existence all around us more easily. Continuing on the path of avoiding its existence is possible, but this might mean having to endorse the continuous onslaught of thousands of businesses shutting down every day while others delocalize in the hope of survival. In the process, we will unnecessarily sacrifice economic, political, and technological leadership, know-how, employment, research, development, and possibly independence.

Fundamental Premises

The Virtus or newly forming evolutionary economic model has underlying fundamental prerequisites built into its genomes, one of these is a premise that has often been taken for granted and encompasses a context that provides a society and its individuals fundamental rights and freedoms, including those of free enterprise, movement of people, ideas, and investments—as these form quintessential traits of the evolutionary concept.

The final "formal" configuration of the BEM^{HESD}(initial) and successive versions cannot but be the result of a collaborative work. In this version, this treatise can only limit itself to introducing the baseline framework and the principles for the steps necessary to arrive at the full, detailed solutions. Of noteworthy importance is the fact that different from existing models, Virtus, is not an exclusive model. Free from ideological impediments, it fosters the development of business and private enterprise, as well as the achievement of value generating structural solutions to biosphere preservation, sustainability, evolved governance, geopolitical stability,... and so on.

The realization of any significant feat or project can only be accomplished through the contribution of numerous professionals from many walks of life. It is only reasonable especially in lieu of one of the worst economic impasses the world has faced.

But how does this all bring about evolution from the current status quo in real life? To best accomplish this we must leverage on precedence.

Redefining and Evolving Existing Elements, and Creating New Ones

What actions then might we need to take, where can we begin, how do we find new solutions to allow us to uncover new dimensions that hide potential? In essence, how can we find new alternatives in addressing the plethora new variables that impede proper advancement and the systemic and structural revival of the economy?

Fortunately we do not have to look too far. As always, one of the first logical places to look is that of viewing at the problem through a different set of glasses. *As evolution has taught us many times over we need to set in motion those levers that will allow the modernization, advancement, renewal, redefinition, and realignment of the paradigms and elements making up current economic model to meet new, continuously changing requirements and challenges if we seek to discover the potential and opportunities each level of advancement produces.*

To provide an initial example let us then begin with one of the most crucial of these elements—cost. Note, many other variables will also need to be redefined. In fact the more variables are redefined, and realigned to address newer, ever evolving needs, the greater the number of potential opportunities, revenue streams, and dimensions will come into view.

Redefining Cost: A Self-Consuming Paradox

In seeking answers and solutions to the new challenges we face, we need to be able to develop perceptive appreciation for possible new dimensions in different areas. The more detailed and comprehensive this activity is the better. The more elements this involves the greater the chances of discovering new ideas, modalities, models, and so on. As we mentioned earlier, one of the fundamental elements or building blocks of the existing models is cost.

Should we examine our current economic models with professional detachment, we would gain a new perspective. What will be noticeable is that though declared as market-based/driven, the existing models are predominately also based on the notion of cost—so much so that cost has even influenced language and human behavior.

Cost is the fundamental building block/base of the current economic models and has been so since the beginning of recorded human economic activity. Cost also directly affects another variable: profit—the ultimate motivational and driving factor behind any economic thought process. How much any item costs versus its perceived benefit is what makes or breaks any decision (at least an economic one):

- We cannot compete because of a cost structure we cannot replicate.

- We cannot be profitable because of a certain cost issue.

- We cannot lever certain investments, research, projects, programs, etc. because of cost concerns.

- We cannot exploit growth-producing potential in many areas because of how much it costs.

- We cannot benefit from many vital strategic initiatives curtailed purely due to economic considerations even those that could prove to have substantial spill over potential in many fields.

- We cannot afford, maintain and/or renovate key strategic infrastructure, services, and education due to cost impediments; etc.

Cost centricity, cost focus, cost vortex, and the self-consuming cost paradigm render, for example:

- innovation, maintenance or refurbishment of critical or useful infrastructure or assets (roads, railroads, dams, electrical grids, fleets, water protection and distribution, water purification, ICT, parks, agriculture and food supply, etc.) noneconomic or economically unattractive; upkeep, enhancement and modernization of fundamental services (hospitals, emergency services, security and policing, education . . .) due to a focus of repetitive budget cuts; etc.

- critical projects and programs, economic development, success, competitiveness, etc. uneconomical or not viable

- research, development, and advancement in many fields, including those *vital to our own health* and survivability, financially unattractive due to cost

- systemic environmental cleanup economically unattractive

As we contemplate on the above list, could cost in reality hide unfathomable potential? As with all the step level evolutionary advancements of the past, we need to open our perception beyond current boxes and become aware of potential new dimensions.

If we investigate closely, it appears that what has to-date been seen, considered and defined as single all inclusive element called cost can in reality hide at least three distinct value generating elements/states/potential, namely those with:

(1) *immediate value generating capability*: those elements that can immediately be transformed into value generators,

(2) *intermediate value generating capability*: those elements that may be transformed into value generators at some time in the near future, and

(3) *latent value generating capability*: those whose value-generation possibilities are as yet unclear.

The immediate *value-generation capability* elements/states/potential are those instantly identifiable as being able to produce benefits. For example, in the case of the maintenance cost of an aircraft engine, the benefits of proper maintenance include passenger and crew safety, increased operation of the aircraft, a positive impact on sustainability, increased revenue generation possibility, efficiency, savings in fuel consumption, reduced risk of failure, and maybe savings on insurance, etc.

The redefinition of just one element i.e., maintenance, and its applicability to all economic sectors hides incalculable new potential.

If the same axiom is applied to strategic initiative components such as: infrastructure modernization; water protection, management and its smart distribution; next generation waste management, and in general all other improvements that can impact lives, businesses, markets; vital life-saving next generation medicines, treatments, and machinery the number of potential opportunities rises considerably.

These aspects have been seen as costs thus far, but as these concepts are redefined as having the potential to generate value and evolve over time, they would in reality create real business, investment, and employment opportunities. In the case of next generation waste management and particularly hazardous materials, for example, the opportunity to reduce, neutralize, recycle, etc. represent capability in generating research, investment, business, and job opportunities.

In the case of _intermediate elements/states/potential:_ currently indefinable, value-generating elements such as the cost associated with wages, taxes, etc., while considered mere expenses today, need further investigation.

Over time, we may find new intrinsic value-generating capabilities as the economic model evolves, as we will see in later chapters. It is not the first time that evolution of economic systems relied on a redefinition of single or multiple variables such as cost. In short, basing our models more and more on value rather than cost may lead us to a more productive paradigm.

As evidenced by historical facts, the redefinition (not for semantic purposes) or a new way of perceiving existing elements has led to significant evolutionary jumps and the opening of significant new plateaus of opportunities.

Extrapolating these notions to more elements that are currently seen as pure costs, new dimensions become perceptible. How many opportunities these may hide then become the real question and the true enterprising quest.

In the next chapters, we address these aspects more exhaustively. For now, we could say that just by adding this small perspective on the make-up of cost and its redefinition, we open a new set of possibilities. Segregating and leveraging the positive elements of costs will provide new, innovative modalities in many additional areas. Just to mention a few, we go from accounting for cost to attributing value to positive aspects of incentivizing virtuous behavior, new opportunities, and business models.

In many ways the redefinition of cost has constituted one of the key elements in the upward migration and evolution of economic models since the barter system.

Yet so far we have only touched on just one of the many elements making up the current model. Cost is not the only aspect worthy of consideration in coming up with a solution.

Other dimensions and elements need to be addressed and considered. To do this we need to migrate to a higher plateau(s).

Migrating Up to a New Development Plateau

The best way to explain this concept is by learning from the past. Humankind made a step-level evolutionary improvement when we evolved from the hunter/gatherer model to the food-maker model as a new set of needs emerged. In taking this step, humans found themselves on a new socioeconomic plateau of opportunities and civilization that were previously unfathomable. As they did, additional new ideas took form because of this step-level evolutionary transition.

New needs gave way to the adoption of a new model. They led to even newer requirements, which in turn fed continuous cycles of new opportunities and necessities. The step-level evolutionary migration to a food-maker model gave way to new requirements to organize a first nucleus of early society, with completely new, previously inexistent, roles and specializations: farmers, herders, food and material processing experts, etc.

Soon new food storage requirements and those stemming from urban growth in the early villages gave way to new housing needs (e.g., brick dwellings rather than temporary dwellings). These in turn led to new building and storage techniques that provided sturdiness and adequate protection that led to the first baked mud brick production, which led to new specialized professions (e.g., brick makers, construction workers).

New step-level evolutionary plateaus were reached as these first human agglomerations evolved into the first city-states (e.g., Sumer, Ur, Susa, Jericho, Thebes, Ecbatana), _opening the way for a totally new set of specializations, processes, organizations, opportunities, and socioeconomic realities that would have remained hidden had there not been a need that led to a new evolutionary step._

The following are a few redefined or new elements made available by the newer plateaus—all previously unimaginable, unfeasible, or unviable:

- the first rudimentary city planning, agricultural, and infrastructure requirements, that lead also to more complex irrigation, dikes, dams, and under-earth water transport systems to guard against evaporation, port facilities, and embankments; more evolved urbanization concepts, roads, paving, first rudimentary resting stations (caravanserais), etc.

- new farming and herding techniques and tools to increase production also in other areas of expertise

- new uses, tools and techniques for e.g., extracting, managing, casting, molding of iron and bronze; but also new materials in all other areas (e.g., for construction, clothing, etc.)

- new transportation and logistics requirements/means for trade

- social organization of city-states and the rise of professional services required for organization, regulation, policing, defense, discipline, religious activities, schooling, etc.; judiciary and law enforcement concepts, processes and systems

- official social rankings, systems and processes; the first experts/professions (e.g., architects, doctors, scribes, artisans, merchants, soldiers, judges);

- taxation concepts, methods, and means that allowed for the above to be financed; record keeping (e.g., commercial, judiciary, state administration); the birth of intellectual, cultural, and artistic specializations (e.g., sciences, music, literature, etc.)

- the consequent development of schools and formal training facilities for each type of requirement

- invention of remuneration criteria, wages, salaries etc., together with the invention of new concepts such as work day and hours and its distinction from a holiday

- new mercantile/business plateaus

    o commerce, beyond border trade

- o coinage/legal tender/money

- o rules, laws, norms, charters

- o exchange systems

- o measuring and weighing systems

- o ownership, legal rights, contracts, terms

- o lending and financing terms, conditions, etc., new concepts such as royalties, commissions, interest

- o payment facilities (rudimentary letters of credit)

- o enforcement of contracts (within and inter/intra city-states), and application of penalties

- o protection (e.g., goods in transit, contractual, military)

- o transportation costs and services

- central government, planning, management, coordination, bureaucracy and administration; the need for defensive and offensive resources; the invention of new concepts such as formal strategy and tactics formulation

- etc.

Imagine how many new, previously unimaginable, inconceivable Jobs, professions, business models, requirements, products, processes, services, and opportunities this translated into each time a new plateau was reached as innovations added new perspectives. And all this was achieved ex-nihilo (from scratch) by our ancestors with a fraction of today's knowledge and capabilities.

Today we are again in front of a new step-level evolutionary transition and the resulting new plateau(s) of opportunity for business, investments, and employment (which could be termed "life projects"), the likes of which are unprecedented due to the incredible leaps with which technology and innovation have provided us. Seen from this new perspective, imagine how many opportunities this might open up.

Unlike any other time in the past, the evolved plateau(s) will no longer be two or three-dimensional but multidimensional, similar to the agglomeration of all the globules it contains—hence, a globule mass, with the hidden potential being geometric with respect to today's possibilities.

Internet exploitation for business purposes was not achievable until recently. The requirement for the new, evolved model for the step-level evolutionary migration toward the new economic plateau could not be appreciated until now. Similarly, today's economy is shackled by the limits, systemic dichotomies, and blocks of the current legacy and hybrid models—underperforming in terms of the leverage capability of potential opportunities.

The sooner we can lead the evolutionary transition and make the evolutionary passage to the next plateau(s) of economic advancement and civilization, the sooner we can to come out of the systemic block and begin a new chapter in human development, long-term sustainable prosperity, well-being and security, freeing currently blocked potential.

Just as the number of new opportunities brought about by migrating to a new plateau was unimaginable before each new step-level change in history, the same is true here today and for the foreseeable future. There are a few yardsticks or variables we can use to measure a few possible opportunities just beyond the horizon. The following provide only teasers and hints:

- The versatility and fluidity offered by Virtus may allow moving toward relationships among elements and globules in the evolved model that are impossible in current models;

- Networks and synapses can be established dynamically, giving way to possibilities and opportunities thus far not imaginable or achievable through the legacy and hybrid models;

- Leverage—deriving from each of the incredibly large number of innovations in each field (e.g., biology, chemistry, nanotechnology, mocynet, medicine, communication, transportation) that can be used allowing for ever-newer possibilities.

Now factor some of these into the algorithm of obtainable opportunities crisscrossed with possible uses and applications. How many new possibilities can one potentially envisage? Our current impelling needs to find solutions in reviving the economy should foster the awareness and the challenge to evolve to the next step. Accepting this means being able to be equally open-minded in developing, imagining, and generating evolved

- definitions, descriptions, meanings, conversion indexes, etc.;

- levers, avenues, means, activities, modalities, needs, etc.;

- business possibilities, enterprise models, levels of interaction, investments, trade possibilities, etc.;

- employment, jobs, employability, professionalism, expertise, new roles unimaginable until today, etc.;

- organizations, networks, communications, etc.;

- time management, availability, free time usage, etc.;

- long-term/lifelong knowledge progression and enrichment, evolved education systems, organizations catering to new needs, etc.;

- accounting, accountability, performance yardsticks, reporting, etc.;

- attribution of value (i.e., assigning value to human contribution, new forms of involvement, etc.);

- remuneration, awarding, recognizing, motivating, prizing, promoting, valuing;

- perceiving, organizing, modeling, conceptualizing, producing, elaborating, providing, servicing;

- evolved governance frameworks, controls, management, enforcement, audits; and

- etc.

Now factor these into the equation to extrapolate potential new opportunities through new synapses with other globules, components, etc. As mentioned, we might be just looking at the tip of the iceberg. Many facets of our lives have already changed dramatically, while others will modify and impact new areas. They all contribute to the paradigm-changing event that is leading us to break away from the chains of the current legacy/ hybrid models and be free to move into the natural reference model Virtus today. They allow us to develop it further as time goes on, allowing humankind to achieve even greater feats in the long run, most of which might be beyond our comprehension today.

The following will no longer stay the same in the immediate future (some have already changed and those that have not are strapped in place and blocked by the current legacy/hybrid models). They are ready to evolve to a new plateau:

- organizations

- employment, jobs, and work

- business and entrepreneurial models and opportunities

- availability and time management

- education, long-term advancement, and personal enrichment

- retirement and pensions

- banking, financing, investments, and markets

- retail, manufacturing, and services

- national debt, deficit, monetary policy, taxation

- remuneration, valuation, and recognition

- accounting and accountability, and so on

If one factors into the equation the evolved versions of the above, the interconnection possibilities become more apparent. It is easy to get excited by the potential likelihoods of new opportunities, but we need to be able to recognize and *filter out those that are viable and sustainable and set aside false positives* (unless they become viable, given the right conditions, later on in the future).

We need to be cognizant that not all true new opportunities will be visible at the same time. Some will come before others, while some might lead to new variables to provide value, etc. It will be a step-by-step process, and we must comprehend that migration toward the new evolutionary plateau might take effect in some sectors more rapidly than others, due to things such as the domino and spillover effects.

Virtus Economic String Theory

All of this leads to a new concept and theory; the *Virtus economic string theory* which states that under Virtus, net of false positives,[44] a growing source of opportunities can be found through the development of synapses between elements, components, and globules independent of their nature, via conceptual strings. To provide a few examples of how this translates into things we can appreciate today, the following could be fitting:

Elementary example: In coming up with the new fusion trend in cuisine, chef's adventuring in this direction generated virtual string connections (synapses) between distinct, previously separate, nations, cultures (globules) and dishes (components), aromas, and spices, new cooking methods, timeframes, artistic touch, tools and cooking means previously used for specific dishes, weights, mixture amounts (new and old elements), restaurant's atmosphere, setting, furniture, ambiance, décor (components).

By developing another synapse through just one additional string with say for instance, a globule such as entertainment and a component such as competition, you end up with what today is considered as a new trend: cooking shows that are booming everywhere. A less obvious example is Apple's current retail strategy. They developed string connections between R&D, innovation, retail, fashion, style, advisory, and entertainment, to name a few.

We should note, that once this process is begun, some of the effects might be immediate and the general impact on recovery more rapid than we might think. Equally true is that the preparation work is but the first module of an ongoing evolutionary project and that this part can be achieved as fast or as slowly as we wish it to happen.

We also must understand that it might produce a new cycle of evolved needs, requirements, and challenges to be addressed, which might emerge in parallel. The most important discourse here is not about the number of elements with which the migration toward the new

---

44. False positives are to be considered temporary by nature; as conditions mutate and evolve these might become real opportunities.

evolutionary plateau starts out, but about the fact that it has actually begun. How do we wish to address it, leverage it, and start on the road to real recovery?

Priority of Modular Migration and Transition

Starting the right way is a key success factor. Hence, prioritizing which parts among those constituting the current legacy/hybrid economic model might need to be migrated and transitioned first becomes very important. Accordingly, deciding which of the elements analyzed in this book (and they represent only a portion), such as public debt, monetary policy, taxation, investments, pensions, and retirement, should be among the first to evolve to their natural reference model Virtus (BEM^{HESD}) is a key success factor.

Once this prioritization is achieved, how to go about this migration needs to be resolved. In order for each element to transition into the new model, to be able to produce sustained development and prosperity, and to position itself on the new plateau, it should acquire the DNA of the evolved model.

The following indicative table can be used to depict a timeline framework that indicates this shift.[45] It also indicates the first possible modules that might be considered for migration into ^{HESD} to create value by the governing bodies and the transition task force.

[45.] The accuracy of the percentages or terminology is not as important as the introduction of the main points, notions, and concepts.

Virtualization Timeline Migration and Transition Priority

	Level of Virtualization (ie of Jobs, Proccesses, Activities, ...)			
	0-30%	30-60%	Over 60%- 100%	Beyond 100%
1st batch of Migration Modules	Many processes still requiring human intervention	Tipping point as most processes evolve even futher requiring less and less human	Only residual levels requiring human intervention	Possibility for the introduction of new paradigm changing variables such (ie thought controlled atuomation)
Migration and implementations of major Evolved Elements using Alpha-e Protocol assuring adherence to Value Balance and HESD Generation according to	Towards HESD / Mostly HESD / HESD / HESDX			
Public Debt / Monetary Policy / Investments, Business / Banking, Markets / Pension and Retirement / Employment / Personal Knowldege Enhancement / Fiscal Policy / Etc.				

This is why taking on a leadership role is so fundamental in steering events from the outset rather than becoming mere followers and dependents.

Alpha-e Protocol

To avoid losing the capacity to steer this evolution toward a new plateau, a protocol had to be devised—namely, what could be called the Alpha-e Protocol. Alpha, the first letter in some alphabets, symbolizes the initial state of this protocol; "e" symbolizes the evolutionary nature of the protocol. Taking into account the introductory nature of this book, only two sample tools of this protocol have been provided.

Apart from facilitative tools useful in the migration and transition processes, the Alpha-e Protocol deals with aspects such as organization, processes, levers, means, and in general what is needed to facilitate evolution to the next step. Leadership in this stage is fundamental as it will set the first set of new parameters and definitions of the evolved components.

Parts of the chapter you are about to read are probably among the more technical passages in this book. A suggestion could be to read it with the eye of an executive seeking to understand the basic notions, This modality should render the concepts easier to appreciate. The primary objective here is to introduce the wide number of aspects that need to be considered. A final summary has been provided that will bring everything together. For readers who cherish detail, there is sufficient information to introduce new concepts.

Striking the right balance for a wide-spectrum subject as in this book is difficult and its appreciation subjective. I apologize for material shortcomings in terms of diametrically opposing individual (technical) expectations. On the other hand, not including this section would have meant not addressing issues of fundamental importance and presenting an incomplete work. As with the other chapters, to allow for better focus and improve ease of reference and comprehension, primary points have been italicized. Reading this chapter, however, is very important.

The following sections will cover the following components of the Alpha-e transition and migration Protocol:

- o Its set of tools (samples);

  - • Evolutionary Conversion Process;

  - • eVolve Migration Process;

- o Key phases and milestones;

- o Ideas about possible organization models;

- o Implementation and transition strategy to immediately address successive levels of Business models', Work, Jobs, and Employment Virtualization;

Tools: Evolutionary Conversion Process (ECP)

To enable a smooth transition, one of the Alpha-e Protocol tools that can be used is the Evolutionary Conversion Process. *It allows understanding how innovations will continue to transform our lives, our investment and business models, employment, processes, etc. It helps answering important questions such as what the implications and what the resulting elements and relative frameworks look like whilst they continue evolving?* The following diagram provides a simple picture of such a process.

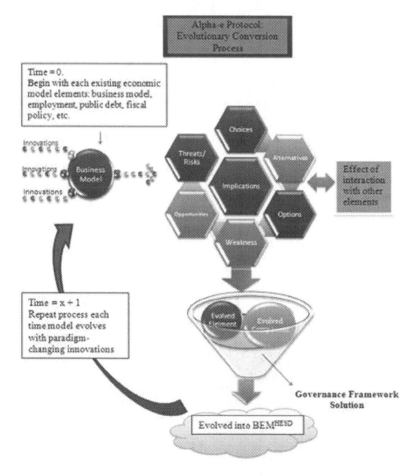

In the preceding example, if a paradigm-changing innovation, one that substantially changes the way things are done at any moment in time, is transforming a particular business model, process, etc., we must ask ourselves what implication this might have on business opportunity and investment generation, intrinsic value, employment, new skill sets, public debt and its financing (taxes), social security, pensions, etc.—in general its "value creation capability."

At each turn, we need to ask if the existing model can address these issues effectively. What are viable alternatives, solutions, etc.? To what degree are these capable of resolving issues? If these solutions produce development of new opportunities in other areas, what evolved governance frameworks might they require? Once the above answers have been identified, appropriate tools covered later can be used to migrate elements to leverage their opportunity generation capability.

Tools: eVolve Migration Process (EMP)

This process is one of the other possible tools pertaining to the Alpha-e Protocol.

In order to start leveraging the newly forming model and obtain results in relatively short timeframes, activating economic recovery and successive sustainable longer-term development, existing elements should transition toward their evolved versions.

In the following paragraphs, a few *simplified examples* shed light on how this might be achieved. *The aim here is to take the variables of the existing legacy/hybrid models, starting with the most important and migrate them toward their evolved versions to liberate them from dichotomies and systemic blocks, allowing them to produce solutions and results.* This can be achieved in several ways. One of these is using a migration process, called the "eVolve Migration Process" (part of the Alpha-e Protocol).

To achieve the intended scope, *existing legacy elements will need to be stripped of all their accumulated complexity, arriving at the fundamental building blocks of each.* For example, with reference to the fundamental elements making up the legacy/hybrid models, this process starts by asking foundation-level questions about public debt, monetary policy, the banking and financial systems, industry and services (e.g., travel, transportation, hotels, retail, construction, waste management), innovation (research and development), pensions and retirement, employment, health care, business enterprise, strategic national sectors, etc. The final objective is to evolve the elements to generate value (elaborated later).

In providing some examples, specifically this means conducting a detailed analysis of each of the following elements:

Public Debt

- What is the current definition of public debt?

- What was its original purpose?

- How does it serve its primary objective today?

- Can this definition still be applied in the worst financial and economic crisis to date?

- Do the current models of incurring more debt to resolve indebtedness make sense anymore? How well do they fit the newly forming evolutionary economic model?

- Have all austerity measures yielded desired results. To what degree have they contributed to suffocating economic activity?

- Will current models of public debt be able to address additional future challenges that are just around the corner (such as Web inclusivity)?

- If the current model is human-made. It was built based on assumptions that might longer hold true and no longer provide the answers and the benefits it was intended to produce in the first place. Should we seek to build a different model?

- What needs will a new public debt model have to address in order to stimulate current and future development of the economy?

- What flexible and evolutionary model can be used to serve current and evolving needs?

Once each element (in this example, public debt) is analyzed in detail and the lowest common denominators identified, these are then evolved through HESD*, providing them with value-generation capability and transforming them into value-creating elements and ultimately value.* The following diagram shows how the Alpha-e Protocol's eVolve Migration Process or a similar one might be used.

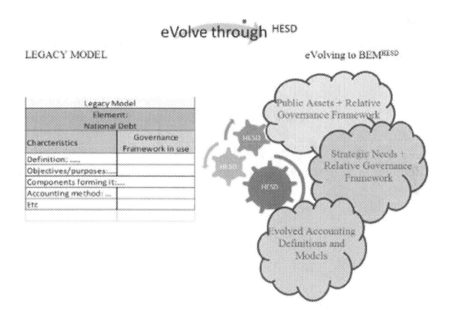

As each legacy element is analyzed, it is evolved into BEM^HESD, acquiring evolved definitions, accounting methods, requirements, etc. Evolved perspectives emerge, changing the way things can be organized, managed, and governed, potentially leading to a totally new set of opportunities and levers geared to confront the challenges of a continuously evolving and value-generating economy.

Let us now see how this can be applied to other areas of interest.

Taxes, Monetary Policy, and Money Creation

The fundamental elements must emerge clearly. Old sacred norms must be questioned and, if no longer beneficial, evolved or simply taken out of the equation. We need to arrive at the essence of the issues and provide answers to hard questions that impede or hinder value generation. We should not be afraid to ask the questions that are being asked by a growing number of subject-matter experts, policymakers, world leaders, and citizens.

What is the true objective of current taxation models? Are they achieving their objectives and at what cost to the citizenry they serve? What tangible benefits do taxes provide the citizenry within the current model? What is the value of fiscal complexity? Does this complexity provide any benefit to the majority? Does it provide more tax revenues in return? If it is to provide new jobs for highly specialized professions, could there not be evolved models that can provide equally challenging tasks and many new professional possibilities without necessarily achieving this through complexity and a dated model?

We need a model that will be able to address the challenges of the financial and economic impasse or the dynamic challenges posed by innovation and future economies that lie around the corner, one based on uncomplicated paradigms that allow fast and effective reaction times, built around today's needs and those of twenty-first century that are not based on the same basic principles and foundations accumulated over four thousand years of history.

This is not about promoting fiscal anarchy but about producing viable results with less complexity, more equity, greater opportunity, and far more benefits to the majority.

Jobs/Employment

Again, also here we must strip everything down to its basic elements. We must be able to answer certain questions. What is the definition of a job? What are the fundamental elements of a job? Is it just for the money? For fun? Is it for passion? Self-esteem? Achievement? A sense of contribution or belongingness? Professional and personal enrichment? Independence? Stability? Is it a base to create a future family? Is it for involvement in and contribution to the community? Or different mixes of these?

Ultimately, do existing models produce growing employment opportunities now and for the future? The definition regarding jobs and the different dimensions making up a job will most likely evolve in their nature and both in qualitative and quantitative terms. Tomorrow's jobs, for example, might evolve into other forms on a continuous basis, as evolution is an ongoing process. The following diagram depicts how the element of "Jobs" is evolved through the eVolve tool.

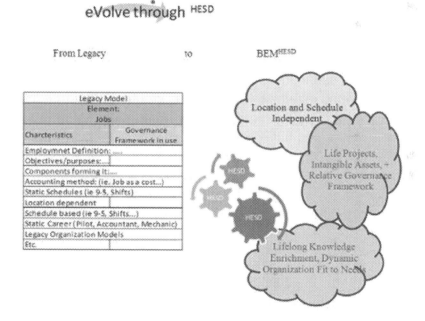

The eVolve process can be run for all remaining elements as necessary in the migration toward the new model. As each element is analyzed, it is not hard to see many new windows opening on new dimensions creating, at the very least, a new perception of reality and new potential.

In the next section we will introduce Alpha-e Protocol's primary milestones in the migratory process toward BEM[HESD] and its successive versions.

Alpha-e Protocol: Key Milestones

It has taken us years since the beginning of the 2008 near-crash and titanic efforts from many people, yet we are objectively still very far away from any deeply rooted systemic and structural recovery. The migratory processes toward a new model that will come about whether we want them or not may take a shorter or longer timeframe than the one we already face and will continue to face for the foreseeable future.

Any successful human feat needs good planning, preparation, and mastery in execution, together with agility, motivation, drive, focus, and ability to overcome unforeseen situations, working in unison toward a common goal. More importantly, it requires leadership and strategic vision.

This is not about haphazard, improvised, or extremist actions, but an evolutionary transition/migration, continuously improving upon what has been achieved. It is an evolution, a byproduct of our own actions from continuous innovations and progress in all fields of human endeavor.

This step-by-step approach does not mean that we should not set challenging goals and objectives or have reasonably challenging expectations of substantial benefits in reasonable yet short timeframes. If we seek ultimate success and accomplishment, we need to approach this migration in the correct manner.

However, this should not require unrealistic timeframes, and implementation depends on how much incentive we have to bring about structural and systemic recovery, how much priority we give to it, and how many resources we put behind it.

An immediate lever, and quick-win result for instance, could be derived simply from the news of the ratification of a new model, spurring an initial revitalization of economic activity, recovery, and renewed trust of markets, investors, shareholders, entrepreneurs, businesspeople and consumers (these words should find a proper redefinition).

Based on the effectiveness of the means and modality of the communication, the positive economic value of this alone could trigger an economic jump-start worth millions of dollars. Whilst in more precise and methodic terms a proper roll-out of the migratory process foresees at least the following steps:

First Step: Acknowledgement—Recognition of the Problem and Transforming the Concept into Action

Recognizing a problem entails acknowledging its existence, impact, hazards, and options, and ultimately a willingness to evolve if the problem is to be resolved. The effectiveness of this first step and those that follow requires the right mix of statesmanship, leadership, resolve, resilience, vision, and a balancing counterweight to generate equilibrium. It is not the first time this particular step has impeded a human organization from looking beyond, coming out of the quagmire.

The adoption of a new viewpoint allowing the focus to shift to a different perspective has always been achieved through the acknowledgement of the existence of a problem, by individuals with vision, sense of pragmatism, and willingness to enact resilience.[46]

Apart from the natural elements provided to us by our planet, every element making the economy is human-made. Equally, the problems and solutions are of human origin. Once consensus is reached in recognizing the problem, it needs to be defined analytically along most of its different major dimensions. This entails

- identification of the key causes of each contributing variable to the impasse and domains affected by it;

- definition of the extent of damage industries, sectors, business types, and governments, municipalities, individuals have accumulated to date and the potential impact under different economic scenarios; and

- the solutions adopted thus far and the results.

Fortunately, much of this work has already been done by many expert analysts in different fields, and it is a question of putting it all together. The better we define the problem, the better we can hone in on the key success factors later on. As the problem is acknowledged and defined, a picture starts to form. This picture forms the underlying framework for the steps that follow.

[46.] e.g., Through people such as Lee Iacocca, Jack Welch, Adam Smith, John Maynard Keynes, Albert Einstein, and Galileo.

Second Step: Call to Action

Once the problem is recognized, the next step is concurring that action needs to be taken by key stakeholders. As banal as it might sound, this is among the most underestimated objectives and one that human organizations often fail to achieve. *Notwithstanding, it is exactly the same type of effort that goes into international collaboration efforts such as G-20 and G-7 Summits, the efforts that went into the Bretton Woods agreement, and the development of the post-war system that we have today. Hence, it is not about science fiction or utopian reasoning but about formulating and enacting protocol that lever on precedence.*

Without acceptance that an action must be taken, any effort, energy, time, and money used to implement it is basically wasted. Many projects reach dead ends simply because of a lack of real commitment at the onset by the key stakeholders. In this case, the situation is an economic crisis of unprecedented dimensions, with devastating effects on a planetary scale, which requires commitment from all participating key stakeholders. Pragmatism and realism might be fundamental prerequisites in this phase.

In retrospect a couple of other analogies might be D-Day or the Apollo program, which comparatively probably took more effort in their preparation. Without commitment and determination to continue in the face of seemingly insurmountable challenges, such unparalleled feats would have never been achieved. One main aspect that might need to be considered for this step is an understanding of the general terms between a nucleus of important countries (e.g., G4, G7) affected by the impasse that have economic critical mass and can manage the gravitas and momentum to generate growing membership after the first tangible results of the understanding are registered.

However many join in forming the first nucleus, the evolutionary steps will achieve a gravitational pull among major businesses, entrepreneurs, and citizens of other nations. Under such circumstances, the question might not be who else will join but how to keep control over the pace. There might be a moment, for example, when a distinct scenario might develop, drawing a momentary line between those countries, regions, or businesses that lead the opening of the new era and those that stick to the legacy models and methods, inevitably missing many new possibilities in the meantime.

Joining in at the initial stages is not necessarily limited to a particular type of economy. Potentially, the more challenges a country is facing, the more benefits it will derive from steps taken toward economic evolution. Less fortunate economies might also be able to leverage new technological enablers, allowing them to jump over gaps that would otherwise have required substantial investments and years to accomplish. This is not the first time such a challenge has been confronted and resolved. As mentioned,

The Bretton Woods agreement and the G-7's have set precedents.

Third and Fourth Steps

The third step is to agree on the fundamental building blocks of both the new model and the governance framework. This step is the one probably needing the highest level of involvement and facilitation. It is the phase requiring the most strategic vision. This step requires high level agreements on the primary building blocks and spearheading—evolving away from a boxed vision toward a new perspective in order to concur on the macro generalities of the fundamental genomes of the new model, because once these find a shared vision, the remaining steps follow logically.

The fourth and successive sub-steps (iterative) are needed to implement and roll out the concurred modules/work packages quickly and in sequence to allow revitalization of the economy. The simpler the reference model, the more flexible the solutions.

Noteworthy is that the key success factor for the implementation of the governance framework in particular is the ability to cover the contours of the continuously changing, amorphous economic model's elements in symbiosis with it as it evolves dynamically.

In other words, it involves developing a dynamic *digital meta-framework* that can mutate and grow in unison with the new amorphous forms into which current and future economies and needs might evolve.

The success of these steps is dependent on many factors. Some of the more important ones among these include:

- the quality of professionals assigned to the implementation phases;

- the ability to deliver results;

- the resources dedicated to the projects;

- sustained commitment from key stakeholders;

- the division of the project into quick-win packets; and

- the leverage of existing enablers.

This step will involve a natural learning curve that, once understood, will be easier to apply, repeat, and leverage to find ever newer versions and opportunities. If the preceding three steps are completed correctly from the outset, the last step may require more repetitions as models evolve to confront new challenges. This will also depend on how well new technological enablers are mastered to aid in this task and the level of simplicity and flexibility.

Alpha-e Protocol: Organization

The previous section is an example of how the Alpha-e Protocol could be utilized with regard to processes. This introductory section describes how this protocol could be used to organize and identify key players. The protocol facilitates the definition of organizational aspects needed to address different phases.

These may include the constitution of *national and international treaty committees* and *transition task forces* to arrive at the definition of the initial evolutionary treaty. They will need to initiate baseline finalization, modular rollout, and the successive cyclical evolutions of the prosperity model. *This can then be relegated either to new, nationally independent, modular and networked organizations, both at national and international levels, or to existing organizations (e.g.: UN), which will need to evolve to meet and address ever newer and evolved needs and requirements.*

To conclude the introduction of the Alpha-e Protocol, it provides different possible alternative baseline frameworks for organizational and other aspects, such as implementation and rollout strategies. It is clear that the implementing organizations will be constituted by and work within the mandates that elected governments, leaders, and parliaments (henceforth *governing bodies*) bestow on them.

On a national level, for example, Alpha-e Protocol's general organizational baseline foresees a scalable, networked, and modular structure of three distinct levels, forming an initial national and international transition treaty committee and task force, each with distinct roles, professional requirements, responsibilities, and objectives. There are several ways this can be achieved. The following could be one of many possible scenarios.

To facilitate evolution and dynamism of the Virtus model, a new or evolved internationally networked organization that supports independent national organizations in each country could promote the continual evolution of Virtus to address new opportunities cyclically at an international level.

In short, the Alpha-e Protocol in its current version is a baseline framework. It will need the contribution of experts to agree and formally to define organization, modalities, processes, milestones, rollout timeframes, and objectives of each phase.

Ideally, the operational transition task force will be staffed by the best (most effective and efficient in delivering results) experts, scholars, economists, government officials, entrepreneurs, businesspersons, and high-level expert technicians, each with strategic vision and each supported, as necessary, by a lean structure underneath to cover domains being treated in a particular phase, module, or milestone with program governance and steering.

Though all team members must have strategic vision, an indispensable professional trait of the *visionary team* will be to think out of the box while remaining pragmatic. The visionary team refers to another concept pertaining to the Alpha-e protocol, i.e., *blue and white teams*—objects of separate and further elaboration.

Value is not generated necessarily by vast numbers of participants, but rather by quality, timely, and successful delivery of results. Having completed the introduction of the Alpha-e Protocol, the next sections will concentrate on providing a few examples of how primary elements of the existing models might evolve toward new a new level, or in other words, what this migration might entail.

Examples: Evolution of Professions, Jobs, and Employment

The history of professions and employment is made of several step-level evolutionary changes and mutations, some of which have been covered in previous chapters. Today, with all the technological advancements, the world faces yet another step-level evolution toward further virtualization of these elements. Data from different authoritative sources and national statistical offices of several nations only confirms this trend, which in its current form is limited to the more service-oriented jobs, especially in developed economies. The data suggests that the more a country develops, the more people move from agriculture to manufacturing to services.

This process can take decades in normal conditions; however, Web inclusivity and technological advancements are speeding up this process, taking us to a new level. Today's developed economies register a growing shift toward services that in some cases outweigh manufacturing and agriculture in terms of numbers.

This by no means conveys that either the former or the latter will cease to exist in the future, professionally less motivating, or that they will be less remunerative—quite differently—it depends how things are implemented. Though the category of jobs (service rather than manufacturing) might still not cease to exist, at least in the near future— what will cease to exist is a growing number of jobs and business models as we know them today as these are automated and or virutalized. Success in employment creation is relegated to the willingness to exploit, seek, steer, and leverage evolutions in innovation, progress, and advancement in the newly forming plateau(s) (NEP).

The degree of success depends on our capability to embrace or resist similar challenges to those that faced by generations before us— seizing evolved concepts, definitions, modalities, remuneration models, organizations, interactions, and dematerialization. This also does not mean that individuals need to have fewer opportunities, rights, earn less or limit the potential to earn more. In more cases than not, if executed correctly, evolution will be more skewed toward increasing the potential, improving conditions, and to earn more rather than less. Sticking to current legacy/hybrid models instead, as it is becoming all too evident, seems to go in the exact opposite direction in curtailing opportunities, possibilities, rights, and earning potential. Each step-level migration to a higher plateau in history has *increased* potential, earnings, and well-being. Evolution will open new windows on more opportunities: from the tedious and repetitive to the more challenging, from the manual to the less manual.

It will invite more possibilities of breadth of movement into new professions. Employment concepts will evolve into what could be called different "*life projects*," rather than mere jobs. Evolution may be more linked to one's passions than one's needs, potentially allowing individuals to benefit from additional sources of income precluded by today's models.

Embracing new ideas also implies embracing new enablers and approaches to education that can be called *personal and professional enrichment and/or knowledge enhancement*, to leverage new opportunities as they emerge. This means an evolution of our education systems to provide lifelong support during different phases, adding leverage and new value to our capabilities.

Consequently, evolved remuneration models for these intermediary periods in which an individual develops or enhances capabilities to add value have to be devised, according to an evolved "*value balance*" concept, described later, which will allow this. There are no free rides, however. Additionally, as will be evident later, this has nothing to do with any of the "isms" of actual or historic reality.

The objective is to find viable new solutions to the paradigm-changing factors we will face and for which new answers must be found. The following are just a few of these challenges, opportunities, and trends we might need to address:

- a transition away from static schedules (i.e., 9–5, shift-based) toward more goal/objective-focused jobs/engagements;

- a different balance between time dedicated to work and total available personal time from which to leverage other new value producing paradigms;

- a more dynamic use of time;

- a shift toward quality augmentation and value generation rather than a set number of working hours—in a growing number of sectors;

- a different concept of long-term personal knowledge enrichment and capability augmentation, enabling /allowing/promoting access new life projects rather than static jobs,

- increasing possibilities toward leveraging one's innate capabilities and passions rather than "doing it because there is nothing else";

- an evolved approach toward formal education (from the earliest years through university and beyond, which may not imply moving only upward, but also sideways and diagonally) to prepare new and existing generations to leverage the continued evolution of future models.

- a shift away from location dependency or physical presence an evolved approach toward a virtual work environment, no longer necessarily requiring physical proximity or presence, but with an equally important shift in promoting, maintaining and fostering real (non-virtual) human relations and interaction;

- remuneration modalities and criteria for personal knowledge enrichment and capability augmentation periods that are a prelude to others that create value;

- a different approach to retirement concepts, allowing natural turnover and rejuvenation (hence real prospects for young generations), while opening the road to new remunerated options available to those who choose to retire earlier—in turn creating other requirements and new business models to fulfill new needs;

- shift toward new merit-based remuneration models that factor-in new variables as they emerge such as value generation potential acquired, knowledge augmentation level, the holistic value of a professional, etc. improving (if merited) ones remuneration level/ potential, with the progression of time;

- a move toward new forms of growing responsibilities not necessarily linked to current criteria such as number of persons supervised or budget managed, possibly generating *evolved* notions of careers and seniority (when this is deserved, useful, motivated, and adds value). If prepared well, the evolved model will work to improve this.

- ever new concepts of rank, level, position, etc. but that not only denote professional stages reached but also convey important motivational aspects such as seniority of a person during their (earned) progression.

- a transformation from static vertical careers (e.g., accountant, mechanic, miner, sales) to new forms of jobs or the possibility of more than one primary type of work experience (hence the evolution from "jobs" to "life projects") or the result of new synapses between new and previously silo-based careers that simply ended as demand for these evolved;

- a move away from physical intervention toward more value-added activities; we need to factor in, for example, the impact of robotics, miniaturization, and automation manufacturing environments as they will increase the tendency toward remote management, process supervision, on-site intervention from the nearest resource, etc.

As it is becoming evident, under an evolved model, at the end of the day and in a not so distant future (closer than many would wish to consider), the world might end up being more open than it is today; one, allowing flow-overs beyond current geopolitical boundaries.

The relevance and importance of where things such as intellect, skills, and capability physically located will probably become of relative importance leaving increased choice and decision making levers to each individual based on his or her preference—shifting the emphasis on key consideration such as proper remuneration, developmental and motivational aspects, together with the availability of proper infrastructure, tools, networks, and means.

A key success factor hence becomes (much more so than today) how to attract, develop, and maintain talent whilst building successful business (or non-business) models that produce value in different locations around the world simultaneously—diametrically opposite from the current delocalization models. This is why these factors need to be resolved through new models. The only viable answers today are conducive to more of the same—producing multiple irresolvable systemic dichotomies.

Finding viable solutions requires at least three things:

1. work from an evolved plateau(s) and leverage new opportunities not visible from the current perspective, leveraging new tools, options, frameworks, ideas, definitions, etc.;

2. be able to see things from evolved perspectives;

3. evaluate new, different interconnections with other elements.

Opening fresh new avenues means opening the possibilities to many more ways of addressing existing challenges that, in turn, will be geared to produce solutions and the basis for additional opportunities. Hence, the jobs (*life projects*) of tomorrow depend on how fast we transition to the next plateau. The job market, the interaction of one's profession with other spheres of one's life, might be based on evolved concepts and new ideas.

Being able to reconcile what is currently not reconcilable via current legacy/hybrid models and finally to liberate blocked potential from current systemic inhibitors and irreconcilable differences allows us to step up to the evolved plateau of development to exploit new opportunities. But this also implies evolving the current system to a new level—one that offers added motivation and evolved teaching and learning techniques.

Technological enablers, for example, might allow people to enrich themselves professionally in substantially different ways than today, not only or necessarily needing to build their expert knowledge base, but rather being able to appreciate subject matter from a holistic point of view (or even more specialist) that is more focused on delivering value. For instance, a lawyer today develops his or her skills over years of education that requires an overwhelming amount of human memory capability and an acute appreciation for semantics.

As improved logic and smarter search-based algorithms allow more accurate and automated responses to search queries, this allows a substantial shift toward more value-added areas of development for the forensic arena, in terms of both augmenting professionalism and opening new spheres of possibilities. An airline mechanic/engineer will most likely be able to place more focus on the global quality and completeness of a maintenance project rather than closing the intervention as quickly as possible due to cost considerations, searching dated, patched tomes of system descriptions that might not have been updated or modified.

We might move from structured legacy-based organization models toward evolved dynamic models based more on professionalism and trust than on hierarchical interactions—from jobs and employees seen and accounted for as costs toward an evolved view, motivation and accountability seen and perceived as value contributors and intangible assets, even more than they are today.

How much time is spent on work might no longer be the real value associated with a job, but the quality and value generated by the activity that will become the focus (which includes respect for quality, milestones, and delivery timetables but also a genuine interest for the person, their professionalism, their skills/knowledge augmentation and their progression).

Evolution towards "life projects" might also mean a gradual shift towards working with a group of professionals gathered to achieve a set of common goals for a specific business enterprise, as opposed to working for a company, a boss, a function and any other similar, increasingly dated concepts.

Surely, the latter might have made sense until now especially within the context of the existing model but these are factually becoming less and less effective motivational factors for existing generations, less befitting changing paradigms and requirements, and growingly perceived as sources of human devaluation.

According to an increasing number of authoritative studies, many companies are objectively facing a challenge in being perceived as offering a coherent model that can still offer true-to-form reward for merit, careers, concrete professional growth possibilities, objective attribution of value to the human element, enriching development . . . and a cost based mind-set does not help.

What might this denote or translate into? Essentially, we must remember that, until a decade ago or so, current models owe much of their success also, to the creation of new business paradigms that factored these new, or previously not-applied elements, for the first time in history. These concepts worked effectively until cost-based logics pervaded organizational strategy. Alarmingly however, the absence of these same human (motivational) factors formed one of the many fundamental systemic flaws that brought alternative models such as communism to its knees. Analogously and consequentially, even more preoccupying, the cost-driven constant devaluation of human and motivational factors will increasingly threaten, and erode at the effectiveness of existing models.

A gradual shift in a new direction might substantially modify the employment paradigm, revealing new possibilities, towards models that allow for example, renewed, deeply rooted, hard-wired paradigms that actively promote/enact sharing common goals, rewards, and success. While concepts such as "permanency", in another example, might evolve towards notions of "continued common interest" in perusing one's "life projects", and or new shared objectives with other groups of "specialized/ professional individual entrepreneurs" that aggregate as enterprises.

The evolution of business enterprises might contemplate scenario's whereby each entrepreneur contributes within a framework of a more rewarding mix between chosen role, and needed capabilities of an enterprise, through contractual relations that might willingly (also on behalf of the individual) be more dynamic, as both entrepreneurs, and enterprises mutate in their interests, continued search for, and adaptation to, new markets, demands, technologies, needs, etc.

As the "knowledge enhancement" paradigm evolves forming an integral part of a persons "life projects" it will create a concrete base for the implementation dynamism; paradoxically, also for the accomplishment of current reforms.

This lays the cornerstone for significant transformations in many areas, as opposed to today's physical, organizationally matrixed, company and its predominantly cost-focused functional, operational, and organizational rigidities and silos. Apart from the introduction of many new notions, a model fundamentally unchanged since the 1950's.

This though does not mean the disappearance of "going concern" types of businesses, rather opening the scenario to new types of scope-specific enterprises and dynamically evolving aggregations and spin-offs of new ventures. This will obviously affect markets, and investments, banking and the financial industry.

As notions are redefined, there might be a need to revisit aspects such as "seniority" for example, which might become increasingly linked to the individuals' comprehensive history, as he/she progressively accumulates a mix of experiences in developing "life projects", as well as achievements, successes, value generation, and referrals during their life.

This evolved notion of "seniority" might constitute an important variable that could considerably modify, augment, and or enhance others such as: level, qualification, career . . . The combined aggregation of all these elements might also become essential in the determination of merit, salary, remuneration, reward . . . throughout an individual's value generation/contribution path (rather than each specific job) providing a sense of continuance and life-time progression as well as a powerful and compelling motivational lever over a prolonged period of time.

Concepts of teams might also evolve to better accommodate and utilize individual potential. More, and more organizational studies are concluding that though team-based concepts maintain their validity, in many specific cases, it is becoming ever more evident that the contribution of the individual is of paramount importance and in many instances a decisive factor of success or failure of initiatives.

Valuing individual capability might also contribute to an evolution of the effectiveness of professionals; appreciated as equally relevant members of a group in reaching common objectives through evolved organizational strategies that promote and enhance individuals' inner driven motivationas opposed currently, predominantly exteriorly induced motivational strategies.

Historically, there is nothing more potent than the inner drive of an individual in reaching the most challenging objectives, achieving the most arduous feats, and accomplishing the greatest improbable, goals. Comparably, there is nothing more destructive to a project, a team, and an organization than a demotivating context, and or an environment kept up through different notions of threat and menace. As each of these dimensions changes, it will impact other elements, allowing them to evolve also. If carried out properly, there will be, for example, a progressive mutation in the search process for talent. Instead of thousands sending beefed-up résumés to compete for a job, there may be a growing number of people being sought out for newer fields. They might be busy doing what they are passionate about rather than taking on the first thing that pays or having to endure the professional devaluation that comes with the existing hollow model and search process in an economy that no longer works or business environments/organizational models that no longer motivate, create positive, dignified preambles, and valid prospective for the future.

Examples: Evolution of Pensions and Retirement

In migrating pensions and retirement to the new plateau, we need to address hard issues such as the following:

What are the definitions of these words? Are they the demons they are portrayed to be or do they hide significant potential? Has the demonization mantra of the last twenty years resolved anything or provided tangible answers? What was their purpose? Do these institutions serve the purposes they were intended to serve originally? Are they adequate? What purpose should they serve in the future? What purpose do we wish them to serve in the future? Our ancestors had the intelligence and the willingness to create these concepts from nothing. Why should we not be able to steer the evolution of these elements to achieve even better results? What benefits do they currently provide the individual and society?

Are current models fair to younger, aging, and retiring generations? Do they provide fair treatment? What benefits do they intend to provide? To what degree are they fulfilled? How are they funded? How could they be remunerated instead? Is there anything that would limit our imagination to think up a better model? Are current retirement models still sustainable? What could reasonable retirement parameters be, from the point of view of all stakeholders (society, business, investment firms, the individual)? What about pension funds? Do current models provide viable alternatives for the current demographic mix of the growing elderly population? Do future models need to be continuously less rewarding, one-size-fits-all or complicated models? Or can there be better models to serve different purposes and benefits for all stakeholders, retirees, pension funds, markets, and businesses?

What new model can best answer evolving needs, creating new opportunities for retirement, while at the same time allowing younger generations to fill a positive natural turnover? Could not added possibilities potentially stimulate the development of new opportunities, ideas, investments, and enterprises? More importantly, how are the needs and expectations of businesses, individuals, communities, and societies evolving?

Do historically consolidated concepts still hold true? Do we necessarily need them to hold true? Are we artificially forcing them into place? Does this create more costs than benefits? Should we let them free to evolve and progress to take the economy forward? Would these not provide new sets of opportunities that would otherwise remain hidden? What if we properly looked into leveraging their interaction with adjacent sectors beyond banking and financial market and even those not currently close once these evolve? How might these opportunities in return influence banking, financial markets, and other sectors of the economy?

Has an improvement in quality of life over history not created new opportunities? Why should we not take this opportunity to improve possibilities for all stakeholders? So far, we have only skimmed the surface of a few of the many new variables, trying to strip them away from the legacy/hybrid models. We can evolve these concepts to their next natural level of utilization and value creation. Could this area finally bring benefits to natural generational turnovers, improve motivation and career possibilities, improve new idea generation, and provide added stimulus to the economy? Seen from the perspective of a new model, yes, and there might be many more than we can currently envisage. If properly devised and interconnected with other components, it may result in the following:

- value-based **pension funds** finally to enable individuals, business, the sector, banking, and markets to count on a more stable/balanced economic model and value generation;

- value-based **markets** to enable new parallel models that are adequately protected from speculative ones; more in line with retirement and pension requirements, generating new business opportunities and [HESD(X)];

- individuals who choose to retire at a reasonable age (but also not beyond a maximum—which will need to be substantially lower than the current unrealistic retirement ceilings—to assure and leverage natural generational turnover) with reasonable income to maintain a standard of living similar to the one they created through a lifetime's work—rather than increasing the number of people that do not have means of sustainment—but that instead create, contribute to, and foster economic development from new evolving needs and necessities;

- facilitation in creating new enterprises and businesses for those who wish to continue their professional lives after retirement, leveraging on the wealth of accumulated experience and expertise focused in generating $^{HESD(X)}$ sources of investments, employment; and

- **governments** and policymakers finally to be freed of one of the many latches that impede them from focusing effectively on addressing economic development and the future $^{HESD(X)}$.

In reality, as the model evolves toward the new plateau(s), many of these aspects might even become of secondary importance or simply irrelevant as evolved models may provide opportunities beyond our current perception.

Generational turnover is not optional; it forms the quintessential building block of any society and its future. It is at the base of an economy's prolonged success and the fulcrum of the most natural of events in human evolution and survival—the creation of a family and procreation—our prosperity and survival as a species.

No human-made model should inhibit this or distort natural processes of generational turnover—and our current models are no exception. *These concepts will need to be applied to all currently curtailed and/or demonized areas of concern blocked by irresolvable systemic dichotomies that could turn into business opportunities and value, such as health care, hospitals, schools and education, public safety and emergency services, and so forth.*

In evaluating the initial version of the new model, the transition task force, mandated through democratically led processes and steered by governing bodies, must constantly remind itself where we stand today and the consequences of remaining attached to the current models.

They must also evaluate what this might imply if elements are not transitioned and evolved to revive and develop employment, business, investments, and the economy and to address key issues such as national debt and the repercussions on the strategic stance of the nation, its independence, its leadership positioning, and its prolonged success.

From our currently limited perspective, we can only start to perceive a few of the new and evolved areas of opportunity, but today we can only see a blocked model filled with unfeasible, irresolvable contrasts that only contribute to exacerbating the economic impasse.

As these fundamental elements are analyzed, transitioned, and evolved through the Virtus model (BEM^{HESD}), each evolved element will start providing many original areas for innovative prospects. *As each new evolved element is put in relation to other elements, allowing them to interact, network, permeate, merge, and influence each other, the number of new ideas that will form is incalculable at this stage.*

Examples: Evolution of Education and Research

This area is of fundamental and critical importance to the proloned and continued success of any future model. Consequently, future learning and personal enrichment needs will most probably push toward an evolving type of education, or what we could call "*knowledge and capability enrichment,*" most likely very different from the forms we are used to today.

Putting the necessary value and importance back into the system will require both the evolution of mainstream educational systems and the introduction of new concepts, paradigms, and educational organizations, new types of expertise, hierarchies, and networks creating a plethora of new opportunities at all levels within academia and businesses directly or indirectly linked to their supply or end-user chains.

There is substantial scientific evidence that each individual has a different way of elaborating and perceiving the information provided by the senses. Depending on the source, some studies indicate that there are at least ten different learning modes, and most of our educational systems for centuries have only tapped into and communicated or provided learning through a few (in most cases three) of these.

This currently leaves an unknown number of potential people *de facto* unable to benefit from education to the same extent, while stigmatizing their *apparent* shortfalls vis-à-vis others who had the luck to be receiving information in a form their brains could easily/naturally absorb with less effort.

Ideally, evolved education will need to begin with the initial formative years. It needs to address such things as bringing back and enrich human needs and experiences with the joy of infancy and childhood, time for natural play with other kids, and for experiencing nature—life and character enriching experiences that only recent generations have been deprived of—with legitimately questionable consequences.

It needs to address the needs of children, teens, and adolescents for natural movement to increase central nervous system maturity, increase cognitive learning rather than relying predominantly on memory, address the individual learning modes, and allow for different timeframes for individual maturity and development of social skills.

This must include soft skills development and improvement of quality of human interactions, a focus on the needs of families, and attention to value of family quality time and relations, quality of child upbringing and experience in its different phases; availability, access and safety of outdoor and neighborhood facilities made for natural play, proper attention to adolescence and positively channeling energies, capabilities, and individual strengths, providing enriching responsibility and social experiences, adapt places of congregation, augmenting such things as self-esteem, sense of belonging, usefulness, acceptability, etc.—whilst having fun, but also allowing and providing for natural, emotional, and physical release of frustrations–appreciating and verifying that this can be achieved naturally without being sought or induced via drugs, alcoholic abuse and so on.

Providng for positive role models, allowing them to freely aquire best fitting, individual strategies to face, manage, and resolve their personal challenges successfully.

It necessitates respect for a child's, adolescent's or adult's innate/ individual attention span and capability and to address important issues such as ADHD, hyperactivity, dysgraphia, dyslexia, autism, and the myriad of other ever more common or new syndromes and inhibitors that are being appreciated, discovered and understood each day, at the core. It needs to create a stigma-free context, reduce unnecessary performance stress and unhealthy non-par competition—which is different from positive motivation and productive competitiveness—identifying and leveraging individual potential and capabilities and making available those assets and progression paths needed to allow maximization of potential.

Importantly, educational systems of the future might probably need evolve to favor de-structured, differently- or dynamically-structured and or tailored approaches avoiding creating forced/predetermined schooling paths from early ages that still exist, also in very advanced countries, with evaluation criteria predominantly based on limited and limiting elements such as grade performance.

It is historic fact that many genius minds and business tycoons had been shunned and or considered poor performers by the legacy educational systems of their time.

Similarly, gifted individuals in all fields and areas of expertise should be able to benefit from educational paths, systems, and tools that could augment, enhance, and allow them to lever their capabilities optimally. In a way this might be the beginning of an evolution toward a more personalized methodology to education providing each individual the best levers and possibilities to succeed in their endeavors.

This represents a significant shift away from current models and toward an approach that sees the individual at the center of the equation, a person theoretically ever more keen and motivated in improving capabilities in his/her areas of interest.

Correspondingly, access to diffusion of knowledge and new findings should evolve to new heights in becoming more open, effective, and efficient than today's extremely limiting fashion of restrictive publication, diffusion, patenting, and copyrighting – whilst assuring rights, fostering and rewarding effort to greater degrees

Personal knowledge enrichment could last over an individual's lifetime, inspiring each to experience other professions and arts (arts as originally intended in Latin to mean all areas of human knowledge). It should be a migration toward an evolved notion, increasingly a willingness to improve one's capabilities rather than today's improvable concepts of study, homework, and testing, recognizing, promoting, and rewarding talent in many more ways than we are accustomed to.

Knowledge and capability enhancement are among the fundamental cornerstones of the Virtus model and the basis of prolonged prosperity— much more than they are today. As such, it is self-evident that proper incentive and remuneration become essential and needed to be addressed to allow them to add value in a virtuous loop.

Closing Thoughts for the Section

The domino effect will occur naturally since the efforts undertaken will start at the lowest levels within each element, changing each paradigm from the inside out. Viable answers can be found by running the options through the Alpha-e Protocol and agreeing on what is best for different stakeholders, nature and our ecosystems, and for the economy.

It will be necessary to decide which option provides the most value if we want to achieve lasting, long-term, sustainable development of the economy, unleashing business and economic potential in currently unfathomable ways.

The adoption of this system will free from latches, no longer requiring straightjacket models, forceful agreements, or one-size-fits-all approaches (some quick wins may be achieved in some very high-impact areas in relatively short times). This is why any new model that seeks to address today and tomorrow's challenges will be amorphous.

As potential benefits emerge, buy-in will most likely ensue at a natural pace, gathering momentum. At the end of the day, one always has to bear in mind the current alternative.

New indicators will be necessary to evaluate progress and address questions such as what is our true *"Problem to Opportunity Transformation Rate Capability"* as a society? In other words, to what degree have we been educated to see, analyze, discuss, waste time, drain money, and complain over problems rather than focus on how to turn challenges into new ideas, opportunities, and benefits?

There is at least one new opportunity behind each challenge equipped with diametrically opposite positive energy. The new model will have one-to-many and many-to-many links and all voids in nature are filled. Our legacy models are no exception.

VIRTUS Key Principles

The following is summary of the Virtus model key considerations, principles, and perceived trends thus far discussed. Each needs further elaboration that goes beyond the scope of this book. The following is a brief outline of the important ones.

Virtus or the newly forming baseline value-generating economic (prosperity) model, BEM^{HESD}, is a reality. It is already beginning to form. It results from innovations and advancements made in recent decades and those that will come in the future.

Not only is the current legacy/hybrid economic model facing systemic inhibitors and dichotomies, but it is also being affected dramatically by progressions and novelties that substantially block it from being effective.

The Virtus model is growing constantly with greater numbers of variables.

Links with legacy/hybrid models are fading and cause-and-effect relations are creating growing systemic and structural inhibitors and dichotomies.

Using remedies and reforms based on legacy/hybrid models in addressing any aspect of the BEM^{HESD} might ultimately yield a neutral, modest, undesired, or potentially virulent outcome.

BEM^{HESD} and its successive version, EPM^{HESDX}, are composed of dynamically changing globules that enclose a temporary aggregation of elements that join for the time required and can, when necessary, connect via a virtual network of synapses. These synapses can be activated or deactivated, forming new connections with other elements and/or components in other globules or even replicating without having to delete the previous globules.

The prolonged success of the BEM^{HESD} and its successive versions will depend on how closely evolved elements introduced into the model maintain the fundamental value-generating DNA characteristics of the model.

Elements of legacy/hybrid models that might still be useful must evolve to respond to new challenges and enable the development of new opportunities.

Holistic value, evolution, the centrality of humanity and ecosystems, sustainability, ecosystems, transformation, change, knowledge enhancement, and adaptation represent some of the constants of the model. Virtus will continuously change its form and connotations, providing new opportunities focused on value creation, providing the possibility to ascend to higher plateaus.

As with any element and component, performance yardsticks can be linked via virtual synapses with other globules and elements.

The BEM^{HESD} and successive versions (EPM^{HESDX}) will need equally evolved governance framework (i.e., laws, policies, norms, protocols) to enable its proper management and steering.

The success of the Virtus governance framework will depend on how well it permeates the model's fundamental components and traits, dynamically covering the model as it evolves and reshapes continuously, modifying accordingly as requirements evolve.

This virtual membrane also provides a necessary balancing agent not only to the single elements and traits contained within Virtus but also to the whole, including the connective synapses.

The evolved governance framework will need to be modeled around Virtus, and future versions will require out-of-the-box thinking and implementation strategies.

Web inclusivity Mobint... and the KES Awareness factor can pose risk and threat factors to long-term prosperity and preventive strategies, so evolved solutions must be developed to steer them beneficially.

Remuneration, money, investments, and financial interests will always move toward ideas, solutions, etc. that offer the best possible returns and least resistance to their inception and growth.

Value generation is key to continued future prosperity and development.

At least for the foreseeable future, innovations and advancements will continue to produce a transition from tangible to intangible, physical to virtual.

We are witnessing a new step-level transition to a new plateau of virtualization of uses, requirements (e.g., customer, employer, employee), businesses and business models, processes, modalities, activities, chores, means, techniques, and work routines.

The not-so-distant future will heavily impact, change, transform, and redefine the following, their business relations and interactions with:

- customers, clients, suppliers, distributors, channels, shareholders, investors, management, employees, and unions;

- time-related matters (e.g., time schedules, shifts, working hours); available free time;

- physical requirements (e.g.: work space needs and requirements, moving away from physical space and moving toward virtual forms and connections);

- plant, equipment, and capital investment requirements; automation of processes, methods, activities, and chores; and

- professions, jobs, and employment; contractual terms; the concept of careers; remuneration and valuation, and measurement yardsticks.

A transition in this direction in so many fields requires finding solutions to fit evolved needs and requirements of different types of stakeholders.

This will open continuously evolving prospects and provide a completely new paradigm for greater challenges in line with our evolving needs and aspirations.

The evolution of businesses, jobs, professions, and remunerated activities, etc., toward a new plateau will require solutions using the tools, models, and methods natural to the new plateau. Instead, using legacy or hybrid models to find leverage will induce new structural/systemic complexity and blocks.

An evolved plateau for new investments, businesses, requirements, employment, jobs, etc., suggests the need for evolved types of elements forming the macro- and microeconomic context (e.g., public debt, monetary policy, taxation, pensions, retirement) that generate value and that can truly address the evolved needs and requirements of the citizenry in a sustainable manner.

It is necessary to find solutions to address an unprecedented number of opportunities to enrich people's lives, permitting the freedom to move from one personal life project to another based on one's passions, capabilities, and aspirations.

In this evolved scenario, it is highly likely that we will need to move away from resources that are accounted for as costs toward an evolved view and consideration of these as essential elements that add *value*.

They have an intrinsic value not only from an accounting point of view, but also conceptually. To be even more exact, fundamentally and substantially beyond this, they provide a true game-paradigm-changing shift.

Evolution of relations between Citizens and their Government

In very generic terms, the axiom in use in today's model is that government incurs costs to produce benefits for citizens who, in turn, are asked to pay taxes to repay them in a closed looped-system.

Under Virtus, the paradigm is reversed, evolved, modernized, and redefined: *individuals, professionals, businesses, corporations, and organizations be they private or public create value across all sectors of human activity in a country, state, city, etc. The sum total of these becomes the total value generated at each level within the system, turning the current relation between government and citizens on its heels toward a more evolved notion of democracy and democratic rule.*

Citizens and constituents of a state or a community become the primary actors in generating value, while the governing body elected and constituted by these rewards virtuous outcomes.

Seen from this different perspective, what a society produces is value (concretely and substantially different from current notions such as GDP, Public debt, deficit, . . . or other emanations of these). In many ways, this might lead to a more natural/proper way of defining the relation between citizens and their government and possibly one that could finally begin to address many of the frustrations and paradoxes the current rapport generates and has generated throughout human history to date.

Evolution of Value Generation for Government and Business

As imaginable, implemented correctly, Virtus will not affect only an economic model. As with any other new paradigm changes in history, it will have significant effect and influence many other dimensions.

It is reasonable and objective to think that value creation will permeate the organization and administration of government, policy and policy making, politics, and the definition of geopolitical scenarios and roadmaps, objectives, and stances. In addition, it will most likely bring about a newly evolved modality of interaction between citizens and business, as well as evolved notions of accountability and responsibility.

Correspondingly, value generation will necessarily permeate the judiciary branch, law making, law enforcement, and their evolution to address more adequately new challenges, efficiency, and efficacy and produce a substantial shift in the enhancement of existing models.

Its effect on business will be even more profound as time progresses, more so than what has been covered so far. In essence, as new plateaus are reached, new versions of Virtus are activated and ever newer possibilities and interconnections become visible, viable, and achievable.

The possible number of transformations, mutations, processes, models, levers, modalities, and opportunities are hard to calculate today.

The same must be said for the effect on the individual, the prime actor in value creation. Theoretically and with the necessary grain of salt, it seems the more value is generated, the more possibilities might become visible. Realistically, though, it will be accompanied by a new series of challenges that future generations will need to address via adaptations to future versions of Virtus.

As mentioned previously, a new model needs to be firmly founded in the real world. To achieve this very objective, Virtus was tailored from grass roots and designed to work at the DNA level, embedding new variables to address an evolving reality. For today's reality, the first version of Virtus evolves from the current market-based scenario with the aim of addressing current real needs, necessities, and challenges and a built-in adaptation to pragmatic requisites of the real world, whether they stem from individuals, business, the banking and financial industry, markets, or government: the current economic model and the growing number of game-changing variables. Different from any other model of the past, Virtus has been conceptualized to be dynamic, adaptable and responsive to future needs, requirements, and challenges.

To be successful, any new model must also consider the different needs and interests of these different stakeholders, starting from today's reality. Thus, if we wish to aim at achievable outcomes and true, realistic results, the different needs of individuals, business, banking, and markets must all be considered, keeping in mind that value creation must be systemic and structural. To explain how to achieve this goal, the next chapters and sections introduce a subset of new concepts that focus on facilitating the accomplishment of such objectives in government, business, professions and at the individual level. The chapters and sections are critical to the proper appreciation of how the model works and its real-world implementation.

Evolved Concept of "Value" and "Value Balance"

So far we have touched a few of the fundamental cornerstones of the new economic model. For purposes of synthesis, in the next chapters we will introduce a few more. As mentioned we are already moving toward a scenario whereby resources, activities, processes, and intangibles in general are slowly moving toward new concepts of valuation and accountability. The imminent evolutionary step is that they might be treated with an evolved notion of assets with real intrinsic value rather than mere costs. As witnessed processes, products, services, and activities that in the past were considered to drain value from a government, state, organization, a corporation, a profession, etc., could become valuable (i.e., R&D, national resilience programs and projects).

As this takes place, the transition toward new plateaus will require a new, evolved meaning of value together with a systemic balancing or equilibrium-generating mechanism that will replace the legacy/hybrid cost concepts. Given the nature of the evolving model, a systemic balancing mechanism for Virtus could be summarized by the notion of "value balance," or equilibrium.

This notion is based on the following algorithm: The value of what is contributed (i.e., input, invested) should be ≤ (less than or equal to) the value and quality of what is achieved in terms of real value (^{HESDX}). In other words, what we (as individuals, business entities, organizations, and communities) get back in terms of value, quality, benefits, and advantages should be higher than or equal to what we contribute/invest.

What we get back in terms of ^{HESDX} is expressed as *real value*, while what we invest in time and resources could be simply known as *"Investment."* In the new Virtus reference model, BEM^{HESD}, the evolved term "value" is seen as a benefit, overriding today's concept of "cost." To achieve a balanced outcome, the real value of a project (e.g., a new business venture, service, dam, school, mass transportation project, remodeled or refurbished business facility) is synonymous with how much overall benefit it produces in different domains.

In another example, real value (^{HESDX}) generated for an individual, a business, a community, society or a union of countries in terms of new and future development, investment, innovation, employment, improvement in quality of life, environment and ecosystems, long-term sustainability, etc., should be greater than or equal to the contribution for realizing a project.

So long as the equation is met, there should be no "cost," as we know or account for it today, to the concern or community (e.g., through generation of public debt and taxes). Any *excess value* achieved becomes a return that can be rolled over or distributed with evolved yardsticks or a simple contribution percentage amongst the various stakeholders to avoid, for example, recessionary, inflationary or deflationary phenomena.

Should the inverse occur, in an unpredictable scenario whereby ^{HESDX} (value) is partially achieved, this could give rise to a penalty or price for generating *damage* to the community in a proportionate manner (applied to those who designed it, made it, approved it, and were mandated with its supervision).

This theoretically should shift the emphasis of the incentive to becoming more virtuous and sustainable, holistically, and to focusing on the true benefits, quality, development of new investment and business opportunities, employment, involvement, sustainability, etc., rather than cutting corners to save on costs, a complete paradigm shift.

Under the new Virtus model, the objective is to achieve value comprehensively and holistically. In all probability, existing/legacy measures of economic success (e.g., sales, turnover, profit, gross margin, return on investment, or other KPI's) will no longer be *the only* yardsticks or be accounted for in the same way. Instead, the focus will be on measures that are more comprehensive and that bring overall improvement, such as increased future business possibilities, new opportunities, better quality of life, reduced human footprint, and the BEM^{HESD} key characteristics (i.e., sustainability, human centricity, development, evolution). Value.

Yet these are mostly seen in the existing models as mere costs—unaffordable, unviable, economically unproductive elements or propositions—as mentioned in previous chapters. Each component of the BEM^{HESD} must bring concrete and pragmatic near, medium, long-term and prolonged results, benefits, and returns and give way to new investment and business opportunities, development, and prosperity.

Evolution from a cost to a value-based model requires equal evolution in terms of aspects dealing with such things as defining value in each different sector, profession, industry, process, and in general any sphere of human activity.

This implies deciding and concurring the redefinition of such things as

- performance measurement yardsticks;

- accounting;

- accountability;

- measure;

- valuation;

- reporting;

- feedback;

- payment;

- reward, remuneration criteria, etc.

along with a price for generating damage (to an investment, business, community, individual, ecosystem, environment, health, consumers, society, etc.). This is why and how humanity (H) becomes central.

If implemented correctly, in theory the incentive of this evolutionary model is centered on doing things right—the investor, the business, and the individual are remunerated for creating value across all sectors of human activity.

No system is fail-proof or perfect. As such, a means has to be created to mitigate shortcomings or damaging extremes and one of the primary ways to achieve this is through the value balance concept.

Let us now see how this might be applied to a real world scenario in the three main domains of which our current system is made up, i.e., government (city, state, country), business/organizations, and the individual recognizing that these also might evolve and be redefined.

Government: Value Balance Valuation

To provide a brief introduction of how this might translate into the assessment of a society's cumulative capability and performance in generating value (as government accounting evolves), new concepts similar to the following *government-level valuation* will need to be factored in to address this paradigm shift.

Government: Value Balance Valuation

Total Real Value Produced $^{(HESDX)}$

+ Net Support Received (contributions rather than taxes, +/- Excess, or Deficit from prior period)

– Incentive/Recompense Recognized and Distributed

= Net Real Value (Excess or Equilibrium or Deficit)

The purpose here is only to introduce the notion/concept, and this is only a possible *starting point* from which a transitional task force, mandated by national governing bodies, will formulate an agreed version of BEM^{HESD} (baseline model) from which successive versions will continuously evolve to address new opportunities.

Before we begin let us see what is meant by each of the new variables making up the aforementioned equation:

Total real value produced: In the above example of government,[47] *total real value produced* is the total amount of ^{HESDX} citizens, businesses, organizations, investors, etc., generate within a certain period. This includes, but is not limited to, things such as business opportunities, employment (life projects), knowledge enhancement possibilities,

---

[47]   Federal, state, city, local

215

sustainability, strategic survival and disaster protection projects, ecosystem enhancement and cleanup, advanced research opportunities, etc., and of course dams, highways, schools, policing, firefighting, emergency services, hospitals, etc.

In essence, it is the total amount of value a community, state, or country receives from its citizens, businesses, enterprises, etc., as a result of their value-generating activity. In return for this, a society needs to recognize, reward, and provide incentives for this virtuous contribution to prolonged development, prosperity, security, and well-being meritoriously.

It must be absolutely clear that here we are not talking about unsuccessful, historically applied models, inflationary models, or any other hypothetical model based on an axiom of simple money generation. Quite the opposite. It is instead about the cyclical, *adaptive evolution* of the current *central/reserve banking system* in use today, *achived through the work of the transition task force*, towards one that addresses current challenges and dichotomies, geared to bring about balanced, systemic, and prolonged economic traction, dynamically.

To be clear, it must address current systemic blocks and contradictions produced by legacy elements such as public debt, the deficit, fiscal policy, by running the Alpha-e protocol, and implementing its findings in a planned and gradual manner, acceptable in form, timing, and content, to the expectations of the public, and in general, the majority of stakeholders. This must be done achieving value, which also means managing, and mitigating undesired outcomes.

Several alternative, or complimentary strategies can be used, and reforms enacted, to achieve these goals, among these: repositioning, redefining, gradual reduction and repayment, scale-down, simplification, and so on. In reality some of these strategies could, if coherently phased, already be implemented towards transition. The onus and responsibility of the transition task force is to define these in line with a governing bodies' value generation mandate.

In itself, this represents a major change of significant proportions, yet it only exemplifies one of the several game-changing elements of the new model. The role of a government, in the new model, is to provide the right environment, policy, governance frameworks, and regulatory value, acting as an independent guarantor of the proper, transparent functioning of system and against fraudulent intent, abuse, etc. to allow value generation.

Net Support Received (contributions rather than mere taxes, +/- Excess or Deficit from prior period): represent amounts received by governing bodies from their citizenry, businesses, and organizations plus or minus any excess or deficit in Net Real Value rolled over from the prior value period (similar to solar of fiscal year). This, as will become clearer later on, will mean a substantial shift away from a model based on taxes and taxation as we know them today toward new evolved notions as these are redefined to fit new challenges and needs.

Incentive/Recompense Recognized and Distributed is the amount that a government[48] recognizes for the value (^{HESDX}) produced by an economy through its interaction with its evolved central and commercial banking system. Among the alternatives, by applying the same levers and facilities used today (see previous chapters)—at least initially, evolving in later stages, as necessary, to fit ever-growing development and prosperity demands—could bring about a smooth transition.

Net Real Value is the algebraic result of the above equation and can assume three distinct states: _Equilibrium_, _Excess_, or _Deficit_ in real value generated over a value period (these will be explained later).

In the evolved model, with the exception of natural elements fundamental to life such as air and water and those sectors[49] each community, society, or country might deem it necessary to be run and or guaranteed by a public concern (government, municipality, etc.) in accordance with its preferences and sensitivities around such matters, almost all remaining activities could theoretically be run by private concerns focused on delivering value and for so long as they are able to achieve this.

This will create a continuous virtuous cycle of possibilities and make them available to a greater number of concerns (that is why the new model is ideologically, politically, and culturally neutral and applicable in any sociopolitical context).

Ideally, the more a society is open, the more it provides its citizenry the liberty to create and leverage new opportunities that generate value and the more it provides potential for prolonged development, responsible entrepreneurship, prosperity, well-being, and security.

Under the evolved model, a governing body's main objective thus becomes the creation of an environment that promotes continuous value

---

48. Local, city, state, federal
49. i.e., public security, emergency services, defense

generation (in all areas), healthy competition, and a level playing ground internally and internationally while the role of organisms such as Federal Reserve/central banking systems are improved and evolved toward a focus on value generation.

Once operational (from the first transition rollout phase of BEM^{HESD} onward), continuously revolving, results focused governing bodies together with an adequate, efficient and effective representative mix of private concerns and stakeholders will need to act as guarantors of the proper functioning of the process in the

- transparency over and identification of the evaluation criteria for value and its remuneration (quantities, modalities, disbursement, etc.) through a demand/ requirement/necessity-driven democratic process and, for example, value index commissions or boards for each economic sector/field (some of these already exist in many fields);

- identification of processes and modalities that curb fraudulent intent and mitigate and or resolve shortcomings;

- continuous generation of traction for prolonged economic development/prosperity.

There are several ways this can be structured and implemented. This includes evolving existing concepts of virtual money generation, its distribution, allocation, accounting, and accountability via evolved central and commercial banking systems.

Many personal ideas and alternatives come to mind about how this may be organized, achieved, and formalized in the first version of Virtus (BEM^{HESD}) and its operations, but this task is best achieved through the governing bodies, the *transition treaty committee*, and *task force*. At an operational level, once means and modalities have been concurred, transactions are triggered/actuated via an "activating algorithm". This algorithm is a string made up of a number of disjunct, randomly produced, highly encrypted blocks, with independent systems of counter checks. The algorithm is continuously updated and evolved as Virtus evolves over time. The activating algorithm is one of the elements composing the operational prerequisites.

Addressing/Resolving Missing Links

One of the fundamental differences under the new model is that there will be no free rides. Value to be produced has to be directly tied to a specific and concurred value-creation goal(s) and once achieved has to be demonstrated, vouched, and certified and its effects have to be tangible, visible, and/or objectively perceivable but what's more recognized and accepted as such by its beneficiaries. This constitutes one of the many "missing links" in today's models and the evolving future value-based model.

Currently, the concepts and means activated through the central banking systems and used by the existing model, though important in their strategic intent, are relegated to very limited aspects (i.e., Quantitative Easing, grants, and in general "facilities" and loan generation process through the banking system and general monetary policy).

Presently they have an increasingly limited permeation to the rest of the economy due to the greater appeal of things such as easier returns form *virtual value enhancers*, whereas their true potential is yet to be unleashed fully—through an evolved banking and financial system.

The effort of the *transition task force* here must be focused in putting the capital B back in the new banking system without the need to jettison thousands of other jobs or hinder the possibilities of leveraging evolved models and interconnections with other equally evolved elements, paving the way to potentially inconceivable numbers of new prospects and interconnections.

Existing limitations, in leveraging such instruments, have potentially contributed to the many systemic dichotomies and multiple unwanted outcomes that can be seen today (i.e., nonproductive polarized liquidity accumulation, credit crunches, improper imbalanced resources seeking only virtual investment possibilities, and resources that do not permeate in creating generalized reinvestment) as reported by a growing number of authoritative government agencies and international organizations, including the Federal Reserve System (2012b) and the IMF (2012). Transition to Virtus might also mean the gradual reduction or end(?) of very controversial phenomena such as: Bail-out's; Bail-in's[50]; and "Bad Bank"[51] measures. Creating value in this context means, being able to address these issues at the core and find viable new ways to improve banking also in terms of its public perception.

Moreover, it is a fact that many economic sectors worldwide have increasingly (since World War II) depended upon subsidies, funding, incentives, grants, aid, concessions, tax rebates/credits, quantitative easing, etc., and many "facilities" similar to the ones used for the financial system's stability (being currently enacted)—without desired and/or lasting results. It has in most cases, only created additional systemic dichotomies, detrimental liability on taxpayers and over-dependence without creating value.

An evolved approach adopted by the transition task force instead must be geared to release the true potential of these instruments or their evolved versions (e.g., instruments that contemplate new notions such as "QVG: quantitative availability/facilities/investments/stimulus for systemic value generation") and unblock this stalemate, putting economic traction, revival, and recovery back into the system, endemically and structurally.

This will help to reestablish the economic loop currently being by-passed by virtual enhancers while an equally evolved governance framework will allow proper balancing of this mechanism while disincentivizing free rides— remunerating, financing, and incentivizing only those initiatives that will create value given the many new ways of generating real value. The most important aspect of this evolved approach and use of new instruments (such as quantitative availability for systemic value generation) will be to enable the transition to, and creation of a new banking system built around value generation and one befit to address the many challenges of the twenty first century.

---

[50] *The Economist* mentions, a bail-in occurs when a borrower's creditors are forced to bear some of the burden by having a portion of their debt written off. For example, bondholders in Cyprus banks and depositors (account holders) with more than 100,000 Euros in their accounts were forced to write-off portion of their holdings);

[51] *"About money"* website defines "Bad banks" as: legal entities created by banks or governments to transfer risky or junk assets from otherwise good banks. By using bad banks, banks can improve their financial statements, investor trust, and strength and stay in business. This practice however, is used by other types of non-banking companies as well.

This could create unquantifiable benefits for businesses, investors, individuals, and an evolved financial system that is linked to the economy, generating the need for the involvement of experts from new ever-more specialized and different fields.

When in equilibrium (*balance*), the evolved model does not produce a *deficit* or *excess* in real value produced in an economy. Theoretically in ideal circumstances, this means all stakeholders have achieved their value-generation goals, or that net effect is an algebraic balance. In the scenario where a *deficit* occurs, reestablishing equilibrium is necessary and this will depend on how equilibrium is defined through the Alpha-e Protocol. Ideally, it should come from an improvement in *total real value* produced in terms of development and prosperity in immediately successive periods or before a "*value-generation year-end*" (ex-fiscal).

A *deficit in real value produced* means that, for example, damage was produced in a certain activity, project, etc. In this case, a penalty will need to be levied on those responsible to reestablish and ensure value. The total of damages produced is netted against *voluntary donations* from businesses and individuals and any *excess value produced* in other areas of the economy, giving *net support received*. Any eventual/residual leftover shortcoming or excess produced in one period will roll over to the successive *value year*.

To conclude this section, we must also introduce the notion of "*strategic value-generating initiatives*." Examples of these initiatives are as follows (part three of the book will examine some of these in more detail):[52]

- mass modernization of key national infrastructure such as next-generation telecommunications, national electrical grids, highways, and water distribution networks

- sustainment of research and development in all fields

- large-scale mass-transit projects

- natural disaster protection programs for large cities, etc.

- structural environmental cleanup programs

---

[52] Many concrete examples involving different economic sectors are covered later.

- enhancement of safety, well-being of citizens and cities

- space-related programs

- recovery of abandoned areas and industrial sites

Based on a nation's or a community's prerogatives, these cyclical programs might need concerted and coordinated steering at the highest levels (involving balanced representations from different stakeholders) through, for example, localized value-generating efforts to ensure that their combined effect and their rollout sequence also translate into value.

Value is not created when things are held up or procrastinated unjustifiably nor is value created by taking on the full effort of strategic initiatives in limited timeframes, creating the paradox of phantomlike useless projects—these generate damage and go against some of the most fundamental traits of [HESDX], such as sustainability and managing inflationary, deflationary, . . . phenomena.

Instead, it is all about comprehensive value generation and careful, modular rollouts. Once evaluated and certified as creating value, their shortcomings will be used as lessons learned in successive phases and rollout packets.

Value here is also generated through things such as respect of realistic but firm rollout milestones, sustainability, and footprint reduction and implementation is achieved according to a concurred action plan with all key players and the involvement of local businesses, workforce, etc., respecting local values and requirements.

The positive implications and interactions of each initiative with other components are potentially incalculable. Just to introduce a couple, they might involve the revival of economically depressed areas, abandoned industrial zones, disaster-affected areas, and poverty-stricken regions,[53] together with impacts on net-positive immigration (rather than uncontrollable desperation-driven immigration) or return to home-countries/countries of origin as opportunities grow and stability resumes locally. Indirect effects might address easing exposure to potential for phenomena such as mass social unrest, regional wars and their spillage, and extremism.

[53.] Zones, neighborhoods, towns, cities, and nations.

This will help address business and employment, especially with regard to the young and those in critical age groups (50-70) who currently are the most affected by the impasse.

Much more can be said about government value creation but this goes beyond the scope of this introductory book. One of the areas thought, that will become the focus of a governing body in its value generation effort, will be in the areas of simplification, streamlined processes, an advisory and customer service orientation towards citizens, business, and all other stakeholders.

Evolution of Democracy and Governance

Policy and policymakers' rapport with citizens are bound to evolve as a result, and this might bring an evolution in the relationship toward increased involvement, accountability, and a more direct link among commitments, promises, actions, results, achievements, election, and reelection to public office, for example, laying the foundations for evolving new democracy model(s) that evolve and adapt continually to new needs, reaching higher levels of civilization.

As is becoming increasingly evident, factual reality and pragmatic necessity call for improvements to governance models. For example, the ambition of becoming an elected official to any public office can no longer remain detached from the achievement of promised goals and objectives, accountability, and responsibility. Though this may be an arduous task, value creation focus and paradigms, at the very least, will most likely help close existing gaps and bridge current missing links.

In many cases, this situation does not arise because of a lack of goodwill. The true implementation of democracy has historically suffered from the impediments and limitations forced upon it by existing models and predominantly cost-based logics that, among other things, fuel much of the cynicism in politics. Realism suggests results will occur progressively and that it will take time before new generations, brought up and accustomed to value-generation paradigms, take over and become more effective in evolving the model further.

The learning curve however, will not forestall the achievement of a fast transition towards a new era. A modular and phased approach and implementation, will enable the activation of the first transitional phases allowing deeply-rooted structural economic recovery from the current impasse and the development of prolonged economic traction as analytically evidenced. If sufficient effort is applied, the first results are achievable in much less time than the duration of the current impasse. Actual implementation times fundamentally depend on resilience and willingness to proceed and the "go-live date" in ushering in transition reforms.

If implemented correctly, Virtus should also lead to the achievement of new levels of civilization and democracy. Human societies have evolved from forms of distributed leadership used in small tribes, to developments that led to the formalization of democracy as a governance concept in Greece, to the realization of the Magna Carta, The Bill of Rights, and The Universal Declaration of Human Rights. All have contributed to the evolution of civilization and democracy throughout history.

It takes human will to develop and implement such concepts as "We hold these truths to be self-evident, that all men are created equal, that they are endowed by their Creator with certain unalienable Rights, that among these are Life, Liberty and the pursuit of Happiness.--That to secure these rights, Governments are instituted among Men, deriving their just powers from the consent of the governed . . .". This dream was achieved by a group of people, facing seemingly insurmountable odds more than 200 years ago. Similarly, today, taking an additional historical step depends solely on will.

Some might ask, "What's in it for me?" This is a legitimate question. Within the context of current world events, the answer might be very simple: theoretically everything. Each living generation (young, middle-aged, or young at heart) is responsible for safeguarding freedom, upholding the sacrifice it took to achieve rights, being accountable for their improvement, and being liable for their safe passing on to prosperity.

Rights and freedom come at a price: sacrifice, participation, and involvement; duties and obligations; and the sincere respect for others—without these, one should not have a moral claim to them.

Evolution of Taxes, Debt, Deficit, Etc.

As is becoming apparent and will become more so as time progresses, it is highly probable that one of the outcomes of the Alpha-e protocol yield a scenario whereby value, value balance, valuation, and certification processes (or similar notions) might progressively evolve and or replace (among other elements of the existing models) the current tax and taxation concepts, notions, systems, and modalities.

Based on the results of the transition task forces, this alone could redefine existing and or produce new and immeasurable number of jobs across the world and potentially add many new opportunities through a plethora of new expertise in increasing numbers of new fields that would have otherwise evaporated under Web inclusivity, innovation, etc.

Increasingly people currently working for ministries of finance or IRS-type organizations, audit firms, etc. for example, might gradually be refocused in the necessarily human-led (for the foreseeable future) valuation and certification processes rather than investigating taxes.

The approach to valuation and certification of value will also need society and these professions to evolve—going from the current "inspect to punish" modus operandi to a "service to guide and advise" modality toward investors, businesses, and individuals to help them refine their propositions and positions in generating and achieving real value goals and objectives. Obviously, the success rate in curbing fraudulent or criminal intent will also need to improve.

A key success factor is implementing continuously evolving processes, modalities, and revolving assignment of responsibility to address the shortcomings of each new version of the model, especially with reference to such things as centralization of power, conflict of interest, independence, revolving mandates, misuse of power, fraudulent intent, transparency, accountability, complicated over-structures of controlling organizations, etc.

As government and banking systems (central and commercial) transition to value balance concepts, they will reach higher levels of involvement in real value creation. Consequently, legacy tax concepts will evolve to new *less* tax-like provisions, conceptually and fundamentally different from today's taxes, toward a theoretical migration and or transformation to voluntary contributions to fund, or even invest in particular areas of interest and programs or generically for the well-being of the societies and economies in which they operate.

This needs to be achieved via realistic (non-utopian) linking of these initiatives to different types of benefits, rewards, return on investment . . ., and plans that can change and mutate as necessary to achieve the maximum outcome in terms of total value generated.

It is useful to remember that many countries today do not have income tax or, in some cases, sales tax. Many more have comparatively limited tax impositions. Should a tax-like provision or concept still be deemed necessary by local transition task forces (e.g., beyond a penalty for damage generation) in an evolved society, this should be tangibly linked to providing not only an appreciation, and a sense of voluntary contribution from individuals for the general well-being of society (e.g., something to give back to fund a particular interest) but also *demonstrate* the value this produced.

As is becoming evident, theoretically, in the evolved Virtus model, there might be no real reason or justification for the existence of today's notions of taxes and taxation. In theory and practice, the evolved model might not require or contemplate the need for such a notion and/or mechanism for its proper functioning.

Realistically and reasonably, however, the evolution in this direction will most probably be a gradual one—which in itself will be a great achievement. This is by no means to suggest a lack of accountability—quite the contrary, it will be one of the value goals of transition task forces.

Should there be consensus among the citizenry, business-leaders, policymakers, and experts (e.g., the transition task force) that this anachronistic human-made model and mechanism (which has become a source of major dichotomies and systemic blocks) should be transitioned after the Alpha-e Protocol is run, at the very least it might be possible for example to: reduce the impact of taxation as we know it today; limit its continence to a modular set of transition phases and or to evolve its application to progressively reduced portions of income and business profits, in summary evolve this notion according to the new requirements and needs.

Value generation and balance will allow evolution of all other currently blocked legacy elements such as debt, deficit, etc., transitioning their elements and components toward value creation through several means, each opening new structural and systemic solutions and perspectives to address current dichotomies and blocks and to provide resolution in the near-term.

The final formal version of concepts such as value balance under Virtus for different themes (taxation, debt, etc.) and sectors will be achieved through the concurrent effort, leadership, onus, responsibility, etc. of the governing bodies and operationally through the transition task force.

There are many solutions for each element and module, but these are only my ideas. These solutions include, but are not limited to, new concepts of *value balance indexing, value rollover, value excess/deficit, and equilibrium strategies, protocol, and policies.*

Evolved Governance Frameworks

As noted earlier, Virtus requires an equally evolved governance framework to work at all levels of the model to generate value balance at each level.[54] The development and evolution of such a framework require the involvement of experts from many different fields, not just those mandated with policy formulation, governance, implementation, and enforcement.

It will not be an overnight event but a process. Out of necessity in finding new solutions, the framework should receive a strong commitment and be designed to achieve rollouts benefiting from modularity, scalability, a small quick win approach, technological enablers (e.g., readily devisable Web-based apps), a natural domino effect, etc. in reasonable timeframes.

Given the weight, effect and impact of the many game-changing variables on all aspects of human endeavor, the fundamental importance of effective governance frameworks cannot be underestimated.

The design, implementation, rollout, day-to-day management, and continuous evolution may open many new ramifications that might not be clear or invisible today. The evolved modular governance framework needs to adhere to certain basic criteria based on a society's preferences (non-exhaustive sample):

- Be balanced (avoid extremes: centralized, inflexible, tedious, bureaucratic, complex, boxed in, and un-evolvable).

- For the most part allow privatizeability, generate new opportunities, and virtuous loops.

- Be simple, dexterous, and intuitive.

- Be sustainable and evolvable.

[54.] Public, private, individual; globule, component, element

- Focus on seeking system equilibrium and value balance.

- Focus on generating value (^{HESDX}) and augmenting value.

- Be open, scalable, and modular and interact with other elements.

As explained in previous chapters, the governance framework applies to all elements, subcomponents, components, and globules that become part of the Virtus model. It follows that this also applies to the value balance concept thus far presented and those that will be discussed henceforth.

So far we have analyzed the value balance concept within the context of government. In the next two sections we will see how this applies to the dimensions of business and the individual.

21 century Corporation/Business: Value Balance Valuation

Many corporations, businesses, entrepreneurs, and consumers have already taken some steps in the transition process toward the new plateau in terms of their sensitivity and by making concrete efforts in bringing about positive change in the direction of value generation,[55] but these notions are currently being greatly affected and limited by dated concepts such as taxation and cost centricity.

The intent here is to take these notions beyond these thresholds to unleash their full hidden potential in developing new business opportunities and revenue streams. Future sources of employment, new *business* ideas, models, processes, *jobs* and investments will be more and more reliant on adopting new notions such as the *Virtus economic string theory,* and ever less on legacy based models.

Evolution toward the new development and prosperity plateau, both within the context of business models and in the remaining domains (the economic reference model, government, and all the other dimensions covered in previous chapters), will finally be able to free the real potential for new possibilities available on a higher-level and increasingly multidimensional model.

Seen from a business, corporation, or enterprise balance valuation perspective, as financial statements mutate toward evolved profit and loss and balance sheet statements (e.g., value-generation notices, *performance and evolution updates*), they will need to factor in the following introductory high-level notions/concepts such as those on the next page (for example).

---

55. Processes, products, services, quality, CO_2 footprint, sustainability, energy efficiency, giving-back initiatives, eco-environmental systems, etc.

Acme Corporation: Value Balance Valuation

Total Real Value created [HESDX]

+ Revenues Realized from Sales

+/- Excess or Deficit from prior period

− Investments in enterprise

− Private Contribution to Community or Otherwise

_____

= Net Real Value (Excess or Equilibrium or Deficit)

Similar to the preceding section, the purpose is to introduce the notion/concept, and it only represents a possible starting point from which governing bodies and a transitional task force will define the initial formal and concurred version of BEM[HESD] (the baseline model). Successive versions will continuously evolve to address new opportunities properly.

Total real value realized [HESDX] for a company or a business concern needs to be approved, valued, accounted for, audited, and certified by much less complex but more qualitatively focused "evolved generally accepted value criteria (EGAVC)," replacing, evolving from, and/or enhancing current versions of accounting standards such as GAAP, GAAS, IAS, IFRS, and other quality certification standards, etc..The modus operandi here will also need to evolve to becoming more "advise to improve" rather than mere inspect to punish—furthermore it must apply increasing levels of sensitivity towards time, need for involvement, resources, . . . a company needs to dedicate / invest in these activities − relieving these of this burden as much as possible—this in fact could be a set of values that certifiers could bring to their customers.

In itself these aspects could provide many new and evolved opportunities for independent consumer and stakeholder guarantors, accounting firms, engineering firms, certification firms, health and environmental protection specialists, etc., in an ever evolving/growing number of fields and subject matters in defining, advising, assessing, tracking and monitoring value models, their implementation, correct application, valuation and conformity (among other things) of companies and individual firms in all economic sectors.

These experts in *new* and evolved professions will need to assess and provide guidance in terms of real ^{HESDX} generated for the societies and communities where companies operate, for example, in terms of:

- the quality of the products and services they produce and market and their real impact, for example, on health and well-being or contribution to improving these;

- the level of adherence to the no-nonsense benefits claimed by producers and service providers (e.g.: evolving away from asterisk based, non-transparent conditions, or pushing non-requested services);

- the value generated and quality of their sales process, channels and modalities of sales;

- clear product longevity, return policies, warrantees and guarantees;

- post-sales support, real proactive customer services conformant to needs, and value these provide;

- CO_2, hazardous material, and footprint reduction;

- energetic efficiency;

- eco-health value and eco-environmental impact considerations;

- increased investment possibilities;

- development of new value-adding products/services;

- advanced research efforts to include beyond own immediate perimeter;

- inventions and innovations;

- contributions to controlling speculatory, inflationary, or similar phenomena;

- cure of premises and surroundings—nature regeneration;

- participation in community value generation and giving back projects; etc.

and also the value-based activation of those sustainable activities that until now have been considered financially nonviable or costly:

- refurbishments, improvements, and enhancements to buildings and facilities

- maintenance of assets, machinery, and tools

- environmental improvement

- new opportunity generation (e.g., business development, trade promotion, etc.)

- new employment (life projects) and quality of company life/ working conditions

- the use of human contribution and involvement

- activities that promote human interaction (business travel, business-generating meetings, project/product development and rollout)

- humanization of the workplace and interaction and dignity augmentation (antonyms to strumentialization, unacceptable behavior, mobbing, discrimination, and similar non-productive practices)

- motivation generation

- professional knowledge augmentation and training, etc.

- sustainability; etc.

Under the new model growing number of the elements of the above list will no longer (according to phased processes) represent costs to a company as conceived in today's models. The focus is value creation. Each of these becomes a potential new revenue stream and source of remuneration for those businesses that create value in these and other new areas.

To avoid systemic overload, governing bodies should devise appropriate policy that enacts a phased approach according to a concurred "value plan"—derived from the yearly democratic processes of governing bodies at all levels (local, state, federal and for some aspects international), leaving even more room for business to define its sustainable growth strategy.

These new sources of value generation and remuneration will need to be focused in compensate/replace loss of revenues derived from, for example, Web inclusivity repercussions, or destruction from severe natural events (substantially different from how it is done today), finalized towards achieving value gernerating objectives, opening new doors and opportunities that would otherwise remain hidden, just as many new types of remunerated or previously non-remunerated activities came into being only at each successive step-level evolutionary ascent to a new plateau.

Whilst remaining objective and pragmatic and looking at the general forward-looking picture over a period of time, it is hard not to reflect on how many new prospects this might generate in different sectors or how many new jobs (life projects) and revenue streams this could potentially translate into for companies, investors, and individuals. And how many more will potentially be derived (net of false positives) as these are crisscrossed with other elements, components, and or globules of BEM[HESD].

Moreover, we need to factor in the positive fallout this might have on suppliers, the economy (local, national, and international), and the stock markets that, among other things, can finally find it pragmatically convenient, for example, to separate highly speculative markets from the real value-based markets.

Could these not have potential positive repercussion on pension funds, on jobs for the young, and on retirement, for example? Or on the travel and hospitality industry (and its supply chain), for instance, as that portion of travel that produces positive outcomes (new contracts, business opportunities, and projects) might be considered value. Augmenting human relations and interaction is value—its virtualization is not necessarily. Humans need not (should not) lose the centrality and importance of this ancestrally humane distinctive trait to a cost-based model.

The prospects are surely exciting, but it is crucial to plan a phased approach and allow evolution of reasonable numbers of elements, at any given time, to avoid systemic excess whilst assuring sustainability and proper balance within the system. Vigilance and assurance of companies' ability to deliver and achieve value objectives become of fundamental importance.

Similarly, systemic dependence, abuse, and/or improper/fraudulent use need to be addressed with rigor and expeditiously. New value generation measurement yardsticks and indicators will be the key in evaluating the performance and credibility of an enterprise in the future. So much so, that based on the prerogatives of the societies where these operate this might also encompass their permit to continue operations in those areas based on, for example, a mix of factors and objective point based system indicative of satisfaction and concerns of different stakeholders.

Investments in Enterprise is what a business (to use today's terminology) pays, for example, in salaries and the purchase of products and services from its suppliers with the substantial difference that if done correctly, many of these "costs," in turn, might lead to the creation of potentially additional revenue streams that weigh on a company's profit and loss statements and evaporate, as mere dead expenses in today's model.

The emphasis on value creation of economic concerns amplifies, evolving further than it is achieving today. It will no longer be focused on producing a widget or a service but doing it in such a way as to create tangible value all around it—putting humans, their well-being, the eco-environment, long term prosperity, and inclusive survival at the center.

Private contributions are voluntary by definition in the new BEM[HESD]. There is no need to force any concern or anyone to chip in simply because the more value created by giving back to the local communities, the more new revenue streams can potentially be generated from these. Additionally, new ways of incentivizing positive contributions can be sought. There are no free rides however. Achieving value is not banal, and it is one of the preconditions for prolonged development and regeneration of other opportunities.

The same principles of balance, deficit, or excess of value creation, solutions, mechanisms, protocols, and the onus of final detailed definition of these, addressing the shortcomings discussed in the previous chapters, also apply here. The only difference is that *excess value generation* here is synonymous with today's legacy concept of profit, but in many ways it will be substantially, qualitatively different, especially its reinvestment in value-generating business activities.

As a final note, it is important to emphasize that *our current perception of what constitutes a company's (or a nation's) performance is strictly linked to current accounting definitions. As these evolve to meet new challenges and needs, the way we conceive a profit and loss statement, a balance sheet and cash flow or for that matter all the KPI currently linked to these notions may no longer have the same weight, provide the same relevance; convey success, returns and profitability or be useful in the same way.*

Individual: Value Balance Valuation

Could this balance valuation apply to individuals and professionals? In the newly forming BEM^{HESD}, this is already contemplated. Theoretically, there is no reason it should not be the case. Moreover, it equally evolves to reap new chances (e.g., identification, approval, valuation, certification, and accounting of an individual's income and those indicated in the previous chapters).

We need to be realistic and pragmatic in this specific area, however, as individual value-generation capability might require a relatively longer implementation and need more time to address adequately. Theoretically, however, how might this work and be applied to a real-life scenario?

Today personal net income is formed from two basic elements: income and taxes. For at least the last two millennia, existing models did not account for the value an individual brings to society during the course of his life. Why? This question assumes greater relevance as time progresses and currently known elements such as jobs, processes, and so on move toward virtualization.

In most cases, people leave legacies and contribute wages, to an improvement in different realms, in providing for and helping their families and their loved ones, communities, businesses, or employers throughout their life span. As the economy sheds millions of jobs without structural, long-lasting solutions in sight and the introduction of new paradigms under the current model only adds complexity and further undermines employment, evolving to a new plateau is as vital as migrating away from the barter system was.

This was the same type of jump achieved by migrating from a rural to industrial, to a service-based economy and from serfdom to democracy. This entailed the introduction of new concepts (most of which we take for granted today) such as the right to liberty, to vote and freedom of speech, but also wages, salary, work hours, holidays, paid vacation, sick leave, and retirement. *Each of these notions was as new to our ancestors as those we will need to face, generate, and benefit from going forward.*

An evolved modality will enhance and leverage on previously non-valued contributions in ways unthinkable and incalculable until today in terms of development of new opportunities. Should we look through a different perspective and factor in an individual's real value generation in the equation, this might add new windows to the next plateau(s).

Let us consider the following balance valuation model for the individual/professional:

<u>Individual: Value Balance Valuation</u>

Total Real Value Created [HESDX]

+ Personal Income Realized

+/- Excess or Deficit from prior period

– Investment Incurred

– Private Contribution to Community or Otherwise

= Real Value: Excess or Equilibrium or Deficit

The first thing noticeable is the striking similarity of an individual's valuation with that of a business. This is because the relation between employee and employer, types of jobs and sources of jobs, is evolving and blurring as we move forward, given the plethora of new intersections between different elements possible in the BEM[HESD] and its future versions.

In a not-so-distant future, some companies might evolve toward a virtual coming together of professionals and/or *micro-entrepreneurs* who, independent of the hierarchical levels and professional seniority they might occupy, seek to achieve a series of common objectives for a specific time, each acting in his or her own capacity, finding it more motivating and economically convenient to remain independent (rather than dependent) in realizing life projects.

Theoretically, this might lead to fewer people wishing to remain mere "employees" as time progresses—at least according to today's notion. To some extent, this paradigm shift, though in its embryonic state, is already taking place so evolution might be a step ahead of us. The problem today is that this shift is not practical (for the majority) under the current model because it has, among other things, only translated into *precariousness, uncertainty, decreasing prospects,* and *devaluation of professionalism,* creating the many systemic dichotomies, and negative impacts on individuals and families (e.g., quality of life, serenity, reasonable sense of continuity and security for the future) we witness today.

Total real value created in ᴴᴱˢᴰˣ not only applies to what today is considered remuneration from a job, a professional activity, or investments, etc., but also incorporates value-based remuneration of things that in the current model are not *valued* (depending on the evolving definitions that it will assume). A few samples might be:

- value creation on the job, remunerated professional tutoring, mentoring;

- certified assistance in many spheres: the family and community (e.g., home management, civil service, home/hospital assistance for the elderly, the sick, veterans, the differently abled);

- professional child care and sitting;

- assistance and support in addressing educational issues such as ADHD, dyslexia, autism, etc.;

- personal knowledge and capability enhancement;

- new business opportunity generation;

- new idea formulation and publication and innovations;

- works of artistic value that can enhance a community;

- professional activities providing training and knowledge dissemination of different types;

- remuneration for use personal data and information—there is no reason why private concerns should use one's private data, its storage, elaboration, . . . and transmittal gratuitously, this should also influence things such as adding tangible incentive to respecting privacy and uncontrolled use of personal data;

- neighborhood enhancement, recycling and enactment of zero miles concepts, etc.

Innovations in many fields provide and facilitate verification of progress, involvement (rather than mere attendance), and extent and quality of contribution through digital means and quality review feedback from users and peers, for example, while continually revolving, impartial/independent value advisors, auditors, and certifiers could evaluate and certify the validity of declared individual value ([HESDX]) generation/improvements or damage and objectiveness of feedbacks.

As with government and businesses, we need to address the shortcomings and problems discussed earlier particularly concerning assuring impartiality, revolving assignments, etc. and curbing conflict of interest, abuse, and fraudulent intent.

In this scenario, the extremely important contributions of homemakers, husbands, grandparents, and a myriad of other people could finally be recognized and remunerated as value-producing initiatives. But it may also create numerous value-adding remunerated *new* professions in many fields, replacing increasingly evaporating and virtualize-able legacy jobs.

This is about the opportunity for individuals to design and develop new ways of creating value tangibly in many new ways and spheres of activity that would otherwise not be possible under the current model. This should produce a model shift of substantial impact and an evolution upward and away, for example, from cost-based, tax-reliant notions of handouts and welfare.

Investment incurred here might be represented by reasonable deductions for amounts incurred in improving [HESDX] and generating value to be defined and tabulated accordingly, whereas private contributions to the community are exactly that, as described in the previous section. Current mechanisms that discourage systemic dependence, abuse, and/ or improper/fraudulent use of our current models will need to evolve to guarantee value-generation valuation, recognition, fair distribution, and the proper functioning of the system.

Furthermore, the above activities will need to evolve toward professions that will become certified through continuous knowledge enhancement of individuals and the evolved learning system to increase the potential for value generation.

In today's economic model, people who lose a business activity or who remain without a job essentially fall out of the system and in a growing number of cases, after a reasonably short amount of time, no longer accounted for in official statistics.

While these efforts only mask these events, the very real problems these generate only accumulate destructive energy. The systemic blocks of the current model are becoming endemic and, in many cases, not only inhibit reentry but also continue reducing possibilities for ever-growing numbers of people. Based upon one's country of residence, there may or may not be social assistance and, if there is, it is only for a limited time. After that, there is only uncertainty.[56]

The new model leverages new paradigm shifts to create new possibilities that will otherwise remain hidden, bringing the centrality of humanity back into the equation, and devloping solutions around a society's needs, sensitivities, and preferences, through the adoption of evolved notions of welfare (e.g., proactive value-creation remuneration), that rather than being based on the hand-out, deficit-generating axiom in use today, is focused on setting the premises for proactive value creation, apt to address currently irresolvable systemic dichotomies in areas such as juvenile delinquency, degradation, crime prevention, and law enforcement, at grass root level.

Theoretically, and based on the efficacy of the measures generated by transition task forces, individuals might be more motivated to achieve life project goals as more and more become professionals and entrepreneurs in a plethora of new fields, seeking to generate value and not just for themselves. There will be no free rides though! Value will also need to be preapproved, demonstrated, vouched . . . and certified.

The same principles of balance, deficit, or excess of value creation and the onus of final detailed definition of these and their criteria and remuneration modalities—together with solutions, vigilance, effective control, advisory approach in providing solutions, etc. discussed in the previous section—also apply here.

---

[56] Headlines report that as of January 30, 2013, unemployment among the young in the United States and Europe reached critical records—an average of 25 percent with peaks of 37 percent in nearly half of the EU countries.

Excess value generation here is synonymous with today's legacy concept of profit, but in many ways, it is substantially different as it goes beyond the mere financial aspects. A deficit, on the other hand, is an indication that something is wrong and needs to be addressed.

Individuals affected by objective impediments and conditions, including injured veterans, are obviously addressed under the new model. If willing, these fellow citizens will be able to contribute and be involved in different life projects and areas respecting their individual passions and strengths, much more than ever before.

The evolved model foresees commensurate means to allow independence and the assurance of the facilities needed to allow a life lived respectfully and in a dignified way through the value balance mechanism.

All too often we are reminded that unfortunate life-changing events and accidents can touch each one of us and or those of our loved ones affecting personal spheres of life unexpectedly. As we evolve as societies, our maturity as individuals and communities is directly linked to how we address these very hard issues. This creates value for our societies, contributing to taking us forward toward higher levels of civilization.

Virtus Prosperity Model and Concept of Virtuation

In the search for a name that could most appropriately enclose all the concepts so far covered—especially those of BEM^{HESD}, EPM^{HESDX}, value generation, and value concept and balance—and could provide a single, less cryptic name to the next economic model, the word "virtus" seemed to provide a good match.

Hence, the *holistic Virtus prosperity model* could be used to define the dynamically evolving economic model thus far presented, while *virtus proximus* represents the next (successive) prosperity model(s) as these evolve over time. The new concept of *"virtuation,"* which includes the essence of words such as virtue and virtualization, encases almost all of the notions discussed thus far, i.e.:

- continuous migration toward newer plateaus and value-generation levels;

- evolution of current (legacy/hybrid) models in all areas but most significantly in the following:

  o central and general banking; government loans, incentives, facilities

  o public debt, GDP, government spending, budgeting (i.e., developing new forms of accounting and accountability for value creation)

  o public spending: pensions, health care, education, civil protection, defense

  o taxation, government revenue recognition, etc.

- migration toward new forms of

- o accounting, accountability, management of what falls under public (government owned);

- o indexing and recognition of value generation;

- o rewarding, payout, and distribution of contributions to value creators, etc.;

- planning, phasing, and road-mapping of strategies that address the phased virtualization of jobs, processes, and models, mutating them into opportunities;

- evolving other fundamental/critical processes in line with needs, such as:

  - o policy making and appropriate governance frameworks;

  - o higher levels of democracy, individual rights and privacy, and civilization;

  - o regulating and managing justice;

  - o education;

  - o free-time leverage, indexing, auditing, certification, assurance of value, advising, etc.

- coordinated phasing and rollout of critical strategic initiatives and projects;

- evolution of legacy concepts such as cost toward separation and exploitation of those elements of cost that denote potential for generating value toward value creation;

- continuous evolution and implementation of appropriate governance frameworks;

- fostering virtuous cycles in the development of economic traction, etc.

Optimal Context for Implementation of Virtus

If we wish the new to produce the *optimal* level of opportunities and results from the new evolved plateau, it needs to have certain characteristics. The following list is just an initial draft of these:

- the context: an open, free, and democratic society where rights prevail (mass social movements, even in democratically led countries, around the world demonstrate how evolution is leading many societies to insist that these fundamental principles be introduced and or evolved);

- resilience in resolving current issues and wishing to step up to the next plateau;

- strategic vision;

- dynamism: being eager to leverage continuously evolving plateaus of development and prosperity;

- Entrepreneurial: grasping new opportunities and using evolved modalities, ways, and definitions to bring about continuous new ideas and confront new challenges that add value;

  o being free and willing to venture beyond dated models and sacred monsters; away from extreme ideological, political thought processes or contexts; outside of excessively centralized or completely anarchical concepts; away from excessive government control and completely unstructured models; away from highly technocratic models and their extreme nemeses; away from highly bureaucratic models and their complete opposites; and preferring/choosing simplicity over complexity where possible, etc.

The essential objective is to achieve an evolutionary, value-centered, balanced paradigm focused around succeeding in value generation [HESDX] in the best way for any society that chooses to leverage and implement it. It must be poised to reach a new level of civilization and civilized society, and it must be focused on achieving value, both tangibly and virtually. In this scenario, balance and equilibrium become sought-after objectives, not because we need to reach them for dry, technocratic accounting purposes or human-distant concepts such as the national budget, but because the balance or equilibrium points represent the best place to be at any particular time in terms of rewards, returns, business, opportunities, investments, employment, and governance over such things as inflation, sustainability, and continuous value (HESDX) generation for humans and their eco-environment. Success and transition toward the higher plateau of development entails considering all aspects thus far covered:

- a focus on HESDX development;

- transition away from legacy/hybrid models and elements;

- evolution toward a resilient, dynamically adaptive, continuously evolving model;

- acknowledgement of a higher plateau and an upward evolution toward it;

- leverage of new perspectives and shift away from cost-based logics; transition toward value balance concepts; new variables, innovations, etc.; evolution of business models, processes, definitions, etc.;

- a value-focused, adaptive, and evolvable governance framework;

- evolution of strategic sectors such as central and commercial banking, financial services, and markets; successful rollout and transition strategies;

- continuous revision of effective strategies to address shortcomings; etc.

Ultimately, we need to start and get on with it.

Executive Summary

To satisfy reader requests and suggestions, the following executive summary provides a general overview of this book, a few examples, and their real-life applicability. First, a few general reflections:

The following overview cannot be considered a substitute for all the new concepts introduced in this book, or provide a full appreciation of the subject. The examples herein can explain a few of the new elements, concepts and instruments. Consequently, these examples will not provide the reader with a full understating and/or perception of the new model or its fundamental elements—and may lead to wrong, incomplete, and or inconclusive interpretations. Furthermore, each new concept in the book needs more elaboration in separate books and papers, with contributions from experts in each field.

Third-millennium epochal challenges, and an immediate, impelling need to address critical issues such as climate change, mass migration and population growth, disruptive innovation, automation and virtualization of jobs, business models, etc., emphasize the need for real change. When combined with current systemic problems such as debt, taxation, structural recovery, unemployment, retirement, generational turnover, the non-sustainability of economic policies based on cost paradigms, the volatility of markets, dangerous geo-political scenarios, and so on— together with the evident impossibility of resolving such issues using current models—lead to a simple, unequivocal, and evident conclusion— the need for a new paradigm.

The evolution of models is a historical fact, and is vital to both progress and survival. Similarly, current models are reaching a tipping point and becoming increasingly dysfunctional. As such, they need step-level advancements to allow new perspectives; sustainable, prolonged economic development, and the achievement of crucial objectives impossible to reach through existing models.

In essence, the twenty-first century requires a new model fit for the challenges of the third millennium. Addressing these vital challenges entails a shift towards models that generate value for all stakeholders and in all fields. Producing value means addressing these challenges and fostering wellbeing, health, prolonged prosperity, structural economic development (as opposed to mini-recoveries), healthy competitive business settings, biosphere preservation, climate mitigation, sustainability, security, protection, stability, serenity, and peace ... but also advancing democracy to new levels and reaching higher levels of civilization.

Value forms the DNA of the new model, and a focus on producing value will allow the opening of new frontiers, perspectives, possibilities, and opportunities. Any new model based on holistic value generation must evolve dynamically along the many different dimensions making up the new economic model. The value-generating evolutionary prosperity model, Virtus, introduced herein, is a baseline, open, modular, scalable, dynamically evolving framework (as opposed to a complete model designed by a single individual), to allow continuous, inclusive, expert and field/sector-specific development. In fact, it requires and benefits from the continued use of expertise in all fields of human endeavor.

The new model requires equally evolvable tools, guidelines, and organizational concepts to assist in the transition to the first and subsequent versions of Virtus. These tools exist within the Alpha-e protocol described in this book. The Alpha-e Protocol governs the detailed inner workings of the organization and operation of this conceptual process—who does what, when, and how—and it is, as mentioned, the result of a consensus-driven approach, continuously updated to address shortcomings, deficiencies, new challenges, game-changing innovations, and variables. The first full version of the protocol and Virtus (and their successive versions) will be the result of the combined work of experts in each field.

Correspondingly, the new model will require a dynamically evolving governance framework that allows effective policy formulation and control. The new model will also need new elements, definitions, instruments, paradigms, measurement criteria, etc., theoretically many more than those in current use.

Under the current paradigm, in very generic terms, governments provide such things as defense, law enforcement, schools, roads, emergency services, and so on, generating debt, which must be paid back in taxes by its citizens and businesses in a closed-loop model, giving way to current notions of public debt, taxation, GDP, etc. The current system, however, is becoming increasingly unsustainable, unstable and ineffective, pressured by new variables that it cannot address, because at best, it addresses the needs of the previous century. Like a dying star, fading economic models, might have moments of relative stability. The current model could continue to lay the groundwork for temporary mini-recoveries as it reaches ever-lower levels of equilibrium before reaching a definitive point of systemic impasse or collapse.

Virtus turns the current paradigm on its heels; the work, output, and achievement of individuals, professionals, businesses, organizations, and so on generate value for the communities in which they reside. In return, the value generated must be recognized and rewarded. There are several ways to achieve this. The way it is realized and it evolves through time, will be the result of the findings of appropriate task forces. As with other major evolutions of economic models, many activities that were previously impractical become possible, while many new ones become visible, viable, usable, and necessary.

Additionally, the advances in many fields and the virtual nature of money lead to many other new opportunities, while new perspectives and notions provide new ways to increase business, job, and investment opportunities: evolution and *redefinition of costs*, redefinition of existing business models, variables, accounting and financial performance yardsticks, processes, the *Virtus Economic String Theory, next-generation banking*, and so on, are just a few of these. Under Virtus, currently inconceivable sources of revenue streams, business models and forms of employment can become achievable.

Furthermore, in today's model, the central banking systems play a fundamental role in monetary policy and, among many other things, make money available as necessary through commercial banks. However, it is now clear that, notwithstanding goodwill, macroeconomic strategies such as quantitative easing, subsidies (according to the IMF News global energy subsidies alone amounted to $5.3 trillion, equivalent to 6% of the world's GDP), facilities, and grants increasingly fail to work in the real world or to produce the desired outcomes (i.e., systemic, prolonged economic traction and development). Under the current model, banking is increasingly separating from the rest of the economy as new variables are influencing and redefining the underlying framework of everything. Yet eventually, without this link, the economy might find ways to distance itself from banking.

To avoid unforeseeable repercussions and to guarantee a smooth transition to the new model, the first version of Virtus will begin with a model that *evolves from the current market-based model*, using for example, such evolved notions as quantitative availability for value generation (QVG) and adapting these as necessary, as needs and variables change over time. QVG *is just one of the many* new instruments that are available.

To be perfectly clear, QVG *is the evolution* of the currently adopted *quantitative easing* concept applied by the most important central banks. Correspondingly, QVG has nothing to do with other existing or historically unsuccessful money-creation paradigms, axioms, or models. It can coexist with other currently used monetary policy strategies.

To address return-on-investment requirements on behalf of the banking system, markets, and investors, several alternative and complementary instruments and strategies are available. The final version of the first release of QVG (including its alternative/complementary instruments) must receive needed assent.

The amount of quantitative availability must meet the approved needs. The sums approved must ultimately equal the value generated in the system. For the purposes of this example, the basis for the availability of the sums will initially be current virtual money-generation models used by the central banking systems, and they will evolve according to needs as their use becomes more familiar.

QVG is an element of Virtus – hence its aim is to embed adaptable governance frameworks and its focus is on delivering value (as well as addressing for instance, unwanted systemic effects such as inflation, deflation, stagnation, and so on). With the implementation of Virtus, the economic development model will finally open, allowing, for example, new strategies for the economy.

Based on the findings of the transition task forces and committees, the components of QVG, or other value-producing instruments, could include investments from private concerns, individuals, pension funds, corporations, and so on, but using value-producing return models. This possibility also opens the door to new, parallel, more stable investment and market scenarios, diametrically opposite to today's volatile, purely debt-generating models.

Initiatives that have been certified as producing value (i.e. strategic value generating initiatives such as climate and geological impact mitigation projects, retirement and generational turnover solutions, key national infrastructure modernization and protection projects, etc.) will receive recognition via this new facility (QVG) or a mix of new alternatives, through the banking system, at least initially and for the most part.

Theoretically, based on the specific objectives QVG must reach, under Virtus, so long as value is generated, the (full or partial) sum of this specific facility, might lead to no increases in taxes, notions of GDP, or needs to adhere to the accumulated restraints of current models (much in the same way as some facilities are currently accounted for under the existing model). Once free from the limitations of the current model, under Virtus, there are many alternative ways to evolve the definition of QVG as necessary and useful.

Under Virtus, citizens (independent of their status), professionals, businesses, organizations, entities, government and non-government agencies, borough/city/town councils, become potential generators of value. Based on the type of activity, public and or private independent certifying entities assess, evaluate, quantify, the value generated by each originator, which becomes the total value generated at each level during a value year, as opposed to a fiscal year.

The value produced by each originator varies according to continually updated value objectives, plans and indexes, which public and private regulatory and advisory types of organizations will regulate, define, and formulate in *much the same way as done for different sectors today*. However, to assure independence, the onus of the definition, development, and design of such practices, regulations, plans etc., will fall to expert committees, whose key decision makers will change periodically, adding new verified and certified members from time to time. These members will add their value contribution history, providing a rotation of experts in different fields whose focus becomes advising stakeholders on the generation and assurance of value (as opposed to today's IRS-like or sector-specific inspectors). Once value produced is certified, the originator of value changes status and becomes a contributor for that specific period and becomes object of deserved recognition and payment through the banking system—among other things, re-creating the link between the economy and banking.

At the end of each value year, each applicant originator of value (a state, county, city, business, individual) that wishes to set new value objectives (beyond what he or she normally does for a living), or continue successive phases of existing project for the new year, can for example, apply via an annual value-declaration form (as opposed to the tax filing forms in use today in most countries). This value objective is assessed against needs and requirements at each level within the system (individual, business, government agency, town, city, country, or union of countries). Those projects that add value will receive approval, those that don't might receive value producing alternative projects or objectives to consider.

In conclusion, the system fundamentally relies on three key phases: (a) the origination phase, (b) the planning and valuation phase, and (c) the recognition and contribution phase. The origination phase includes the activities that formalize the requirements and needs for value creation from the bottom up in a pyramidal fashion. The planning and valuation phase includes the activities allowing assessment of value at each level and formulating, updating, and setting strategic value-development plans. Finally, the recognition and contribution phase includes the activities that allow final payment through the central and general banking system.

To avoid any misinterpretation, Virtus *does not* promote a bureaucratic, highly regulated, intricate, system made of regulators controlling other regulators, certifiers, inspectors…as this sort of system is the nemesis of value creation. What Virtus foresees instead, is the use of the best, most effective…and lean processes to achieve optimal cost/benefit levels of control and outcomes. Based on the continuously updated results of value objectives to be reached, the amount of value generated will vary, and will usually cover the portion of the project cost (as redefined) that produces value. The new model, however, is dynamic and makes room for exceptions. In particular cases, this could reach the full amount needed for a specific value-generation initiative, so long as it results in value generation.

The primary scope is to create ample room for different private initiatives and investments in a growing number of strategic projects, new, previously invisible, and/or uneconomical or non-viable opportunities, creating and maintaining healthy economic traction, motivate virtuous behavior and results, originate new possibilities and redefinitions, and foster value-generating initiatives, jobs, businesses, and entrepreneurship.

It needs constant consideration that *under the current model*, as facts demonstrate, *there is objectively no practical way to address, find structural solutions to, or finance the many challenges* and new variables economies, governments, business, investors, and individuals need to face. Unsustainable public debts and taxation, mass unemployment and precariousness of entire generations, pensions and retirement, generational turnover, the effects of virtualization, miniaturization, general inclusivity, mass-migration, environmental damage and change, mass health risks, ideologically fueled tension, and geopolitical instability are just a few of these problems. Consequentially, existing models will increasingly be misaligned with reality and increasingly dysfunctional in addressing new challenges.

Once again, expert committees at different levels will decide what does and does not constitute value at any given time to make sure that everything falls under an approved general plan derived from a democratically led, consensus-driven approach. These plans will evolve according to the needs of individuals, business, communities, states, governments, and so on. Equally important is that the availability of, and accesses to, next-generation evolved facilities, such QVG, represents a few means by which Virtus can stimulate new businesses, jobs, investments and so on. The availability of these evolved facilities might initially be limited to value-generating initiatives that cannot realistically be achieved through regular means, at least until they become economically viable.

It is likely, for instance, that the first projects to receive value recognition might be of national (or cross-national i.e. EU) strategic relevance (i.e., infrastructure modernization, pensions and retirement, and other strategic value generating initiatives, as presented in Part 3 of the book), as these alone could generate enough economic steam and stimulus to create prolonged economic development with immediate knock-on effects on business, professions, and employment.

But, as time progresses, and according to the need to meet challenges and national value objectives, value-generation projects and recognition for private economic concerns can roll out according to an approved road map. To be clear, apart from value objectives such as avoiding inflation, deflation, strategic international imbalances…, there is nothing to stop the use of parallel strategies to allow value recognition in the private sector (or at the individual level) to allow for example the permeation of value generation or address particular unemployment challenges. It is highly likely that the *Virtus Economic String Theory*, the *redefinition of legacy elements*, and the many other concepts described in this book, will provide the greatest source of new paradigms and opportunities in the longer term future. Correspondingly, as the new model develops, the financing, funding, and development of the majority of these initiatives might be private and use next-generation, value-based markets and financial institutions/networks.

Value producing initiatives could take different forms for different players and sectors, the following are a few examples. For instance, if a small town that lacks necessary financial resources, requests the addition of a new county hospital, and the primary need conflicts with, for example, a mix of value criteria such as sustainability (because other hospitals are in easily reachable towns nearby) and optimal capacity, the request may be only partially approved. An increase in the hospitals' emergency facilities, doctors and expert staff, and improved or updated systems might be preferable, because, according to historical data and expert assessments, these improvements might enhance the hospital's general quality and service levels and address the real needs of that specific community, without having to invest in a new hospital. However, this is not the full process; it may be possible to update the full value assessment and value-recognition cycle after analyzing feedback from, for instance, the hospital's patients, doctors, and other stakeholders. Value generation is project-specific, based on reaching specific objectives/results. Unless value creation is continuous and follows pre-approved plans, the amounts recognized will cease.

Correspondingly, an airline that adheres to stringent safety and security standards along its full-value chain might receive recognition for creating value in the maintenance of its engines and other aero structures. These measures will substantially reduce the risks of loss of life and the consequent loss of business and jobs, together with the company's possible bankruptcy as a direct result of cost considerations which led to unfortunate and devastating consequences.

Virtus, though, *is not* an instrument to bail out bankrupt concerns or to finance bad management, poor market strategies, and unneeded and/or poorly performing products or services . . . quite the opposite, as none of these create value. The same reasoning should be valid for the intrinsic value derived from the need for adequate rest, physical and psychological health, and training for pilots and flight crew, and those measures needed to assure passenger safety, seating comfort, and space that consider/enhance passenger health (currently deemed as cost prohibitive or economically non viable propositions).

Comparably, a particular government agency might demonstrate value by obtaining certified increased satisfaction ratings from its customers for efficiency, timeliness, quality of work, and level of *proactive* service rendered, or by proving it has cut bureaucracy and improved accessibility to address customer issues, and/or improved its procurement. In general, a government agency or municipality must refocus its activities around producing substantial benefits and value generation, in its area of competency, in the best interests of the economy, public and society. Setting virtuous examples will also help to focus private practices and business models on value generation. The true independence and quality of the work of the certifying body must be transparent and guaranteed.

A consumer goods manufacturer might receive value recognition after demonstrating it has achieved increasing standards in substantially reducing unhealthy, artificial additives or has attained healthier food standards or transparency in traceability. A group of agricultural concerns may receive certification for producing according to stringent environmentally and herd-friendly biological practices, models, forage, and processes. A large corporation might become eligible for value recognition for creating a new value-adding distribution paradigm that promotes business via small local distributors and entrepreneurs within larger cities.

A small university lab involved in space exploration facing funding difficulty might receive recognition of value creation for successive phases in the advanced studies in a particular field. A bank might be able to demonstrate the no-nonsense transparency and straightforwardness of its loan conditions and contracts or show how many times it adjusted or renegotiated loans to fit specific customer needs (obviously non-fraudulent ones) in a win-win fashion. A pharmaceutical company might receive recognition to continue its research on the development of a new drug for a malady affecting only a limited number of people or for the development and distribution of a drug needed to cure a multitude that was previously not economically viable.

A city such as New Orleans, New York, Genoa, or Venice might become eligible to go ahead with the phased implementation of environmentally and citizen-friendly protective solutions to mitigate the effects of climate change. A utilities company might be eligible for replacing old and leaking drinking water pipes that pose health risks. A construction firm might receive value recognition for providing the best value for money while implementing challenging anti-earthquake safety solutions in an area historically affected by earthquakes such San Francisco, Tokyo, Valparaiso, or for refurbishing an abandoned manufacturing site by clearing it of hazardous material and disposing of it through value-added waste management concerns respectful of environmental issues. A corner store might become eligible for value recognition for having cleared and refurbished an abandoned county lot that posed security risks to the neighborhood, turning it into a basketball court (with the prior consent of, and project approval from the county, and in line with neighborhood needs). A person looking after the elderly in the comfort of their homes, or a home-/family-administrator, based on different parameters, could achieve value objectives, and be recognized for this important, previously non-remunerated effort.

It is important to state that in most cases, certification of value is not permanent, and must be repeated each year, cycle, and/or period (or other criteria) as defined by expert committees for each specific sector. Similarly, apart from particular cases, originators can claim payment for value produced once feedback from stakeholders, users, and customers, and then only in a measure commensurate with the rating received.

Appropriate governance entities and frameworks preside over the curtailment of misuse, abuse, and systemic dependency. The objective here is to enhance an economy's general state of health, enable originators to achieve value objectives, foster virtuous outcomes and behavior, and so on. There will be no free rides and no handouts!

Realism dictates that for any new model to work it must consider the return for the majority of stakeholders (not only individuals, employees, and businesses, but also banks and markets as well as the biosphere(s) we live in). One of the primary aims of Virtus is to factor-in these dynamically-changing equilibriums.

Depending on the outcome of the expert evaluation, for an initial period, the current municipal, state, and government accounting systems might remain unchanged and run in the background in parallel as experts redefine, adapt, and transition more elements of the current model to the first version of Virtus and run it in the foreground to allow a smooth transition.

How successful the new model will be and how quickly it will be possible to switch-over depends on resilience, willingness to find new solutions, and, in essence, the use of the fundamental suggestions presented in this book. Applying the *Virtus Economic String Theory* to create a new business model without developing its governance criteria, for instance, will not produce the desired outcomes. Nor will introducing a new organizational model without making value its focus. Similarly, using the current models' measurement yardsticks to assess a company or the effectiveness of its products or services might not convey how successful they really are, and/or their true potential, and or their return on investment.

Transition to the new model is as easy or as hard as any other migration to a new model. The following set recent precedents: the global Internet revolution; the planetary diffusion of mobile telecommunications; dissemination of social networks; the overnight interruption of the gold standard and the implementation of the "Nixon shock" reforms; the international adoption of the Bretton Woods criteria, the nascence of the United Nations organizations, and the successive cyclical G4/G7 reforms that set the basis for today's economic model, and touch many aspects of daily lives, jobs, business, taxation, and the fate of entire economies. Yet, these are just a few examples. Think of what it took to develop the backbone infrastructure necessary for the distribution of utilities to each household in entire nations.

Therefore, the question is no longer about whether an evolution to a new model is necessary, but when to initiate the switchover. The shorter the trajectory to transition and its modular roll out, the faster the achievement of outcomes. Dealing with a new paradigm means being willing to think beyond the known, the layers of standard assumptions, and the boundaries and restrictions imposed by current models. Virtus helps in this shift, because it evolves upwards from the current model.

In reality many elements of the new model are already forming around us, what Virtus tries to attempt is to provide a comprehensive framework that among many other things, introduce possible solutions, and connect the dots.

Finally, systemic and structural economic recovery from the current impasse will not require the full activation of all initiatives simultaneously. As shown by recent economic data, the agreed-upon and planned implementation of just a few of the strategic value generating initiatives, described in more detail in Part 3 of the book, could activate a virtuous domino effect on most (if not all) sectors — net, that is of business models that do not evolve.

PART 3

Applicability: 19 Examples

Strategic Value Generating Initiatives

Though it is understandably tempting to jump to this final part of the book, the reader is advised that without an proper overview of the material covered in the previous chapters/sections, which provide the necessary foundations and logic behind everything, reading the following chapters alone, will not allow a full appreciation or understanding of how: jobs, employment, business, and investment opportunities can be generated; further new possibilities become visible; nor new levers be identified.

In this part of the book, <u>a total of nineteen</u> real-life examples of immediate applicability of the concepts so far discussed are disclosed. The samples used represent lower-hanging, more proximate opportunities[57] that can be leveraged, yielding multiplier effects. The following is just a list of teasers from a plethora of strategic value generating initiatives that can be activated in regenerating, prolonged structural economic traction cyclically, and evolution toward new plateaus. A choice was made to present the following examples in random order with no reference to priority, or relative importance.

An important premise: None of the issues covered so far, and those developed henceforth should be interpreted as, or confused with, a preference towards conservative, liberal, or progressive, a pro or con: military, green, or environmental stance, a left or right issue—with all the challenges discussed thus far, limiting our choice of strategies to few options is one of the biggest impediments and mistkes that can be made especially in seeking viable solutions, resolving the numerous systemic blocks we face, creating new opportunities, and in moving forward. Virtus, is an ideologically-free paradigm.

[57.] These are a subset of the previously mentioned, critical, strategic value-generating initiatives.

Natural Disaster Protection and Mitigation

The word "mitigation" is used here because we currently cannot prevent natural disasters from happening, but we might be able to increase predictability, mitigate their effects, improve survivability, and possibly reduce exposure to damage and importantly rebuild under safer standards and conditions. The number of projects and the titanic efforts required might need years just to design and initiate phased implementation. They will need to be continuously updated and maintained—with most providing new opportunities cyclically.

Value and opportunities here are generated by addressing the full spectrum of dynamics and issues that occur prior to, during, and after an event.

- In pre-event: the emphasis of value generation could be on advanced warning, protection, and mitigation projects as well as structural refurbishment and phased smart relocation and construction of appropriate infrastructure, neighborhoods, and communities in lower risk areas;

- During the event: the emphasis is on first responders and emergency services, emergency access creation enabling rapid arrival of necessary assets, intervention, activating casualty and damage reduction solutions.

- In post-event: the emphasis of value generation mutates toward structural cleanup, reconstruction of not only individual lives but also businesses and infrastructure.

Generating value against the effects of cataclysmic or devastating consequences of recurring natural events such as drastic snowstorms and rainfalls, flashfloods, inundations, forest fires, tsunamis, earthquakes, tornados, massive soil movements and soil erosion, etc. means being able to design, undertake, develop, implement, and *maintain* numerous very large projects in just about every country around the world every time these emerge.

Limited examples of similar projects are already under way in some countries but face the restrictions posed on them by current models. Under the new model, concrete, structural examples for the immediate future could be:

- evolved ecosystem and human friendly disaster mitigation systems against inundation and rising water levels for areas such as: New York, Venice, Southern Louisiana, Holland;

- flash flood mitigation systems in places such as Italy, Bangladesh, China, Central/Eastern Europe . . .; urban areas such as Washington D.C., Las Vegas and Toronto; along the Mississippi and other major river systems around the world;

- pre, during, and post-earthquake mitigation systems and structural projects in California, British Columbia, Chile, China, Iran Turkey, Japan, Indonesia, Italy, etc.; In a recent study conducted by the USGS and other scientists, it is said that "nearly 150 million people in the US are threatened by possibly damaging shaking from earthquakes". "Authorities calculate that the financial average financial loss from earthquakes is roughly 4.5 billion dollars a year". The total number of persons living in earthquake prone zones around the world, the total number of fatalities and injuries, and the average yearly damage they produce is staggering.

- autochthonous flora replantation and reforestation in Brazil, Australia, the many sub-Saharan Africa and the Congo Basin . . .;

- drinking water protection, sanitation and smart distribution projects in many parts of the world;

- topsoil erosion and desertification mitigation projects;

- etc.

Life as we know it exists within a delicate and well-balanced mix and range of parameters. These include temperature, seawater salinity, exposure to ultra-violet rays, atmospheric composition, CO_2 and chemical release in ecosystems, and rainfall. They also include still poorly-known geological, atmospheric, oceanic, and cosmic cycles . . . and localized earth-crust pressures in micro areas that may start to be affected by century-long oil, gas, and mineral extractions, etc. There are enough telltale signs to begin a process of addressing these issues and to develop many business, employment, investment, and value-generation opportunities.

Next Gen Cities & Infrastructure

There are many ideas and opportunities here, and we have not even touched the surface of the otherwise submerged ice-continents. Before we get there, we need to refresh our baseline paradigms, philosophy, and pragmatic approach to designing a new evolutionary model based on value generation that will be affected by different things such as the following non-exhaustive suggestions:

- Evolved mass transit and traffic management concepts:

    o next-generation mass public and private under/over-ground transportation projects that can be increasingly personalized, increasing frequency, and providing adequate "salubrious," health-focused, space for individuals even during peak hours, eliminating extremely crowded and unhealthy conditions for travelers and commuters;

    o with the rapid growth of airline passengers, mass transit in today's and tomorrow's world might include airline travel. It has a unique opportunity to leverage and evolve in providing value through no-nonsense individual health focused comfort, seating space, privacy, and new on-board services, incrementing business returns and rewards rather than focusing on a destructive cost-based logics and seeking new ways to providing unique travelling experiences. This in no way implies the possibility of coexistence of purely no thrills low cost business models. As the economy picks up, more and more people will be able to choose and purchase among better degree of services and value based on preferences;

    o structural eradication of urban and sub-urban, no longer necessary non-intelligent lighting, substituting them with *virtual* and/or smart and energy-saving public and traffic lighting, urban lighting and green solutions;

o   intelligent traffic management and traffic reduction concepts.

- Structural safety, maintenance, and introduction of evolved building concepts that focus on health and safety of living and working environments; of industrial facilities, office and retail space, and residential housing:

    o   redevelop, refurbish, and restructure according to safety standards based on exposure to geographical natural events (e.g., hurricanes, earthquakes, inundations, fires) affecting each area;

    o   upgrade and maintain: enact value-generating concepts in buildings, residential homes, industrial sites, etc.

- Structural city infrastructure redesign and modernization. This regards everything from waste management, water and sewage management, utilities, telecommunications, roads, etc.

The potential immediate windfall from the construction and maintenance industry sectors alone will be incalculable (*note: governance and* ^HESDX *mean avoiding real estate balloons and must mitigate the exposure to purely speculative phenomena[58] to generate value!* The focus is on long-term continued development and prosperity).

Naturalization and humanization of urban settings:

- Increased natural settings (i.e., more green areas). The many green initiatives undertaken by Singapore set a positive example.

[58.]   Realism suggests that it is highly unlikely that any model could make speculation disappear as a phenomenon. Under Virtus however, this must be addressed or at the very least mitigated by creating, for example, parrallel totally vitual markets that are sealed, firewalled and separted from real markets.

- Evolved paving that increase optimal fruition on behalf of the disabled, families, joggers, . . .

- Refurbishment, cleanup, and maintenance of abandoned/ neglected sites, areas, roads (e.g., industrial sites, public housing, parks, viaducts, etc.).

- Redesign of community areas, such as piazzas, to improve utilization and usefulness, neighborhood aesthetics, events, entertainment, local shopping, and social gatherings and interaction possibilities. If done well, this might impact many other areas such as reduce serious crime and increase business possibilities. London and some other cities provide examples of where this concept is seeing its renaissance and being implemented in different boroughs with varying degrees of success, reclaiming otherwise abandoned and unsafe areas and creating, consciously or unconsciously, also a new wave of micro-tourism (among Londoners and non- residents) in search of new experiences.

- Increased walk, people, children, and bike-friendly neighborhoods, whilst allowing for evolved access and traffic reduction strategies (yet what is mentioned here is to go beyond current efforts creating, for instance, distinct separation of bike and vehicle traffic).

- Reconversion of unused office spaces into better uses (e.g., private or individual entrepreneurs, microenterprises, leased business services).

- Intelligent next-generation alternative energetic sourcing and distribution, ever more based on zero-mile and proximity concepts.

- Alternative next-generation data and communications transmission systems that substantially reduce potential damage from electromagnetic smog (under a new model growing number of stakeholders will be motivated to seek ways to reduce/avert exposure to anything damaging to humans or ecosystems).

- Neighborhood-friendly business solutions.

- Urban quality of life improvement and abandoned area reutilization for new purposes.

There is a growing move away from 9–5 job schedules and the need for physical offices toward new types of business models and office concepts. This alone will impact many dimensions of our lives and many business sectors.

For example, effective working hours, the way we interact, potential flexibility, free time, transportation, logistics, augmenting neighborhood and community interactions (i.e., places where people can meet, congregate, play, shop, eat, and find entertainment, reconverting unused spaces to other creative uses such as unique hospitality models and evolved hotel concepts), and value-based city redesign and planning, could generate a plethora of potential new businesses and value-enhancing opportunities.

The rehumanization of urban settings, increased use of outdoor facilities, and healthier lifestyles might also have positive effects on values, violence, crime rates, and business models able to leverage them. Examples of these concepts can be witnessed in certain areas of large cities around the world, such as Melbourne, Vancouver, and Arezzo in Italy.

As with the preceding chapter, the objective here is to make better use of what we have within our cities, towns, industrial sites, etc. If this is executed correctly, with all the projects mentioned thus far and their numerous intersections with other possibilities, this may be more than the construction industry (and its entire supply chain) can handle for many decades to come. Speculation-driven additions of billions of cubic square meters of new cement will not create value but damage. Value ([HESDX]) will need to be not certified but produce tangible benefits and projects and programs rolled out according a value generating master plan.

Waste and Natural Resource Reutilization

Our miniscule planet is a delicate, closed-loop system; theoretically, only those objects that have been ejected out of earth's atmosphere have reduced the total available resources. Extrapolating the same logic, the amount of waste created in each nation is bound to be enormous. In need to address shortage and scarcity of resources, population growth, growing demands, etc., this might become the first place to look for natural resources.

While a recently extracted steel bar from a torn-down building might be recycled immediately, a dumped washing machine from years ago might not hold its original consistency, but that does not mean the remaining rusting material might not be useful for other ends. However, it will not be until we seek opportunities to use it.

The magnitude of the total resources involved is stratospheric—in the billions, if not trillions, of dollars in the case of developed nations. Theoretically it is equal to all the resources consumed since the beginning of human activity, less the comparatively miniscule tonnage of materials that have left earth's ecosystem, being transformed, for example, into energy or burned (while the same is not true for the resulting gases, which may have been reabsorbed by other elements within the ecosystem).

The intrinsic value of each element making up each disposed product could even be greater than its value when it was first produced. For example, this could be due to an increase in the price of the raw material, growing scarcity, greater extraction and processing costs, greater transportation costs, or commodities market speculation (under the current model). Under Virtus, its value-generating capability may be substantially higher.

Yet, for the most part, waste is still seen as such in many parts of the world. It is something to get rid of. Ironically and paradoxically, we are reaching a stage where we have trouble finding places to get rid of it. Maybe this also indicates that a tipping point has been reached and that evolution is waiting for us to find new ways forward.

While awareness is growing and new opportunities are being seized in this area, no significant attempts at structural mass recuperation of old mega dumping sites have been made at least not in systemic modality. The primary reason for this is practical. It is not as remunerating as it could be, seen through today's legacy/hybrid model.

The moment this concept is run through the new model, it assumes totally different connotations.

This is not only about waste accumulated on land. Much waste covers our riverbeds, lakes, seas, and floors and the low-orbit space around our planet. Waste includes storage of unusable weapons, military hardware, and hazardous minerals such as depleted uranium and thousands of square kilometers of land and sea used as weapon testing ground. In Kazakhstan alone for example, according to a NATO article (Monitoring Contamination in Kazakhstan), between 1949 and 1989, a total of 456 nuclear tests (some sources claim more) were carried out at Semipalatinsk, the former Soviet Union's premier test site, involving an area the size Wales, before its closure by presidential edict.

In addition, according to many sources there are said to be floating islands the size of some states in different oceans and seas across the world while other sources mention that much of the material making up these islands has decomposed releasing unknown quantities of noxious chemicals into different ecosystems that also cause tremendous damage to the oceanic biosphere and to our health. In whatever form these might be, they are sources of waste reutilization.

It would be interesting, for example, to understand the amount and the value of different noxious gases (useful in productive processes) that could be recovered from the atmosphere. How much potential value (^{HESDX}) resides in this is probably not clear.

For now, these possibilities are perceived only as "costly," economically non-viable cases. Some argue about the economies of scale of such operations and deem them disproportionate to their returns. To be fair, they may be right—under current circumstances.

As mentioned, humankind has not created waste on earth alone but in the orbital space around earth creating many potential security hazards also for space flight and operations. The number of satellites in disuse and tonnage of orbital debris and junk is impressive.

Only when this paradigm changes will it be possible to transform things such as structural, space and oceanic waste recuperation and recycling into an opportunity of considerable proportions. If one goes further and includes the result of possible interactions with other elements, the amount of possibilities could increase.

Just to provide one idea among many using the *Virtus economic string theory* the interaction of two simple elements such as waste and food production within Virtus—fishermen and/or other hard-hit maritime transportation sector concerns, who today are subsidized to keep them unproductive and away from the oceans, barely enough to allow some natural rebirth of oceanic life (much lower than that needed to guarantee proper regeneration and equilibrium)—could produce real value by supporting the waste-collection effort by using specifically dedicated assets (such as purpose built barges) or ones refurbished for dual use—via value generation—to ensure refitting for both fishing and cleanup to address health concerns.

This will allow a cleaner, more salutary environment for the natural repopulation of species in our oceans and waterways. In this very small and elementary example, new revenue stream can be envisaged not only for the sectors immediately concerned (waste management, and fishing) but also, metallurgy, plastics, and other raw material processors, shipping, ship-building, coast-guard, maritime and port services, satellite and telecom services, trucking, warehousing, and suppliers of these sectors such as electronic hardware, software, radar manufactures) just to mention a few.

Petroleum existed in nature before the arrival of humanity and was readily available in many parts of the world, as it spewed out naturally from the ground, forming big pools in some areas (e.g., the Khuzestan region in southwestern Iran).

No one saw a true business in it until technology and the combination of the right conditions produced a new business model, generating an economically viable need for it. Once the model changed, the product and a plethora of new services became an overnight bonanza for many.

A multitude of individuals started prospecting for petroleum in many parts of the world. They drilled wells without any science to back them up and sold gasoline in canisters to a market that still had to produce cars in large numbers and build roads, bridges, highways, interstate roads, and fueling stations—anything that would be needed to make the business model work, as we know it today.

This analogy is used to confirm that with today's technological enablers, waste alone, if looked at from a different perspective, has the potential to provide a wealth of opportunities for a very long time, surely adding to value (^{HESDX}).

The same general concept is applicable to all other natural resources independent of whether they have reached their tipping point in their availability. New, previously impossible or non-viable perspectives could become opportunity generators and rewarding in ways we could not contemplate or would not consider until today, and this includes the possibility of evaluating new horizons and reaching new frontiers such as beyond earth sustainable natural resources utilization.

The ability to see outside the obvious is allegedly said to be what makes the difference between Steve Jobs, Bill Gates, and John D. Rockefeller and the rest of humanity. Humbly, though they were/are geniuses, the shortcoming in numbers of these gifted individuals might not necessarily be due to a scarcity of such people around the world. Rather, they were among the few who made it against the many odds that our current models produce.

A new model could allow more ideas to be considered and leveraged and more people to achieve greater results, be awarded and recognized for their efforts. That is another reason why Virtus has been devised to be an open framework allowing the contribution from all those willing to contribute to its current and future development, continuous enhancement, and improvement.

Space

Sooner or later, humankind will need to seek an alternative place to call home, be it for economic motives, depletion of or need for new sources of natural resources, to mitigate socio-demographic and sustainability issues, extinction risks, to address currently unknown mutations to earth's ecosystems, natural cyclical mega-events, or catastrophic natural disasters, or simply space exploration, exploitation, and even colonization in an age of value creation, these two terms will need more appropriate words/modalities such as beyond earth sustainable development and value based habitat creation and habitation to better convey value.

There is objectively no feasible way for these feats to be achieved through the current model, as it is stratospherically cost-prohibitive. The only way to address and accomplish these kinds of mega-feats is through an evolved model. Tapping into the opportunities that are synonymous of space alone will create more opportunities (both direct and along the full value chain) that we might be able to handle for generations to come.

That is why a value-based strategy will be fundamental in the phased and modular roll-out of the many projects that will need to be implemented sustainably.

Space should not be interpreted here to denote a single element but as a very large subset of globules, components and elements. One capable of developing a theoretically unlimited number of synapses and connections with a myriad of elements, components and globules much beyond its immediate proximity.

It is not limited just to the Virtus string theory applied to everything dealing with aerospace, defense, propulsion and so on, but all other fields of science, and human knowledge.

It will for example involve, currently perceived far away notions such as entertainment, hospitality, gardening, education and cosmetics.

It will surely involve genetics, hibernation and completely different modes, modalities and means of communication, navigation, propulsion, life sustainment, and terraforming. It will also need to find solutions to long-term isolation, socialization, procreation, food production, medical care, hull protection, self-sustained maintenance, and much more.

The need to find and develop space related, solutions, alternatives, contingencies and mitigation strategies might in reality not be postponeable options. Though we might be able to estimate, with growing precision, weather patterns, mitigate their effects, and do much more in the future, our presumption over the perduration of the ideal conditions for the sustainment of life of our planet, in general our solar system and interstellar phenomena is at best a theory based on our current knowledge.

Research, Development, and Innovation

A plethora of programs and projects need to be revitalized, especially those out in left field—blue-sky projects and those beyond the immediate horizon—as they are the ones that will continue creating vital lymph and a virtuous cycle for nearer-term innovations. This is not limited to low-hanging next-generation products and services (e.g., the next version of a tablet), but things that today might appear on the outer margins of the innovation radarscope in all sectors. The following provide mere examples of what is meant here for different sectors:

- pharmaceuticals and healthcare: projects that ended in the valley of death (not enough patients to justify an investment when these might hide solutions to other maladies affecting also many more, or those requiring considerable investments)—*going beyond curing the symptoms toward the root causes; Within healthcare many new concepts can help save lives and increase patient quality of life.*

- construction: next-generation materials, designs, concepts, buildings, houses, etc.;

- energy and propulsion: *going beyond the hot water or spin paradigm*. In this realm we still rely, for the most part, on millennia-old legacy models such as the production of hot water to generate steam to run a turbine that finally produces energy or other sources to spin a magnet. It is time we sought new axioms, better ways, or put in action and assess those solutions that have been stopped due to cost concerns—to produce, distribute, and use energy. Additional areas, for example, where we can start working through a different non-cost-focused perspective are: breaking the cold fusion barrier—tapping into and harnessing a theoretically unlimited source of power; and levering hydrogen-based solutions; etc.

- next generation engines and propulsion systems that lever new concepts such as: *natural-energy absorbing sensors and material* that cover the outer layer of different transportation means and machinery that can covert natural background energy into kinetic energy; *directional vacuum generators* that induce propulsion via suction; plasma activated propulsion and so on.

- advanced technology, aerospace, defense, etc. Many useful programs with multiple-use applicability in different sectors here have been frozen due to cost considerations;

- eco and bio system and other natural sciences innovations and research;

- advanced studies and investment in actions and systems to protect against unwanted effects of strategic experiments in advanced physics (e.g., un-controlled propagation and chain reactions, mini black holes, etc.), biology, nanotechnology, cyber-science and artificial intelligence, Web awareness and control, etc. Recent declassified data suggests that when the atomic bomb was first detonated, there was inadequate knowledge of the possibilities of the uncontrolled chain reaction that could propagate beyond now know limits; In essence, under Virtus, going forward, research and development activities should undergo as much testing as deemed relevant, to avoid or mitigate the long-term fall-out of negative effects on the biosphere and humans. The logic here is also backed by historical evidence, which suggests that the costs to health, the biosphere, environmental clean-up . . . far outweigh the costs of initial experimentation. Systemic dependency, fraudulent intent, and abuse, however, do not create value.

- development and research in the arts (all sciences and fields of art); *This should include not so evident subject matters such as economic related fields such finance, banking, markets, management, HR, procurement; but also in policy-making, political science, diplomacy, democratic process, state and public administration; prevention, justice and the application of the law, law enforcement and policing; protection of civil liberties, rights, and privacy; together military doctrine and intervention strategy, etc.—all in dire need for modernization and advancement to new levels.*

Hopefully, at least in the initial years, a by-product of all this activity (unfortunately we need to be pragmatic) can also mean finally being able to address tough issues, such as poverty and famine, structurally across the globe through evolved value-based and enhanced versions of programs such as the ones being adopted by various non-government organizations;

- creating local possibilities and proper conditions in poor and war-torn countries provide the fundamental cornerstones for a number of critical issues such as mass migration, terrorism, piracy, belligerence, exposure to proliferation of pathogens, propagation of war into neighboring countries, geopolitical concerns, etc.

- reduction of exposure to dangerous viral strains and diseases across the globe;

- structural eradication of underdevelopment;

- next-generation, smart, right-sized infrastructure projects that are manageable and maintainable locally respecting bio-diversity and diversification strategies.

If we look beyond all existing legacy boxes, we might find a world that has been hidden from our eyes in each area, just as the example of the vast pools of naturally gushing petroleum pits had no apparent value to our ancestors.

Just to provide a final thought for this section, the sun and the moon alone create enough energy to run most all biological, meteorological, tidal, atmospheric, and marine current systems. To some unknown extent, they influence even the geological and natural electro-magnetic systems of our entire planet, yet we seem to be convinced that they (or the energy they generate in nature) cannot be tapped into, and or complement, and or intelligently replace most of our current sources of energy.

Next Gen Agriculture and Food Production

Current agricultural/food models rely mostly on automation that has largely taken the human element out of the equation, but they still use legacy models to run the rest. They use the same underlying model that humans have used for centuries—namely, the exploitation of increasingly large parcels of land. Many reports from different UN organizations suggest that the amount of land being seized and used for agriculture has increased exponentially in the last few decades, replacing valuable woodlands and rainforest.

Erosion of topsoil and fertile land is also of grave concern. The public, farmers, and a growing number of agricultural concerns are becoming very sensitive about practices negatively affecting soil quality and availability, not to mention the devastating and prolonged effects of herbicides and pesticides on many ecosystems, including the extinction or near-extinction of several useful species (insects such as bees needed for pollination and flora).

In the fishing industry, data suggests that natural growth and balances in fish stock and their regeneration capabilities in streams, rivers, lakes, seas, and oceans are being negatively affected at alarming rates (United Nations Food and Agriculture Organization 2003). In other areas of the world, large-scale fish farming techniques are being implemented with varying degrees of success; however, some business entities have become the center of attention due to the type of food they use to feed the fish in captivity (that might expose these species to mad cow-like consequences or pose yet-unknown effects on animal and human health). Other studies focus their attention on the damage to both local ecosystems and the fish themselves in amassing extremely large numbers in fixed geographical areas for extended periods.

In the animal stock industry, living conditions for some animals are improving. However, the vast majority of cattle, sheep, and chickens are still brought up in many areas of the world in extremely stressful and unhealthy conditions that could create health hazards to humans directly via food or indirectly via the development of new or mutated viral strains that could lead to epidemics. Recent studies also indicate a growing concern over things such as the gas production of large herds and exceptional food and water consumption requirements that, in some cases, outweigh the benefits they produce putting us on an unsustainable paths. There is much controversy around genetically modified organisms (GMO), products, and strategies. Without the archaic cost consideration that drove industry to develop and mass-produce GMOs, the development of new alternatives that will address these concerns may bring the potential for better, natural solutions, rewarding bio business propositions, well-being, and returns for all stakeholders. There are, on the other hand, numerous successful non-GMO-based business models (e.g., in Israel, Italy, France, Spain) that can testify to many evolved qualitatively higher capabilities that can provide a baseline for even more improvement in each of the above areas. Recent evolved concepts and ideas include:

- protection of the qualities intrinsic to localized denomination of origin and uniqueness of natural characteristics—specific to geographical areas;

- naturally fed, regenerated, and grown herds;

- next-generation, intelligent, right-size farming, breeding, and stress-reduction solutions;

- next-generation fishing moratoriums and natural fish farming solutions that do not require physical boundaries or human produced/sourced mass feeding;

- next-generation agricultural and bio-friendly solutions;

- elimination of nitrates and in general any health-damaging, addiction, dependency and allergy producing, minerals, additives, colorants, and substances from the food chain (of humans, animals, and vegetables).

Under a new model, these add value to all stakeholders and, hence, will need to be remunerated. These new strategies are all going in the right direction but need to be developed even further. Through a new perspective, every idea potentially produces a myriad of new possibilities. Much more can be done to augment value generation for these sectors, rendering them even more attractive and remunerative.

Next Gen Healthcare and Medicine

Many public and private hospitals and, in general, many in the field of medicine and health care have the opportunity to improve their paradigm completely. The cost vortex should no longer impede going beyond the boxes of what is economically viable today. Evolving the paradigm further—in the unfortunate case of sickness or malady a person (no longer a patient)—becomes the focus of greater value to doctors or a hospital (not just a source of income or cost) and vice versa.

The resolution of a malady, no matter how rare, is value, not only for the additional knowledge it brings in curing many other aliments, but possible impacts in other medical areas and on things wich have nothing to do with medicine! The efficiency of emergency rooms and availability of adequate levels of staffing, state-of-the-art machinery, and beds is value. An environmental ambiance that provides courtesy, privacy, cleanliness, and a natural setting (beyond what is expected today) is value. The doctor-to-patient ratio and doctor availability is value. Family support facilities for those who need to watch over their loved ones is value (independent of the time and sustainable resources required). Finding a diagnosis through a network of expertise without having the individual need to waste years in searching for the right doctor in different geographical areas from the comfort of home or the closest hospital is value. Not prematurely discharging individuals for cost reasons, or its exact opposite is value. Pristine, clean, sanitized settings and systems (air conditioning, life support, food production and distribution, hazardous waste management, rooms, washrooms, etc.) create value.

Obliviously, taking advantage of the system or abusing it produces the nemesis of value. In advanced research for cures, value is derived from shifting the model to finding root causes and focused cures that do not have or substantially reduce bad side effects. Rather than simply curing symptoms, healthcare should be open to holistic and or evolved approaches rather than predominantly chemical or invasive ones. Creating more opportunities than the current model allows.

Great strides and advancements have been made in recent decades, but much more can be done. The hospital-doctor-individual rapport must be allowed to evolve to new heights. All of these examples form the premises for areas where value can be generated indefinably and, with them, new sources of revenue streams for this sector, its immediate supply chain, and adjacent and/or inter-connectable economic sectors.

Climate Change Economy

Further opportunities, in this area, lie in programs and projects that, under current legacy models, form the set of already-achievable next generation solutions that cannot be implemented due to the extremely limited investment appeal and their reduced capability of producing acceptable economic returns.

Under the Virtus (BEM^{IIESD}) the same or previously not-contemplated developments have greater leverage and a tremendous impact on new and long-term development, investment, business, life projects, sustainability, ecosystem survivability, and environmental recovery. They finally find investment appeal and viable economic returns, adding opportunities and augmenting long-term prosperity.

Many books have been written on the new subject matters, such as the green economy, smart cities, zero miles, etc. but all these are borne out of and suffer from cost-based logics. The emphasis here, however, goes beyond these. It is about redefining each of these using a comprehensive strategy to exploit, lever, and unleash their true potential in broader scope programs such as systemic/structural ecosystem cleanup, revitalization, carbon emission reduction, re-naturalization, and all those other initiatives needed to address epochal challenges such as climate change. It is about finally shifting toward the analysis, development, and enactment of structural projects that might have seemed economically non-viable until very recently. The fundamental paradigms are changing and, through evolved models, allowing us to reach beyond them.

For an increasing number of authoritative scientists, climate change is no longer a probability but a certainty. Data and undisputable daily events and facts confirm that de-glaciation, geological events, super-fires, and extreme weather conditions (excessive heat, abundant snowfalls, flashfloods) are increasing in frequency, intensity, and destructive power, causing among other things, increasing unnecessary loss in human life, devastating effects on natural settings, impacted economies, damage to many concerns, and exposure to risks.

What these hide as secondary effects and unquantifiable consequences are things such as:

- out-gassing and release of noxious gases, such as methane, that were until recently imprisoned through millennia of natural cycles in large quantities in permafrost all around the Siberian tundra, some oceans, and some other regions of the world affected by global warming;

- the potential for exposure to unknown variables, e.g., the release of pathogens and viruses possibly captured in the melting polar ice that could revive and proliferate;

- oxygen reduction in oceans and the alarming proliferation of certain species such as algae, jellyfish, squids, etc. that may generate the collapse of entire ecosystems in our oceans and beyond[59] and millions of dollars of damage to entire economic sectors.

- rising sea levels. The area of land that is only slightly higher than current sea level is phenomenally vast—much beyond general perception. The number of cities exposed to this very real risk is impressive. Most of these areas are occupied by an impressive number of very large centers of human agglomeration, vital economic activity, strategic centers of governance, mega-cities, and human settlements of strategic agricultural importance all around the world; and

- a currently unknown tipping point toward a long-term shift in weather patterns and maybe geological aspects with effects on all ecosystems.

Seen from a new perspective, the projects and programs here are not only needed but are also enough to generate opportunities for investments, business, and employment for many years to come.

[59.] According to UN data and other sources, currently 150 such areas have been identified around the globe.

Terra Curing / Healing

Terra curing or healing refers to all those initiatives in recreating lost natural equilibriums in the earth's biosphere. It is a planetary project involving the effort of all countries in addressing the numerous challenges that affect environment, climate, geology, water, atmosphere, sand movement, topsoil, flora, and faunain essence, life on earth.

Recent studies by different UN and specialized independent organizations have stressed the gravity of the current state of health of our planet. For example, a recent report commissioned by the World Wildlife Fund ("Reviving The Ocean Economy: The Case For Action"), which saw the involvement of The Boston Consulting Group and Professor Hoegh-Guldberg, lead author of the report and director of the Australia-based Global Change Institute, depicts a dire picture of the state of our planet's oceans and provides strategies to begin addressing the problems. According to *The Guardian*, the report warns about the start of the collapse of fisheries, record levels of pollution (CO_2, plastic, chemicals, etc.), acidification, and rising temperatures and indicates the shocking rate of change in the world's oceans' chemistry, faster than at any point in the past 65 million years, as illustrated by the latest UN report by the climate science panel. Professor Hoegh-Guldberg goes on to say, "The changes we are making will take 10,000 years at least to turnaround," adding, "This generation of humans is defining the future of 300 generations of humans." What is important here is not the preciseness of these estimates but the underlying messages conveyed. There is an objective need to undertake very important steps to remedy the current situation.

The combination of all initiatives covered in the book and those that could not be included purely because of space limitation will influence everything from gradually but structurally improving the biosphere, the quality and naturalness of our food to addressing poverty, famine, and mass migration in a more effective way, while creating many opportunities.

Next Gen Markets, Banking, and Financial Services

This sector, which includes investment funds, pension funds, equity and private venture banking, M&A, insurance services, and so on, is as it is becoming evident of pivotal importance. If designed implemented and operated correctly, this sector can be the source of several new next-generation business models and opportunities that go beyond the Bitcoin and peer-to-peer credit network revolution and prepare this sector to address the plethora of new variables and challenges (technological and non) and possibilities that will be necessary in the near future.

Each enhancement applied to this sector has potential to translate into new business opportunities and the creation of previously unthinkable, new revenue streams. The knock-on effect on employment and investments possibilities will also affect companies operating in the supply and value chain of these sectors.

The number of new possibilities that can be implemented and leveraged is theoretically linked to a multiplier effect; it is directly linked to the number of new synapses created with other elements and components and indirectly to currently unpredictable new requirements and revenue streams.

In order to provide a concrete example, just the separation of markets into two distinct primary markets (at least to begin with) i.e. a) value-based market, and b) virtual market; each capable of further subdivisions will be able to open new perspectives and possibilities. The focus of the value-based market could for example, include new types of enlistments such as entrepreneurial initiatives which could be both of public, or private interest with specific, publicly-declared, tangible, and auditable programs, projects, value plans, propositions, products, services...and/or objectives carrying specific implementation deliverables, results, time frames, and primary milestones.

Such an evolutionary paradigm shift will translate into different sets of valuation criteria for business, and non-business concerns, but also specific initiatives; equity valuation, assessment, and measurement yardsticks; more stable conditions for critical investors such as pension funds; a different value focus, and remuneration models of senior executives and management; new strategy and business plan formulation criteria…while more perspectives, and possibilities can become visible through new synapse connections with other elements via the Virtus economic string theory.

The premature or incomplete realization of such game-changing, disruptive models, without that is, the necessary frameworks, and preambles should be avoided though.

Similarly, the insurance sector has much room for evolution, especially with regards to true evolved value-based protection plans that are transparent, easy to understand, and truly comprehensive and inclusive rather than confusing, exclusive, and in most cases limited, as they are under the current model. As these are linked, for example, to the same areas of synapse evolution of the banking sector, to other adjacent and non-adjacent sectors, the number of possibilities grows.

If this is extrapolated to all other economic sectors, many more avenues open up. There is no doubt that all of this will have incalculable knock on effects on markets and investment opportunities. And this does not even consider the effect of what might hide behind a simple examination of impacts on other dimensions and plateaus. What is certain though is if no action is taken, these sectors are among the most exposed to disruptive technology and paradigms.

Next Generation Services

This area includes, but is not limited to, what today can be defined as consulting, advisory, think tanks, system integrators (ICT or otherwise), strategy, identification, certification and assurance, facilities management . . . legal and professional services sectors, and so on, and those that will be generated ex-nihilo.

Many of these currently hard-hit sectors could, using the appropriate business model, potentially see new renaissance and revival in terms of requests for their value-added services, employment, and a recuperation of lost margins.

The true potential for innovative opportunities and forms of services in this sector is currently inestimable. With each interaction in all other domains (and we only touched on very few) there is theoretically at least one new dimension that could open up in this sector to other possibilities.

As it was with the shift from industry to services, evolution here might mean an aperture toward currently unknown types of mutations toward ever newer frontiers, dimensions, and domains.

Next Generation Retail

This sector is one of the most affected by the current impasse, and it will need new strategies to address the many trials it will face. In the short term, there are several possibilities to leverage on current problems, transforming them into opportunities and creating new connections with different elements, most of which reside in other globules.

Some of the opportunities possible are already visible in new adjacent sectors, such as those that gave birth to the social Internet networks and domains, but many more are hidden by current models.

These opportunities will become more evident as thought processes evolve toward identifying and testing new synapses with other elements, components and globules, and or even creating new value producing elements.

Already some important manufacturers in the electronic fields, for example, are successfully applying (consciously or unconsciously) business models that combine different elements of current models. Apple, for instance, has begun a journey in this direction, using just four elements: innovative products, entertainment, customer relationship, and customer experience, evolving their business model by converting their in retail outlets to showcase their products rather than merely selling.

The logical question that follows is: how many more possibilities might be developed under new models?

Country Stabilization and Mass Migration Mitigation

The issues relative to international stability and mass immigration are becoming of primary concern, of growing relevance to public opinion in many hosting countries, the subject matter of heated debates, the rise of xenophobic sentiment, and one of the main topics on political agendas. Cost-focused paradigms, a general strategy of enacting reforms and policies to replicate cost-based models in developed countries or allegedly address long-term retirement funding issues, are not generally considered to be helping. Rather, in many cases, they are only adding layers of complexity. Who is right or who is wrong is no longer the main issue. The fundamental focus, instead, should be on how to effectively and pragmatically address these phenomena before they become inhibitors to development and social time bombs.

One of the ways to address the diversified challenges and risks associated with mass migration from grass roots is by re-establishing adequate living and working conditions and opportunities in the countries of origin. As recent events have shown, this solution cannot be achieved with one-size-fits-all strategies; instead, local, country-driven initiatives meeting local requirements and respecting indigenous cultures are needed.

Authoritative demographic data from the 1950s through the 1960s and from the 1980s indicate, in countries experiencing economic growth, not only did emigration to other counties drop considerably, but these countries actively sought a natural evolution in their relations with other states, opening possibilities for foreign investments and labor and interaction with other cultures, progressively creating positive common grounds for a growing number of projects and initiatives. At least, such was the case during those earlier times more than it is currently for the same subset of countries.

Similarly United Nations data suggests, in theory, as countrywide projects and initiatives commence, a varying mix of positive outcomes occur, for example, renewed economic development, reduction of social tensions, resumption of entrepreneurial activity, and—in some cases—a return of migrants. Such countries as Peru, Chile, Ireland, Poland, Croatia, and Albania are recent examples to differing degrees—but which, in the absence of evolved value models, will most likely remain in-bilico.

However, returning to such growth presupposes pacification, normalization, and resumption of economic activity; instead, in a growing number of countries are experiencing wars, systemic collapse, social tensions, and so on. As *indigenously-led* efforts and initiative towards normalization and peace resume, these create value and, in turn, states, regions, factions which protectively enact normalization policies become the focus of value-based investments fostering a virtuous, pull (as opposed to push) cycle of transition toward stability. This scenario is substantially different from the current self-destructive and suffocating debt-based models and paradoxically more beneficial and remunerative than the current situation for all stakeholders.

If additional new concepts of value creation are factored in, the number of possible opportunities for each country rises both internally and internationally. As secondary effects, hypothetically, levels of international tensions and exposure to extremist actions would gradually subside or, at least, through increased coordination and international cooperation become more manageable. Correspondingly, as counties develop and more developed countries systemically recover, they might discover new needs for foreign expertise, reversing the paradigm and becoming net importers of expertise or possibly fostering an open movement of people and enterprises.

In aiding normalization, "Terra healing" projects—and for example, value-generating famine, health, food production, reforestation, and water-cycle projects that previously never benefited from enough funding—might gradually be planned, phased-in, and implemented, positively and systemically contributing to the improvement of local conditions. A third outcome might be a beneficial domino effect on collaborating nations and economies. Furthermore education-related initiatives that generate value, gradually opening to different subject matter, will help reduce intolerance, improve literacy, and foster sharing of a growing subset of positive values.

Institutional value generation, created by a country's institutions (e.g., parliamentary, judiciary, law enforcement, governance, and so on), might help gradually reduce such systemic phenomena as corruption, which plagues many countries under the current cost-based logics, impeding them from truly advancing and finding necessary stability and governance. Finally, the adoption of Virtus by any country and its membership among nations adhering to its fundamentals must be the result of a democratically led value-based process prompted by the deliberate and free choice of its citizens.

Next Gen Traffic Solutions

This entails identifying and prioritizing city road systems according to traffic flow and congestion generation capability. This might entail, for example (at least in the near future and until better solutions are found), moving an increased number of critical urban road segments underground together with parking facilities for both commercial and private uses.

These are not science fiction projects, and they are currently being implemented on comparatively important scale[60] in cities around the world such as Chicago, Sydney, Boston, Moscow, and Amsterdam (where the municipality is taking a few roads and their parking spaces below its famous canals).

The implications of a structural strategy, instead, are immeasurable today. As major arteries above ground are liberated from congestion and traffic, some of these areas can be put to more friendly uses as they have been in many cities around the globe, offering unique hospitality, shopping, and entertainment facilities that may increase possibilities across different sectors. The impact on extremely congested cities that had never been developed to accommodate previously unthinkable masses of persons such as Jakarta, Manila, Tokyo, Rome, . . . will be remarkable not only in alleviating traffic flow but its effects on health, smog, and so on.

People, for example, may wish to move back into redeveloped neighborhoods or remodel unused office space for living purposes, adding to a revitalization in the real estate and construction industry but also in environmental, art and entertainment, health and hospital, high tech, defense and aerospace, telecommunications, and a plethora of other sectors that may be affected in a domino-style positive economic revitalization.

As with the preceding section, the objective here is to make better use of what we have within our cities, towns, industrial sites, etc. Implemented correctly, with all the projects mentioned thus far and their numerous intersections with other possibilities, this may be more than many affected economic sectors can handle for some time to come considering that these are cyclical projects by nature.

---

[60] With respect to what is optimally needed—note: taken singularly they are big projects worth millions of dollars, but they only address the issues in a limited way.

Next Generation Mobility

The technology is here already and ready to be implemented. It could probably benefit from a few more tweaks, but this evolution, even in its current state, has the potential to become another mega opportunity generator. The current technology allows for driving a vehicle requiring substantially reduced human intervention - when this option is chosen. In its private vehicle version, it has already been tested in most traffic conditions in northern California.

The vehicle stops when it has to, drives at the speed limits, maintains safe distances, and allows for cars behaving erratically, safely making space and keeping distances. It keeps watch on the conditions in a 360-degree hemisphere around the car (much more than a human can do, especially with blind spots and on long, tedious drives).

Under a new model, the potential number of opportunities this creates is vast. These go from the structural impact this technology could have on the look and physical refurbishing of highways in the near future to opportunities to design new cars or evolve roads, potentially cleared of *most* physical road signs, since they could become visible on head-up displays or be prompted directly onto smart navigators, leaving only those physical road signs that are considered of absolute necessity. It could also mean new types of entertainment stopovers.

Each element gives rise to yet another set of opportunities that were not possible until recently. For those professionals who make a living on the road, it might mean a totally different way of pursuing their dreams and improving their quality of life, while for others (travelers, commuters, etc.) it could mean stress reduction, reduced accidents or road rage events, having more rest and entertainment opportunities, leading also to new insurance and novel business models.

Though there is never certainty about anything, it is highly probable that the technology will arrive on the roads eventually. A growing number of elements of these technologies are already in our cars (assisted parking, anti-drowsing solutions, etc.)

The question is whether we wish to leverage new opportunities, to what degree, and how fast do we wish to start a new chapter in economic evolution. Or do we want to wait until more car manufacturers go out of business, creating further financial disaster that propagate to other sectors, slashing thousands of other jobs in their wake?

With regard to potential opportunities available in redesigning, refurbishing and/or implementing new smart road/highway infrastructure solutions, the possibilities are countless as is. Current literature and studies provide abundant examples, however, if we were to factor-in the result of new synapses development within Virtus the number of possibilities assumes a totally different connotation.

So the true question is, do we want to wait for the demise of related industries, or continue on the path of degradation and reducing our cities to slums? It is important to understand that value is not created by building bridges and highways all the time, simultaneously, and all over the place, but in the majority of cases, improving upon what we have and producing $^{HESD(X)}$, where value is certified. Otherwise, we are potentially looking at unsustainable models and projects.

Next-Generation Pollution-Free Concepts

Not long ago, pollution was mostly assimilated with smog. Today this concept is evolving with advancements in many areas, allowing us to perceive and develop a better awareness for these phenomena and their impact on many aspects. Hence, this notion includes pollution from and increasing number of sources: vehicle braking systems, industrial processes, animal farming gases and agricultural pesticides, chemicals, radioactive substances, medical waste and expired medicines, water and sewage treatment, and food and biological sources. This is also valid for jet fuel pollution which, according to many studies, is becoming of critical environmental and health concern. Our oceans and waterways are also filled with extremely hazardous artificial pollutants such as fertilizers that are already heavily impacting health and ecosystems.

The number of sources of electromagnetic pollution alone is growing exponentially (e.g., digital and satellite radio, cellular phones, electrical wiring, and machinery), many of which have been deemed potentially damaging to human health by different studies while their combined effect probably still difficult to assess. Being able to confront these opportunities from a different perspective will allow us to undertake important developments in many areas.

An immediate obvious example would be the burying and safe insulation of literally millions of kilometers of electrical grids, for instance. Different than today, as human centricity and value become central under the new model, industry has finally the real incentive to produce healthy and environmentally conscious products and services.

It took the Earth's ecosystems literally millions of years to liberate the atmosphere from its primordial toxic and noxious chemical elements (i.e., CO_2, methane, etc.) to levels that allowed life to spark and prosper as these elements settled on the surface and covered by layers of sediment as a result of millennia-long erosion processes or trapped in permafrost or under oceanic floors around the world. Yet it has taken humankind only a few decades to displace millions of tons of toxic minerals and gases over delicate life-supporting environments and unleash preoccupying levels of these back into the atmosphere and in general ecosystems again. It is time some of our efforts went into recreating necessary equilibriums.

Uniqueness

Why do individuals dream of going to places such as Paris, London, Rome, Venice, Madrid, Tokyo, or Egypt? How about Yellowstone National Park, Rio de Janeiro, the Grand Canyon, Crater Lake, Monument Valley, or the Amazon River, or the Caribbean, Thailand, Mauritius, or the Seychelles? Why dive in the Maldives or at Sharm el-Sheikh?

In many cases it might be because they carry uniqueness. They are one-of-a-kind places that naturally attract us. Tourism and adjacent industries (concepts and business models that did not exist or make sense until only a few decades ago) are suffering from the effects of reduced economic traction, yet they provide business and investment opportunities and development potential for millions of people around the world.

Should we choose to think of curing our rainforests, seashores, etc. and managing the places and habitats in which we live in sustainable and unique ways (^{HESDX})—just as our ancestors did with a fraction of our capabilities in the past, leaving an incalculable wealth in terms of legacy—we might find a multitude of new opportunities.

In the travel and hospitality sectors and their supply chain alone, apart from value models in airlines discussed previously, other travel and hospitality concerns could benefit considerably from the evolved model.

Uniqueness, however, is not a concept connected only to the travel sector, but it has applications in just about all economic sectors, products, and services and even in an evolved financial market. It is all about creating propositions that generate value in particular ways.

Furthermore, if we look at the different interconnections, dimensions, and plateaus that this might impact, uniqueness also influences far-fetched, not necessarily obvious areas such as policy and policy-making. The more a community, region, or country adopts measures that respect and are in line with their particular set of environmental-socio-economic circumstances, culture and sensitivities, the more successful the possible outcomes theoretically and potentially in as many areas policy and policy-making touches.

To provide a real life example, countries in Europe, such as England and Switzerland that maintained a certain level of uniqueness be it by maintaining their own monetary system, legislations, code of civil rights and liberties, etc. in line with the expectations, requirements, views consummate with those of its citizenry, have de facto and historically resulted in increased resilience and success.

Whereas countries that have after the 1980's (to use a set of specific examples) left their natural course, in some cases, toward going out of their way (sometimes revolving several non-elected governments until specific legislature was not passed) in adapting to and/or blindly copying different policies in vogue at the moment that seemed to provide varying degrees of success in other nations have factually broken what constituted the backbone of an otherwise enviable economic/naturalistic/cultural environment with great levels of potential in many sectors in many, very unique ways.

One size fits all, not only it is utopic and counterproductive but also it does not create value. This again has nothing to do with such things as a pro or contra-EU stance but about the intelligent design and application of policy that can produce the best mix of levers and benefits for a country or a community.

"Web Uniqueness" and Cyber Protection

Extrapolating this concept also to other dimensions is valid and applicable also to the Web. Web uniqueness is the positive response to Web inclusivity. The amount of information to be elaborated here is so extensive it will need to be the focus of a specific paper. Anything that generates

Web uniqueness can counteract the effects of Web inclusivity at least for a while. There are several ways to achieve this, but for the purposes of this book, it is important to convey the fact that different business propositions and models are possible.

Cyber-protection initiatives instead, represent strategic projects aimed at protecting critical national infrastructure and data, but also those projects that, though led and enacted by private concerns are needed to protect private data, assets...and assure privacy of all stakeholders and need to adhere to value producing policies.

Lifelong Knowledge Enhancement Education and Learning

This area represents one of key success factors and fundamental cornerstone of any society and its prolonged prosperity in the future. It will be one of the major contributors to a continuous ascent toward new levels in civilization, revival of economic traction, and new opportunity generation.

The prospects here are numerous, limited only by imagination. Success in generating new jobs, higher-paying jobs for professionals, and jobs in new academic areas/fields will derive from new requirements emerging for different types of educational services and models in both public and private institutions addressing new needs beyond the scope and capabilities of current models.

Theoretically, as new variables are produced in the Virtus model and these give rise to new opportunities, modalities, processes, etc. they might introduce new disciplines, specializations, and areas of scientific or intellectual interest. Additionally, the investigation of potential new synapses with other elements and components could lead to new areas of advanced research and development.

Each of these might in turn require different value assessment procedures, indexes and benchmarks, and or new differing specialist capabilities for certification and or advisory services. Accordingly, each subset of similar new variables can potentially lead to an evolution of education requirements, tools, needs, and services. These may in turn need proper diffusion, transfer of knowledge, and training.

Other Examples

The list of opportunities lying ahead of us on the new plateau(s) is unfathomable. Many other examples can be added and elaborated in many other sectors—aerospace and defense, transportation, logistics, telecommunications, real estate, energy, utilities, etc., but as stated this is only an introductory book to a new concept and only envisioned through one initial perspective: the author's. *Imagine how many more there could be through other perspectives (e.g., yours)!*

What is even more interesting are the plethora of new sectors that might be generated under the new model . . . *Only our will, imagination, sustainability, and true value generation might pose the limits. It does not matter if things are undertaken exactly according to what has been introduced thus far. The modalities, processes, tools brought as examples should be taken as teasers and ideas on how to develop new perspectives, because at the end what is important is that we understand that what we are facing is a step-level need for change toward new models and plateaus.*

It is important to consider that so far we have only investigated possibilities in a few sectors and this has been done keeping a natural focus on predominantly hybrid legacy models (as we know them today), and for the sake of pragmatism and realism. However, new opportunities, dimension and frontiers lie beyond these known thresholds, and horizons, and will be generated levering on the creation of incalculable synapses via an open model and variables such as the *Virtus economic string theory*, rendering visible what today might be inconceivable.

Epilogue

As we approach the imminent and inevitable crossroads and step-level events in the evolution of existing socioeconomic models, hard evidence and facts force us to acknowledge our legacy models are becoming increasingly less usable and responsive to our changing world and evolving needs.

In finding a solution, we should avoid wasting more time focusing on or demonizing the current state of affairs; after all, it is of our own making. In many ways, we owe the living standards we enjoy today to the old models. Furthermore, it is not the first time economic models have evolved to meet new requirements, and address new challenges. We should welcome constructive disagreement on views because they will continue to provide needed corrections and rebalance the previous models from time to time.

Fundamentally, however, it is necessary to come to grips with the brutal reality of the current, prolonged global economic impasse and vacillating geopolitical equilibriums: uncertainty and volatility; *apparently* disconnected or unpropagable ideologically fueled regional wars; growing intolerance and social revolts; real unemployment; and exposure to growing numbers of risks to individuals, businesses, entire societies, and economies.

New disruptive and paradigm-changing variables (especially those beyond our current perception and knowledge) are pushing the limits beyond the envelopes of our existing legacy/hybrid models and have changed our ways of interacting, doing business, and providing for our loved ones. As with other similar times in history, there is an undeniable need for an evolved set of baseline assumptions, models, modalities, and approaches to address these new variables.

Policy makers, businesspersons, or simply living generations can decide to postpone the inevitable evolution and continue the strife of paying the consequences or decide to embrace it and benefit from it. A growing number of individuals and businesses are already developing evolved solutions based on a mix of models as discussed herein in different sectors. These solutions range from green concepts, carbon reduction, to usage-sharing business models, from bitcoin to peer-to-peer credit, and so on.

A noteworthy consideration is that innovation and virtualization of jobs, processes, and business models of entire economic sectors force us to address an existing reality with increasing urgency. Should we wish to achieve prolonged, structural economic recovery, open a new chapter, and migrate to a new plateau of long-term development and prosperity, we must be able to embrace and leverage new concepts and ways with the same courage and resilience as our ancestors have throughout history with much less knowledge and capability than we have today.

Like them, we must not be afraid to let go of dated, archaic, no longer performing concepts, allowing them finally to join their parent reference models in an honorable and well-deserved retirement and noteworthy remembrance in history books before any additional unnecessary damage is done.

As we step back, we can appreciate how and why, as long as we work within the boundaries of existing economic models and their relative cause-and-effect theories, any remedy a legacy or hybrid model has produced may be short-lived, have little or no effect, or worse, have a drastically negative effect on the economy with unknown virulent effects—failing to provide valid answers. If we look carefully, businesses, organizations, policy, and initiatives that are successful in the current scenario are those that, in some way, are applying a few of the elements and strategies discussed thus far. What this treatise suggests is that application of its elements should be done structurally and systemically across all domains, and sectors. Many times change does not materialize because it does not address the specific needs of different stakeholders—Virtus however, factors-in and addresses these different requirements; from employment to business, from banking to markets, and government.

What Can Individuals, Businesses, and Organizations Do?

Wherever we live in the world, whatever citizenship we hold, and whatever we do in life, if we want to proceed, the first question is how we—as individuals, businesses, organizations, political parties, groups, and so on—can do anything to activate the transition towards a new

model such as the value-generating evolutionary prosperity model—
Virtus? Whatever evolutionary path a society might choose, the first step
is up to each of us: increasing awareness of the possibility of a solution,
sharing information, and *disseminating* knowledge through the incredible
number of modes and media offered by today's technology. It starts by
asking our policy makers to *spearhead* and lead evolution toward a higher
plateau of prosperity and civilization.

If results are sought, these processes must be *repeated* until desired
outcomes are achieved. Fortunately, innovation allows us to do so even in
ways unthinkable until today, even from the comfort of our own homes.
Thus, you could contribute to making a difference.

Nothing should ever be imposed though. The Americas, Switzerland,
Sweden, Australia, or other places and communities people might cherish
or idealize have been achieved though the will and dreams of their
people. Whatever evolved model you might prefer, it needs to be shared,
evaluated, improved, completed, tested, verified, accepted, and ratified
through a democratic process and only then implemented systemically in
phases.

It is important to appreciate that any next model *must address the
very real needs* of people, businesses, and society and the challenges we
face. Legitimately, entire economies, businesses, and billions of people
can no longer be expected to afford, survive, or continue through
implementation of patchwork, unlikely or ineffective policies or reforms,
slogans, precariousness, austerity measures, and or structurally empty
temporary mini-recoveries. Rights and freedom constitute the *sine qua
non* foundations of successful societies and form the key success factors
for progress. Historically, reforms that reduce, cut, curtail, or endanger
these rights and freedom, will ultimately erode the foundations of
successful societies and nations; negatively affect employment, business,
and markets; and especially, continue impeding addressing the many
challenges we face.

Extreme haphazard approaches produce equally similar results, and
revolutions only lead to horrendous unjustified fratricide, bloodshed, and
economic degradation that lasts many decades. Instead, choosing and
implementing a winning strategy will make the difference.

Reasoned, democratically led transition and evolution is a much
better strategy, the one with the greatest potential for success. However,
any initiative requires a sense of direction toward its achievement, and

having this sense of direction requires a will and an appreciation for the essence of time.

Resilience, perseverance, diligence, determination, and resolve—drive successful transition. Every major human achievement in history is the result of repeated efforts, not a one-off exercise. The business returns, the scale of the momentum generated, and the sense of urgency will determine the substantial reduction of time scales needed for transition.

The motion of a single water molecule interacting with others creates a momentum that generates waves in the largest of oceans. Quantum vibrations and interaction of the smallest particles of matter led to the formation of our planet, our solar system, and the vast universe that surrounds the miniscule spacecraft we call *Earth*.

In terms of human achievement, much larger feats act as precedents, and have been achieved with infinitely greater energy and resources than will be needed for the transition to a new model (Virtus). As with any other twenty-first century paradigms based on innovative technologies, once the first nucleus of the new model is formed its rollout, propagation, distribution…will be achieved geometrically.

We are more than the sum total of our physical cells, and there is more to life than what we might limit it to be. As our awareness of our increasingly complex interconnected societies, organizations and individuals grows, we will should come to realize that we have a growing individual responsibility and a choice: doing what we can in the best way we can or surrendering to complacency and accepting we might in some way, directly or indirectly, be unwillingly contributing to the status quo and many other things we might lament, dislike, or fear to consider. After all, they are the cumulative result of our choices, decisions, initiatives, and interactions.

Every step we take, every word we communicate, every thought we contemplate, and every action we undertake can make a difference. Each resonates in the world and leaves an indelible trace of our existence and affects many things, far beyond the horizon of our limited perceptions.

Smog and pollution produced in one country cause damage not only to its communities but also to its neighbors downwind. Delocalizing investments and production in one area creates the setting for dangerous geopolitical imbalances that induce turmoil, transfer of wealth and financial resources, mass migrations, and instability. Forcing people to work in inhuman conditions in one part of the world induces business closings in other countries, causing unemployment; it weakens local economies, affects debt and deficit, exposes investments and wealth to financial risks, infringes on rights and liberties, and causes desperation, fueling violence and criminality. Everything is interconnected—probably more than it has ever been historically, and even more so in the future. We can use this interconnectivity to grow virtuous outcomes or become prey to the propagation of undesired systemic effects of current models.

As we confront the inexorable question of our legacy and purpose, it might simply be about being able to look inside ourselves with sincere honesty and through the eyes of our sons, daughters, and loved ones and feel we have contributed our share, just as our ancestors did before us though great sacrifices, leaving a legacy of themselves in humble recognition of a gift called *life*.

It is time we brought hope, optimism, a can-do attitude, positivity, resilience, the right to realize dreams, a sense of perspective and relativity, happiness, and smiles back into our lives, whether we are young, middle aged, or young at heart. As someone once said, "Today is the first day of the rest of your life."

Today can be what you wish it to be. We each have the irreplaceable chance to fill the magnificently empty pages we have each been granted in this uniquely valuable moment and ephemeral mystery called *life*—our moment of life.

Perhaps we have reached a unique stage in evolution as a species, society, and civilization: a stage and an age in which individuals can begin a process of focusing on what their positive natural, innate abilities, gifts, or essence would lead them to do in realizing their aspirations and dreams; of generating value all around us unselfishly; of reaching new levels of awareness free of fear, intolerance, and hatred, not only resolving the immediate problems we face but also addressing *critical* challenges, such as mitigation strategies for *climate change,* famine, war, and *sustainability* and initiating the long search and journey toward new *frontiers* and places beyond our planet that one day we may call home as our Mother Earth evolves toward new cycles in its sustainability of life.

We could bring in a new era in which economic models, priorities, and necessities increasingly address, foster, and complement human needs, priorities, and requirements in a virtuous cycle of developing opportunities, assuring prosperity for current and future generations as responsible and respectful custodians of the planet and biosphere we have been granted.

Fundamentally, *this evolution has already started*. The sheer breadth, complexity and resources needed to address the numerous challenges ahead cannot but be managed through a new paradigm and there is little more to add other than the obvious: Those individuals, businesses, markets, organizations, economies, and nations that embrace progress will be able to advance. Those who do not will fall behind.

As with everything else, we have a choice—an alternative. Given the challenges awaiting living generations, each individual, business, or organization can choose its role: a catalyst; a contributor to a new era in writing one of the important chapters of human history; or one who disseminates and enhances knowledge by sharing, informing, and prompting key decision makers and policy makers to evaluate and consider new options, discussing how all this affects one's business. Just as importantly, one could choose to play no role at all.

There is one certainty, however: if no choice is made or no action taken, nothing will change, except for what will be decided for you by others—your job, business, wealth, endeavors: your future and those of your loved ones.

In today's fast and dynamically changing world, the outcome of such a decision by an individual, a business, an organization, a society, a nation, or a union of nations is of strategic and vital importance and defines all of their fates.

Will you be among those that contribute to making your world a better world and leave a legacy of yourself to prosperity?

What you do next will make the difference and determine your future, but also impact the lives of those that will follow.

Addendum

Chart 1

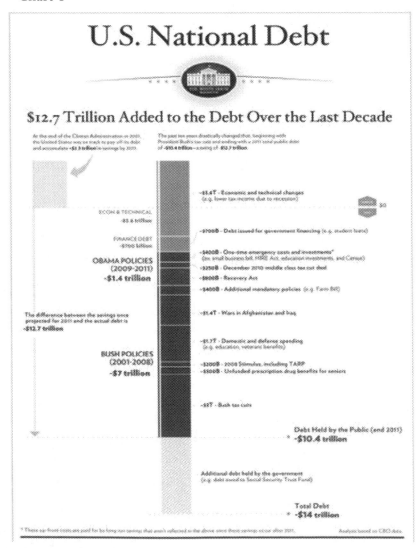

Source: The White House.

Chart 2

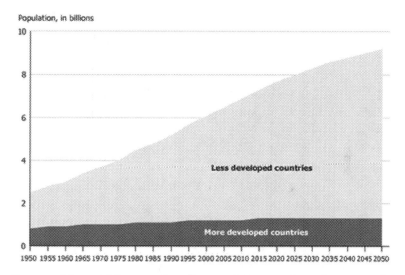

Population, in billions

Less developed countries

More developed countries

Source: United Nations Population Division; Population Reference Bureau.

BIBLIOGRAPHY

Bremmer, I. 2009. "State Capitalism and the Crisis." *McKinsey Quarterly*, July. http://www.mckinsey.com/insights/public_ sector/ state_capitalism_and_the_crisis (accessed June 5, 2014).

"The Caribbean: A Chinese beachhead?" 2012. *Economist*, March 12. http://www.economist.com/node/21549971 (accessed June 3, 2014).

Carlson, Mark. 2007. *A Brief History of the 1987 Stock Market Crash with a Discussion of the Federal Reserve Response*. Washington, DC: Divisions of Research & Statistics and Monetary Affairs, Federal Reserve Board.

Central Intelligence Agency. 2011. "World Fact Book." *http://www.cia.gov* (accessed April 30, 2012).

Chaudhury, Shoma, and Shantanu Guha Ray. 2010. "For a Few Pieces of Silver." http://archive.tehelka.com/story_main45.asp? filename=Ne260610coverstory.asp (accessed June 6, 2014).

"China's Growing Investment in the Caribbean." 2011. *Business Journal*, June 28, 5–6.

Colvin, Geoff. 2010. "Desperately Seeking Math and Science Majors." http://money.cnn.com/2010/07/29/news/international/ china_engineering_grads.fortune (accessed April 27, 2012).

Cooper Ramo, Joshua. 2004. "The Beijing Consensus." London: Foreign Policy Centre. *http://fpc.org.uk/fsblob/244.pdf* (accessed June 3, 2014).

Davies, Martin. 2010. "How China is Influencing Africa's Development." http://www.oecd.org/development/pgd/45068325.pdf (accessed June 3, 2014).

Dodd-Frank Wall Street Reform and Consumer Protection Act, H.R. 4173, 111th Congress (2010).

Eckerman, Ingrid. 2005. *The Bhopal Saga: Causes and Consequences of the World's Largest Industrial Disaster*. Hyderabad: Universities Press.

Economist Intelligence Unit. n.d. "Global Debt Clock." http://www. economist.com/content/global_debt_clock (accessed February 18, 2013).

Epstein, David. 2006. "Quality vs. Quantity in Engineering." *http://www.insidehighered.com/news/2006/03/03/engineers* (accessed April 27, 2012).

Federal Reserve System. 2012a. "The Federal Reserve and the Financial Crisis Lecture 4: The Aftermath of the Crisis." http://www. federalreserve.gov/newsevents/files/bernanke-lecture-four-20120329. pdf (accessed Aug 6, 2012).

————. 2012b. "Monetary Policy Report to the Congress." http://www. federalreserve.gov/monetarypolicy/files/20120717_mprfullreport.pdf (accessed July 17, 2012).

————. n.d. "Monetary Policy and the Economy." http://www. federalreserve.gov/pf/pdf/pf_2.pdf (accessed Aug 7, 2012).

"Friend, Enemy, Rival, Investor." 2012. *Economist*, June 30. http://www. economist.com/node/21557764 (accessed June 5, 2014).

Galbraith, John Kenneth. 1975. *Money: Whence It Came, Where It Went*. Boston: Houghton Mifflin.

Galloway, James N., Hiram Levy, II, and Prasad Kasibhatla. 1994. "Year 2020, Consequences of Population Growth and Development on Deposition of Oxidized Nitrogen." http://www.gfdl.noaa.gov/ bibliography/related_files/jng9401.pdf (accessed June 4, 2014).

Greer, Thomas H., and Gavin Lewis. 2001. *A Brief History of Western Man*. 6th ed. Fort Worth: Harcourt Brace Johnston.

"Group of 7, Meet the Group of 33." 1987. *New York Times*, December 26. http://www.nytimes.com/1987/12/26/opinion/ group-of-7-meet-the-group-of-33.html (accessed June 4, 2014).

Halper, Stefan. 2010. "The China Model: The Beijing Consensus is to keep quiet." *Economist*. http://www.economist.com/node/ 16059990 (accessed June 3, 2014).

Hutchinson-Jafar, Linda. 2011. "China woos Caribbean with Offer of $1 bln in Loans." http://in.reuters.com/article/2011/09/12/ idINIndia-59302220110912 (accessed June 5, 2014).

IHS Jane's International News Briefs. n.d. http://*www.janes.com* (accessed October 17, 2012).

International Monetary Fund. 2012. "World Economic Outlook Update." http://www.imf.org/external/pubs/ft/weo/2012/update/ 02 (accessed July 16, 2012).

Investopedia. n.d. "Fiscal Policy." http://*www.investopedia.com* (accessed Aug 8, 2012).

Katzenbach, N. 1987. *An Overview of Program Trading and Its Impact on Current Market Practices*. New York: New York Stock Exchange.

Maddison, Angus. 2012. "Mis-charting Economic History." http://www.economist.com/blogs/graphicdetail/2012/06/mis-charting-economic-history (accessed July 3, 2012).

McKenzie, R., and Gordon Tullock. 1978. *Modern Political Economy: An Introduction to Economics.* New York: McGraw-Hill.

McLamb, Eric. 2011. "The Day of Seven Billion." http://ecology.com/2011/09/day-seven-billion (accessed April 12, 2012).

McLellan. n.d. "The McLellan Oscillator & Summation Index." http://www.mcoscillator.com/learning_center/kb/mcclellan_ oscillator/the_mcclellan_oscillator_summation_index/ (accessed June 6, 2014).

Princeton University. n.d. "Wordnet: A Lexical Database for English." http://wordnet.princeton.edu/ (accessed June 3, 2014).

Reinhart, Carmen, and Kenneth S. Rogoff. 2009. *This Time is Different: Eight Centuries of Financial Folly.* Princeton, NJ: *Princeton University Press.*

United Nations Department of Economic and Social Affairs, Population Division. n.d. "Population." http://www.esa.un.org/ undp/wpp/Excel-data/population (accessed September 14, 2012).

United Nations Food and Agriculture Organization. 2003. "General Situation of World Fish Stocks." http://www.fao.org/ newsroom/common/ecg/1000505/en/stocks.pdf (accessed June 3, 2014).

UN University and UNEP. 2012. "A New Balance Sheet for Nations: UNU-IHDP and UNEP Launch Sustainability Index that Looks Beyond GDP." http://www.un.org/en/sustainablefuture/pdf/New%20balance%20sheet%20PR%20%20FINAL.pdf (accessed June 4, 2014).

U.S. Congressional Budget Office. 2010. "Historical Data on Federal Debt Held by the Public." http://*www.cbo.gov/sites/ default/files/cbofiles/ftpdocs/117xx/doc11766/2010_08_05_ federaldebt.pdf* (accessed May 15, 2012).

———. 2011. "CBO's 2011 Long-Term Budget Outlook." http://www.cbo.gov/publication/41486 (accessed February 15, 2013).

———. 2012a. "The Budget and Economic Outlook Fiscal Years 2012 to 2022." http://www.cbo.gov/sites/default/files/cbofiles/attachments/01-31-2012_Outlook.pdf (accessed August 7, 2012).

———. 2012b. "Understanding and Responding to Persistently High Unemployment." http://www.cbo.gov/sites/default/files/ cbofiles/attachments/02-16-Unemployment.pdf (accessed August 7, 2012).

————. 2012c. "The United States is Experiencing the Longest Stretch of High Unemployment Since the Great Depression." http://www.cbo.gov/publication/42977 (accessed June 5, 2014).

U.S. Department of the Treasury. 2012. "Reforming Wall Street, Protecting Main Street." *http://www.treasury.gov/connect/blog/Documents/20120719_DFA_FINAL5.pdf* (accessed August 2, 2012).

————. n.d.a. "Data and Charts Center." http://www.treasury.gov/resource-center/data-chart-center/Pages/index.aspx (accessed February 15, 2013).

————. n.d.b. "Debt Limit." http://www.treasury.gov/initiatives/ Pages/debtlimit.aspx (accessed June 5, 2014).

————. n.d.c. "History." http://www.treasury.gov/about/history (accessed July 8, 2012).

————. n.d.d. "Treasury Direct." http://www.treasurydirect.gov (accessed July 3, 2012).

U.S. Financial Crisis Inquiry Commission. 2011. "The Financial Crisis Inquiry Report." Washington, DC: Government Printing Office.

U.S. Government Accountability Office. 2010. "Nanotechnology: Nanomaterials Are Widely Used in Commerce, but EPA Faces Challenges in Regulating Risk." http://www.gao.gov/assets/310/304648.pdf (accessed Aug 10, 2012).

————. 2011. "Debt Limit: Delays Create Debt Management Challenges and Increase Uncertainty in the Treasury Market." http://www.gao.gov/products/GAO-11-203 (accessed June 4, 2014).

————. n.d.a "Fiscal Outlook and the Debt." *http://www.gao.gov/fiscal_outlook/overview* (accessed February 15, 2013).

————. n.d.b "What factors make Treasury securities attractive for investors?" http://www.gao.gov/fiscal_outlook/understanding_federal_debt/interactive_graphic/what_makes_treasury_securities_attractive (accessed June 4, 2014).

White House. 2010. "G-20: Fact Sheet on Sustainable External Imbalances and Orderly Global Adjustment." *http://www.treasury.gov/resource-center/international/g7-g20/Documents/G-20%20Seoul%20Fact%20Sheet%20-%20Sustainable%20External%20Imbalances%20and %20Orderly%20Global%20Adjustment.pdf* (accessed August 7, 2012).

————. n.d. "U.S. National Debt." http://www.whitehouse.gov/infographics/us-national-debt (accessed June 20, 2012).

Williamson, John. 2003. "Appendix: Our Agenda and the Washington Consensus." In *After the Washington Consensus: Restarting Growth and Reform in Latin America*, ed. Pedro-Pablo Kuczynski and John Williamson, 323–31. *http://www.piie.com/publications/chapters_preview/350/ appiie3470.pdf* (accessed June 6, 2014).

World Bank. n.d. "World DataBank" http://databank.worldbank.org/ data/home.aspx (accessed April 30, 2012).

Additional Bibliography and Recommended Reading

The following is a very brief list of resources (Web-based or otherwise), a bibliography that can be consulted for a more detailed analysis, additional reading, complementary and alternative views, and continuously updated information:

American Recovery and Reinvestment Act of 2009
Austrian Economics
blogs.worldbank.org
Bloomberg
BBC
CNBC
CNN
CIA World Fact Book
Economist
Emergency Economic Stabilization Act of 2008
European Central Bank
European Union websites
FAO
Federal Reserve System
Glass-Stendall Act, Economic Stimulus Act of 2008
GAO
Harvard Business Review
Il Sole 24 ore
International Monetary Fund
International Red Cross websites
IRS
Keynesian Economics
OECD
SEC
Troubled Assets Relief Program (TARP)
UNHCR,
United Nations
U.S. Congress
U.S. Department of State
U.S. Department of the Treasury
U.S. Federal Reserve System websites and documentation

U.S. Government
U.S. Senate
White House
World Bank
Wall Street Journal

Afonso, Antonio, and Ricardo Sousa "European Central Bank: The Macroeconomic Effects of Fiscal Policy." Frankfurt: European Central Bank.

Bilal, Sanoussi, Isabelle Ramdoo, and Quentin De Roquefeuil. 2011. "Europe, G20, and South-South Trade Insights from European Approaches to Regional Integration in Africa." *Economic Policy Papers*. Washington, DC: German Marshall Fund of the United States.

Bloomberg. n.d. "Nasdaq Composite Index – CCMP:IND." http://www.bloomberg.com/quote/CCMP:IND/chart (accessed July 3, 2012).

Burnette, Ed. 2006. "U.S. vs. China vs. India in Engineering." ZDnet.com. http://www.zdnet.com/blog/burnette/u-s-vs-china-vs-india-in-engineering/125 (accessed April 27, 2012).

Federal Reserve System. n.d. "Flow of Funds Accounts of the US—Estimated Ownership of Debt Held by Public." http://www.federalreserve.gov/apps/fof/ (accessed May 2012).

Heyne, P. T., P. J. Boettke, and D. L. Prychitko. 2002. *The Economic Way of Thinking* (10th ed.). Upper Saddle River, NJ: Prentice Hall.

International Monetary Fund. 2012. "Taking Stock: A Progress Report on Fiscal Adjustment." http://www.imf.org/external/ pubs/ft/fm/2012/02/fmindex.htm (accessed June 5, 2014).

Kinder, Caroline. 1998. *The Population Explosion: Causes and Consequences*. New Haven, CT: Yale New Haven Teachers Institute.

Larch, M., and J. Nogueira Martins. 2009. *Fiscal Policy Making in the European Union: An Assessment of Current Practice and Challenges*. London: Routledge.

McNicoll, Geoffrey. 1984. "Consequences of Rapid Population Growth: An Overview and Assessment." *Population and Development Review* 10, No. 2 (June 1984): 177–240.

PriceWaterhouseCoopers. 2009. "Junior Mine Survey." Toronto: PriceWaterhouseCooper.

Reinhart, Carmen, and Kenneth S. Rogoff. 2008. "The Forgotten History of Domestic Debt." *Economic Journal, Royal Economic Society* 121(552), 319–50.

Schiere, Richard, and Alex Rugamba. 2011. *"Chinese Infrastructure Investments and African Integration."* Working Paper No. 27. Tunis: African Development Bank Group.

U.S. Congressional Oversight Panel. 2011. "March Oversight Report: The Final Report of the Congressional Oversight Panel." http://cybercemetery.unt.edu/archive/cop/20110401232213/http://cop.senate.gov/documents/cop-031611-report.pdf (accessed March 16, 2011).

U.S. Department of the Treasury. "Tax Policy General Explanations of the Administration's Fiscal Year 2013: Revenue Proposals." Washington, DC: U.S. Department of the Treasury.

U.S. Government Accountability Office. 2010a. "Financial Audit: Office of Financial Stability (Troubled Asset Relief Program) Fiscal Years 2010 and 2009 Financial Statements." http://www.gao.gov/new.items/d11174.pdf.

White House. 2010. "G-20: Fact Sheet on U.S. Financial Reform and the G-20 Leaders' Agenda." *http://www.whitehouse.gov/the-press-office/2010/11/12/g-20-fact-sheet-us-financial-reform-and-g-20-leaders-agenda.*

Williamson, John. 1990. "What Washington Means by Policy Reform." *http://www.piie.com/publications/papers/paper.cfm? researchid=486* (accessed April 10, 2012).

Recommended Reading of Published Works by the following:

Robert Altman
Ben Bernanke
Warren Buffet
Joshua Cooper Ramo
David Epstein
Milton Friedman
Francis Fukuyama
Timothy Geithner
Alan Greenspan
Stefan Halper
Randall Kroszner
Paul Krugman
David Laidler
Michael Lewis
Roger Malcolm
Richard McKenzie
Bill Mitchell
Warren Mosler
Robert Murphy
John Nesbitt
Joseph Nye
Murray Rothbard
Nouriel Roubini
Anna Schwartz
Michael Spence
Joseph Stiglitz
Gordon Tullock
Paul Volker
Vivek Wadhwa
Randall Wray
Fareed Zakaria
Mark Zandi
Zhao Qizheng

Index

A

B

C

D

E

Fifth-dimension asymmetric strategy 74
Fifth dimension of warfare 74
Financial reform 87
Financial services 247, 284
Financial Stability Facility 90
Fiscal policy 84, 100
Fishing 104, 270, 277, 278
Forensics 193

G

Gama, Vasco de xxiv
GDP 61, 62, 63, 209, 244
General inclusivity 19
Globalization 13, 44, 60, 80
Globule 148, 151, 152, 153, 167, 169, 205, 206, 230, 287
Gold 35, 66
Governance framework 132, 139, 140, 155, 156, 169, 177, 185, 206, 216, 220,
        229, 230, 245, 247
Greece 94, 108, 109, 147
Green economy 265, 281

H

Health viii, xiii, 18, 31, 32, 34, 35, 42, 45, 52, 53, 57, 58, 59, 68, 70, 71, 84,
        86, 94, 100, 101, 118, 149, 157, 161, 177, 199, 202, 214, 218, 227, 232,
        233, 244, 264, 267, 269, 270, 274, 277, 279, 294
HESD xxvii, 131, 142, 147, 148, 151, 153, 154, 155, 156, 157, 158, 172,
        179, 198, 199, 200, 205, 206, 212, 213, 215, 217, 218, 222, 230, 232,
        233, 235, 236, 238, 239, 240, 241, 244, 246, 267, 268, 269, 271, 281,
        293, 295
Holistic 149, 206
Holistic value-generating model 143
Housing 61, 86, 164, 265, 266
Human centric 149
Humanization 234, 265, 267
Hybrid economic model 137, 138, 141, 142, 147, 153, 154, 155, 167, 169, 172,
        177, 189, 192, 198, 205, 207, 212, 247, 269

I

J

K

N

O

P

Q

R

S

V

W

ABOUT THE AUTHOR

The author is an executive with diversified international experience acquired in top-three consulting firms, Fortune 100 conglomerates, leading investment banking, top ten aerospace multinationals and tier-one financial services corporations, such as Arthur Andersen, Accenture, American Express, and Siemens, through twenty-seven expatriate assignments and relocations in different continents around the world. He has developed expertise in different functional areas, especially in strategy and innovation, and nurtures a passion for economics, international policy, and foreign affairs, with years of experience providing C- B- and G- level advisory for important government, public and private concerns. His curriculum is complemented with an international education, an MBA, and the Italian Naval Academy.

During his lifetime, he has experienced several exceptional, life-changing scenarios such as revolutions, disruptive regime changes, and collapses of socio-economic models--starting anew, and as he puts it: "developed a particular appreciation for this uniquely marvelous gift called life."